GUIDE TO BETTER BULLETIN BOARDS

TIME AND LABOR-SAVING IDEAS
FOR TEACHERS AND LIBRARIANS

by Kate Coplan
Former chief, Exhibits and Publicity, Enoch Pratt Free Library

and

Constance Rosenthal
Artist and illustrator

1970 OCEANA PUBLICATIONS, INC. / DOBBS FERRY, NEW YORK 10522.

© COPYRIGHT 1970 BY
OCEANA PUBLICATIONS, INC.

LIBRARY OF CONGRESS CATALOG CARD NO. 76-102937

ISBN: 0-379-00369-4

MANUFACTURED IN THE UNITED STATES OF AMERICA

TO PHILIP F. COHEN

OCEANA'S ENTERPRISING PRESIDENT,
THROUGH WHOSE VISION AND
ENTHUSIASTIC SUPPORT
THIS BOOK BECAME A REALITY.

Books by Kate Coplan

EFFECTIVE LIBRARY EXHIBITS:
    How to Prepare and Promote Good Displays
POSTER IDEAS AND BULLETIN BOARD TECHNIQUES:
    For Libraries and Schools
THE LIBRARY REACHES OUT:
    Reports on Library Service and Community Relations by Some Leading American Librarians (Edwin Castagna, co-compiler and co-editor)

Books Illustrated by Constance Rosenthal

POSTER IDEAS AND BULLETIN BOARD TECHNIQUES:
    For Libraries and Schools, by Kate Coplan
KENNY AND JANE MAKE FRIENDS, by Elizabeth Vreeken
MY BOOK OF TIME, by Marshall Hagan

CREDITS

Designer . . . . FINTAN O'HARE
Photographer . . . . LOUIS MARINO
Calligrapher. . . . . CHARLES CIPOLLONI

ACKNOWLEDGMENTS

Grateful thanks are due many people for their gracious and invaluable assistance. Leading the list is Philip Rosenthal, husband of this team's junior member, whose prodigious services —always cheerfully rendered—ran the gamut from studio construction to design conferences.

The authors were the beneficiaries, also, of useful ideas, helpful suggestions, constructive criticism and/or strong moral support from a host of other interested and knowledgeable individuals, among them: Mr. G. Alfred Helwig, former director of curriculum, Baltimore County (Md.) Board of Education; Mr. Edwin Castagna, director, Enoch Pratt Free Library, Baltimore (Md.); Mr. Lewis Lyman Bowker, Sr., art supervisor, Shrewsbury (Mass.) School System; Mrs. Mildred Cook, librarian, Old Saybrook (Conn.) Junior High School; Mr. Joseph De Gange, principal, Kathleen E. Goodwin School, Old Saybrook; Mrs. Jane Barton, librarian, Essex (Conn.) Elementary School; Mrs. Beryle Owings, art teacher, Elementary School, Ann Arundel County (Md.); Mr. P. Timothy Owings, head, art department, Southern Senior High School, Ann Arundel County; Miss Dorothy A. Ciliano, teacher, Montville (Conn.) High School; Mrs. Beverly Wiseman, assistant principal, Cecil Elementary School, Baltimore; Miss Helen Hermon, former area director, Baltimore Public Schools.

Also, members of the supervisory staff, Area F, Baltimore Public Schools; Mrs. Sandra Stebbins, Mrs. Joan Wendler, Mrs. Dorothy McCarthy, Mrs. Evelyn Orman, Mrs. Henny Olsen, Mrs. Norma Diamond, Miss Nancy Hawkins, Misses Fannie A. and Edith H. Coplan, Mr. A. Rabinowitz, Mrs. Dorothy Ginn, Mrs. Stanley Herbst and Mrs. Joseph Levy.

Mr. Mike Ferdinand, Oceana's able production manager, gave service over and beyond the call of duty, while Miss Betty Adler, Baltimore bibliophile, added her competence to the reading list and index.

We express warm appreciation to the Conde Nast Publications for the use of some of their photographs appearing in *House and Garden Magazine,* and to *McCall's,* for their generous blanket permission in connection with photographic reproduction.

Last, but not least, we tender best thanks to a group of very young Connecticut artists, collectors and writers whose work is represented in this book: Toby and Lisa Diamond, Andrew May, Susan Olsen, Benjamin and Jonathan Rosenthal and Curtis Wendler.

—K.C. and C.R.

CONTENTS

ACKNOWLEDGMENTS / viii

LIST OF ILLUSTRATIONS / x

INTRODUCTION / xiii

BULLETIN BOARD BASICS / xvii

PATTERNS FOR DRAWINGS / 173

APPENDIX (Commercial Suppliers of Display Materials) / 217

RELATED READINGS / 219

INDEX / 221

LIST OF ILLUSTRATIONS

FRONTISPIECE, BOOK WEEK
    (see also, Page 166)
AFRICA .... Page 89
ALL LIVING THINGS NEED AIR ...... Page 145
AMERICA, AMERICA .... Page 62
THE AMERICAN INDIAN .... Page 71
ANIMAL HOMES .... Page 94
ANIMALS, FLOWERS AND BIRDS .... Page 111
ANIMALS WE DESIGNED .... Page 61
ARMCHAIR TRAVEL .... Page 83
AUTUMN (Also, Halloween,
    Thanksgiving) .... Page 162

BABY .... Page 76
BACK TO SCHOOL
    (With Hanger People) .... Page 131
BALANCE THIS SCALE .... Page 40
BANK DAY .... Page 139
BE A MOTHER'S HELPER .... Page 79
BELGIAN CONGO, LAPLAND,
    SAHARA DESERT .... Page 120
BICYCLE RULES .... Page 113
BIG FACTS ABOUT LITTLE THINGS ... Page 129
BIN STRIPS .... Page 134
BIRD WATCHING .... Page 122
BIRTHDAY CAKE .... Page 22
BLOW YOUR HORN .... Page 100
BOOK WEEK .... Page 166
BOOKS ABOUT HOLLAND .... Page 82
BOOKS ON CHILD CARE .... Page 78
BOOKS ON NATURE .... Page 121
BROTHER .... Page 75
BUILDING A HOUSE FOR THE FAMILY Page 53
BUON NATALE, GLADELIG JUL,
    JOYEUX NOEL .... Page 11

CAN YOU SOLVE THESE
    MEASURING PROBLEMS? ..... Page 38
CAN YOU SORT THESE? .... Page 24
CARING FOR OUR PETS .... Page 93
CIRCLES ARE EVERYWHERE ...... Page 52
CIRCUS DAYS AND WAYS .... Page 118
CIRCUS WORKERS .... Page 59
CLIMB INTO THE SKY .... Page 49
A CLOSE LOOK AT NATURE ...... Page 122
CLOUDS .... Page 129
COME TO STORY HOUR .... Page 72

COMMUNICATION .... Page 70
COWBOYS ... TALES AND TRAILS . Page 45

DENTAL HEALTH WEEK .... Page 137
DID YOU CHECK YOUR WORK? .... Page 130
DISCOVER AND EXPLORE .... Page 126
DO YOU BRUSH AFTER EVERY MEAL? Page 15
DO YOU KNOW THESE
    FAMOUS PEOPLE? .... Page 41
DON'T FORGET .... Page 142
DON'T LEAVE TOYS ON THE STEPS . Page 44
DRESS FOR THE WEATHER .... Page 144

EAT .... Page 135
ENJOY NUMBERS:
    THEY GROW ON YOU .... Page 39
EXOTIC READING FROM
    ROMANTIC LANDS .... Page 87
EXTRA CREDIT .... Page 130

FAMILY LIFE TOGETHER .... Page 57
FATHER .... Page 73
FEBRUARY BIRTHDAYS .... Page 153
FEED OUR WINTER FRIENDS ...... Page 170
FINGER PAINTING .... Page 101
FLOWERS THAT BLOOM IN MAY ... Page 95
FOLLOW THE LEADER—
    KEEP YOUR SCHOOL CLEAN .. Page 150
FRANCE .... Page 3
FRESH FROM THE GARDEN ...... Page 163
FROM THE FARM TO THE TABLE ... Page 34
FROM SEA TO SHINING SEA ...... Page 154
FUN WITH NUMBERS .... Page 108

GARDEN IN A JAR .... Page 96
GATHER NEW WORDS .... Page 54
GEORGE WASHINGTON .... Page 168
GET READY FOR WINTER .... Page 67
GETTING CLOSE TO NATURE ..... Page 127
GO SOUTH FOR THE WINTER ..... Page 123
GO: THE STORY OF
    TRANSPORTATION .... Page 123
GOOD FOOD BUILDS
    STRONG BODIES .... Page 35
GOOD GROOMING .... Page 149
GOOD TEETH .... Page 143
THE GREAT OUTDOORS .... Page 18

GREECE	Page 88
HALLOWEEN (Also, Autumn, Thanksgiving)	Page 162
HAPPY CHANUKAH	Page 158
HAPPY HOLIDAY!	Page 12
HAPPY VALENTINE'S DAY	Page 30
HAVE A GOOD, SAFE SUMMER	Page 106
HAVE A HAPPY NEW YEAR	Page 28
HAVE A HOBBY	Page 58
HAVE A SAFE VACATION	Page 63
HAWAII	Page 171
HEARTS AND FLOWERS	Page 32
HEMIDEMISEMIQUAVER: A 64TH NOTE	Page 98
HERE COMES THE CIRCUS	Page 60
THE HISTORY OF AFRICA	Page 90
HOLD ON TO YOUR HAT	Page 68
HOLIDAY COOKERY	Page 29
HOLIDAY FUN	Page 27
HOLLAND	Page 81
HOW TO GIVE A PARTY	Page 42
HOW TO USE YOUR LIBRARY	Page 119
HOW WE USE MEASURING	Page 107
HOW WE USE MONEY	Page 157
IN FEBRUARY WE CELEBRATE THE BIRTHDAYS OF GEORGE WASHINGTON AND ABRAHAM LINCOLN	Page 153
IN THE DAYS OF LINCOLN	Page 165
IN DAYS OF OLD WHEN KNIGHTS WERE BOLD	Page 164
INDIA	Page 86
INDIAN STORIES	Page 47
INSIDE FUN FOR A RAINY DAY	Page 80
ISRAEL	Page 160
IT'S CIRCUS TIME	Page 51
IT'S FALL AGAIN	Page 20
JAPAN	Page 156
JOIN CLUB 100	Page 133
KEEPING OUR COMMUNITY IN GOOD CONDITION, A and B	Page 110
LETTERING	Page 133

LET'S BE PROUD OF OUR HOMES	Page 23
LET'S NOT LITTER	Page 17
LIGHT READING IS FUN	Page 163
LIGHT SUMMER READING	Page 116
LISTEN—WHAT DO YOU HEAR?	Page 99
LOOK	Page 134
LOOK AT ME—WHAT DO I SEE?	Page 148
LOOK AT OUR WILD LIFE	Page 126
LOST AND FOUND TREE	Page 114
LOVE	Page 135
MAKE SPRINGTIME SAFE PLAY TIME	Page 5
MERRY CHRISTMAS	Page 11
MERRY CHRISTMAS, HAPPY CHANUKAH	Page 26
MEXICO	Page 160
MR. TURKEY	Page 33
THE MOODS OF THE SEASONS	Page 7
MOTHER	Page 74
MOVING AIR	Page 124
NATURE NOTES	Page 40
NATURE STUDY	Page 169
NEWS	Page 104
... NIGHT ... and ... DAY ... NIGHT ... and ... DAY	Page 21
THE NOVEL 100 YEARS AGO	Page 109
OCEANS AND CONTINENTS	Page 66
ONE WORLD	Page 84
OUR CITY AND HOW IT GROWS	Page 92
OUR FOREST FRIENDS	Page 9
OUR NEW VOCABULARY WORDS	Page 105
PAINT WITH STRING	Page 16
PARADE OF CHILDREN (United Nations)	Page 85
PEACE * PEACE * PEACE ... JOY * JOY * JOY ... PEACE ON EARTH	Page 25
PICTURES MADE OF WOOL	Page 4
PLEASE DON'T SPREAD GERMS	Page 141
PRACTICE GOOD WRITING	Page 138
A PROGRAM OF CHRISTMAS MUSIC	Page 102
PUZZLED? ASK QUESTIONS	Page 66
RAIN—SUNSHINE	Page 128

RAINY DAY FUN TABLE	Page 49
REACH THE SKI LODGE	Page 42
READ ABOUT YOUR HOBBY	Page 68
READ ALL ABOUT IT	Page 155
READ BEFORE YOU SKI	Page 64
ROMAN NUMERALS	Page 38
SAFE PLAY	Page 43
THE SEASON'S BEST	Page 77
THE 7 BASIC FOODS	Page 36
SHAPES	Page 157
SHIPS THAT SAIL THE SEA	Page 164
SISTER	Page 75
6TH GRADE EXHIBITION	Page 19
SOME BLACK AMERICAN AUTHORS	Page 14
SOME BLACK AMERICANS— HOW MANY DO YOU KNOW?	Page 13
SPAIN	Page 161
SPRING RAIN BRINGS FLOWERS	Page 65
SPRINGTIME IS SAFE PLAY TIME	Page 5
STOP—OBEY LIGHTS	Page 59
STORM WARNING	Page 125
THE STORY OF ELECTRICITY	Page 115
TAKE GOOD CARE OF YOUR PET	Page 132
TAKE ONE	Page 140
THANKSGIVING	Page 159
THANKSGIVING (Also Autumn, Halloween)	Page 162
TO STAY HEALTHY	Page 151
TOUCH AND FEEL	Page 97
TOWARD A BETTER TOMORROW, TOGETHER	Page 50
T.V. SET	Page 172
THE TREE	Page 55
UNDERSTANDING EACH OTHER	Page 48
USING MATH IN THE KITCHEN	Page 167
VALENTINE	Page 153
A VISIT TO ARIZONA	Page 10
A VISIT TO A MUSEUM	Page 9
WAS YOUR BREAKFAST GOOD AND HEALTHY?	Page 12
WASH YOUR HANDS	Page 147
WE PLANT OUR GARDEN	Page 127
WE READ AND LEARN ABOUT EACH OTHER	Page 103
WE USE OUR LIBRARY	Page 41
WE VISIT A DAIRY FARM	Page 37
WE VISIT A SUPERMARKET	Page 117
WE WORK AND PLAY TOGETHER	Page 57
WE WRITE ABOUT SPRING	Page 112
WELCOME BACK TO SCHOOL	Page 136
WELCOME TO 5TH GRADE	Page 106
WHICH ONE ARE YOU?	Page 146
WINTER FUN	Page 6
WITCH	Page 31
WITH THESE RESPONSIBILITIES COMES THE GIFT OF FREEDOM	Page 71
THE WORLD NEWS	Page 91
WORLD TRAVEL	Page 1
WORLD TRAVEL WITH BOOKS	Page 2
WRITING LETTERS	Page 69
YOUR FLAG AND MINE	Page 46

INTRODUCTION

To borrow an overworked phrase from show business, this book was written by "popular request." It was in the spring of 1967, while on a visit to my beloved Enoch Pratt Free Library in Baltimore, that I stopped to chat for a few minutes with the late Miss Katherine E. Conger, a member of the Fine Arts Department, whom I encountered in the second floor corridor.

As on several previous occasions, we discussed the continuing active demand for my books, EFFECTIVE LIBRARY EXHIBITS (Oceana, 1958) and POSTER IDEAS AND BULLETIN BOARD TECHNIQUES: For Libraries and Schools (Oceana, 1962), which classified in her area. And, as before, Miss Conger mentioned that these works were seldom available on the shelves, leaving numbers of teachers and librarians frustrated in their efforts to check them out at times most needed.

Facetiously, I suggested that Fine Arts might acquire 25 more copies, boosting the Department's circulation and at the same time swelling my royalties. But this feeble attempt at humor fell flatter than the proverbial pancake. Miss Conger simply ignored the remark and asked, "Why don't you write another book on Bulletin Boards? Teachers and librarians are always asking for it."

Thus the seed was planted. On returning home that afternoon I gave considerable thought to what type of book dealing with visual communication might prove most helpful to teachers and their associates, librarians. Reflecting at length on the manifold professional duties and responsibilities falling to this dedicated group, I recalled that throughout my long career at Pratt, teachers and librarians had complained repeatedly that they found the planning and preparation of Bulletin Boards a heavy additional burden.

Particularly where there was a lack of formal art training and experience did teachers and librarians dread implementing and executing displays. Sometimes, they pointed out, it took several agonizing hours just to come up with a catchy caption for the display. Further, the prospect of creating an original design of proper import and good quality was a frightening one, indeed.

Without too much trouble, therefore, I came to the conclusion that these hard-working, hard-pressed people could use to advantage a practical book of "quickie" displays—offering a host of lively, easy-to-do ideas and adaptable suggestions likely to relieve them of the worrisome, wearisome details of planning and producing meaningful Bulletin Boards.

Because of their predominant numbers and needs, it seemed sensible to direct the main emphasis to teachers. Ideas proposed, I decided, should often permit the involvement of children, affording them both the pleasures and benefits of a shared learning experience. But many of the designs could be dual-purpose, I reasoned, serving librarians as well as teachers.

Once the theme and goals of the volume were settled in my own mind, I consulted with my publisher and gained instant approval. Then I enlisted the cooperation and multiple talents of my young artist colleague of Pratt Library days, Constance Rosenthal, who had so capably illustrated POSTER IDEAS AND BULLETIN BOARD TECHNIQUES. Mrs. Rosenthal—though she now makes her home in Connecticut and consent inevitably would mean almost constant consultation with me in Baltimore by mail and telephone, as well as a heavy share in the sweat-of-brow labor—needed little persuasion. Rather, she entered into the project with tremendous enthusiasm, immediately recognizing the opportunity for performing a useful service to the nation's forward-looking educational segment.

Together we agreed upon our primary purpose: to put at the disposal of teachers and librarians everywhere those techniques and design elements which would assist them in producing constructive visual aids easily and swiftly. In so far as the former were concerned we envisioned not teaching a lesson to the students, but rather helping their mentors acquire a knowledge of pleasing, effective Bulletin Board design that would stand them in good stead when related to general topics discussed in the classroom during the school year.

In today's fast-moving world Bulletin Boards are pertinent to the instructional program, a definite link in communication between student and teacher. Good Bulletin Boards enhance the room and enrich the curriculum. Also, they make the environment more pleasant, giving children a growing awareness of beauty, as well as a general appreciation of the esthetic. Multiple Bulletin Board colors, if well coordinated, can unify a room. If properly handled, the Bulletin Board is a focal point of the classroom. Moreoever, it can be a valuable teaching tool, motivating students to learn more about any given unit.

The wise teacher will not maintain the *status quo* for too long a period, but will keep the display flexible, changing certain portions, taking away, adding to, or moving items about from time to time. If it is a long-term Bulletin Board, it is valuable only so long as the children are contributing to it. For whenever the

Bulletin Board remains exactly as originally installed beyond two or three weeks, it becomes a familiar fixture, an integral part of the classroom which youngsters eventually fail to "see," and its effectiveness is thereby lost.

We strongly advocate pupil participation in the formulation and presentation of the majority of classroom Bulletin Boards. Not only is it desirable to involve children in the planning and execution of the displays, but their work in the classroom should be shown whenever possible. This lends added interest and incentive, affording youngsters deserved recognition and a gratifying sense of achievement. Now and then children in the higher grades may be invited to assist teachers of the lower grades in preparing Bulletin Boards.

With the teacher's encouragement and guidance, students may help gather a variety of odds and ends for a treasure chest of display materials (more is written of this subsequently); cut, paint and attach caption letters; clip newspapers and magazines; mount pictures, maps, drawings, and other articles.

When teachers and students combine their imaginations, resourcefulness, ingenuity, energy and talents, they are bound to resolve the most formidable display problem. Even the greenest novice will acquire facility with experience. And in a relatively short time what was formerly regarded as a difficult chore, will become a spirited exercise in fun and adventure.

Of course, it goes without saying that regardless of the extent of pupil participation, the ultimate responsibility for creditable classroom Bulletin Boards falls on the teacher. It is the teacher who must provide leadership and supervision, sometimes more subtle than direct, in order that best results may be obtained.

Incidentally, principals and supervisors frequently use Bulletin Boards as a measuring stick to assess a teacher's creative ability, and the degree to which he projects bridges to better understanding of the curriculum. For classroom Bulletin Boards, without doubt, yield significant clues to a teacher's personality, imagination, vision and objectivity—some of which traits, hopefully, will be developed in his pupils.

Though intended mainly for teachers and librarians in the elementary schools—public, private and parochial—many of the ideas presented in these pages may be adapted with minor changes to the needs of the higher grades, as well. (Because Bulletin Board measurements vary greatly from school to school, classroom to classroom, and library to library, those who work with the materials and illustrations listed should make any adjustments necessary to suit their respective projects). In addition, workers in public libraries, museums, art schools, book stores, religious schools, and other book-oriented establishments, should find the concepts depicted here useful in developing their own exhibits skills for their own particular purposes.

Mrs. Rosenthal and I shall be very happy if our displays serve as a jumping off place for more sustained effort anywhere in the broad spectrum of visual communication. For we are convinced that effective display programs can contribute materially to the widening of youthful knowledge and awareness of today's complex world.

Readers will find in these pages no flossy literary flourishes, no superfluous verbiage. The aim is to provide simple, practical, direct information and instructions for speedy, stimulating Bulletin Boards.

Inevitably, in such a work, there is a certain amount of redundancy in words and phrases. We ask forgiveness if this treatment bothers some purists, but readily acknowledge the use of repetition wherever deemed necessary. In every case, of course, teachers, librarians and others having access to this volume, should exercise their own good judgment as to whether they wish to follow directions precisely as given. Latitude is taken for granted. When we suggest pinning items to Bulletin Boards, for example, workers must decide for themselves whether small, medium or large pins would be best for the purpose, depending on their material. Or they may prefer to use thumbtacks in matching colors, inconspicuous staples, carpet tacks, paste or glue to fasten pieces to the backdrop. The important thing is to employ whatever tools and techniques will best achieve the objective—neatly, attractively, inexpensively, and with dispatch.

—K.C.

May 30, 1970

BULLETIN BOARD BASICS

It is essential to remember that one need not be an artistic genius to prepare successful Bulletin Boards. Rarely does a member of the teaching or library profession lack innate good taste and discriminating judgment, both of which are invaluable factors in creative Bulletin Board composition. Possessing these, any teacher worth his salt can master the skills of interesting design arrangement and pleasing color combinations.

Aside from personal preferences, the alert display worker will find innumerable suggestions while viewing store windows, museum exhibits, bus cards, magazines and newspapers, television commercials, travel posters, book and pamphlet covers. One idea leads to another, and anything is fair game if it can be adapted to constructive educational purposes.

Millions of dollars are spent annually on various types of visual promotion. Whenever possible, therefore, teachers and librarians should capitalize on this fact, borrowing adaptable advertising ideas and putting them to work in behalf of their respective programs. As one learns to recognize advertisements that do their job well, "selling" the prospective buyer efficiently and persuasively, one gains an increased awareness of how to apply similar methods and techniques to one's own field of endeavor.

It goes without saying that, to accomplish their objectives in communication, Bulletin Boards must be neatly "packaged," attractive and eye-catching. Otherwise, regardless of their message, they will fail to win attention or excite interest. The emphasis should be on simple, effective arrangements of maximum visual value, attained with minimum effort, time and expense. Appearance of clutter must be avoided. Sufficient "white space," to use the advertisers' term for blank space, should rest the eyes at intervals, serving as a sort of frame to set off individual and group display items.

Here are some general tips on producing lively, well-organized, well-designed classroom (or library) Bulletin Boards:

Choose a pertinent topic.

Whenever possible, build a display around one central theme.

Consider carefully the overall meaning of the unit and its concept.

Narrow thoughts down, and put idea into its simplest form. (Ideas have a way of popping up at odd times, even during wakeful moments in the middle of the night. A pad and pencil should be kept handy, to jot them down immediately, so as not to forget them).

Determine which symbol or symbols will best interpret the idea in art forms, using basic design qualities shown in the examples contained in this book.

Keeping the size of the Bulletin Board in mind, decide on the materials to be used, their proper colors and placement.

Lettering must be planned as an integral part of the design, not added as an afterthought, or extra.

Caption letters should usually be large and easy to read from a distance.

Clutter must be avoided. Crowding the Bulletin Board with too many elements at one time will confuse viewers, and distract them.

The message and meaning of a Bulletin Board should be immediately apparent on visual contact. If the display requires deciphering or interpretation, it is bound to puzzle, frustrate or confuse, and the desired favorable impact will be lost, or at best, substantially reduced.

Teachers and librarians should bear in mind that children particularly, are attracted to color. The liberal use of bold color is especially recommended, and unusual color tones, when used in combination, draw like magnets. One needs only to consider nature in this respect, recalling how handsome and decorative is a multihued floral arrangement. (See illustration, FRESH FROM THE GARDEN).

The perceptive worker will find agreeable color clues in department store windows displaying wearing apparel, art posters, transit vehicle advertisements, book jackets, fashion magazines, television commercials. If one is alert, these may also serve as design resources waiting to be tapped. Eyes and minds must be kept wide open always, ready to seize any opportunity for adding to the storehouse of ideas adaptable for present or future use. Teachers, especially, must learn to be observant, and to make good use of what they see. Imagination, individuality, ingenuity, will enable them to put together thoughts and ideas stemming from various sources, with gratifying results. It is well to remember that many successful modern artists studied and learned from cave drawings of the Stone Age.

To save time and energy, a supply of simple shapes may be cut from paper or other materials and kept readily at hand for use over and over again, in different ways. Included may be trees, birds, animals, hands, the sun, flowers, boats, airplanes, trains, boys and girls in silhouette, and stick figures. (See section of suggested patterns in this book). The periodic employment of such pieces will help develop the worker's own distinctive style.

Some teachers find it helpful to outline a Bulletin Board schedule at the beginning of each semester. Working materials may be collected throughout the year—fabrics, wallpaper ends, newspapers, colored construction and tissue papers, shopping bags, decorative wrapping and foil papers, egg and tomato cartons; cake, hat, dress and shoe boxes; discarded magazines; old music books; ribbons, hats and gloves no longer serviceable. Almost anything is grist for the display mill. A large carton, to contain the conglomeration, should be easily accessible. This will permit the preparation of striking displays by imaginative students at little cost.

Mothers who do the family sewing will be glad to save scraps of cloth for their youngsters' teachers. Brown paper bags from the supermarket often provide just the right color and texture for lining the Bulletin Board. Rug remnants are sometimes on sale for five cents a square foot, and these make excellent backdrops to set off display items. Bamboo poles can be pressed into service when a nature scene is involved (See illustration, OUR FOREST FRIENDS). Boxes, open or flat, may occasionally be used as part of the Bulletin Board design. In fact, this book abounds in pictures showing how many discarded odds and ends may be tied in with quality displays.

Depending on the effect desired, shapes and objects on Bulletin Boards may be oversized or diminutive, brightly colored or in soft, muted tones, bold and exaggerated, or in simple, silhouette form.

Display arrangements should be varied, with some well balanced, others showing contrived imbalance. When a Bulletin Board is excessively large or too unwieldy to work with, it is advisable to use only a portion of it for the main design (see illustration, LOOK). A decorative border may supplement the exhibit, or the principal display may be placed off center, with the remainder of the space closed off with complementary colored paper.

Occasionally the Board may be divided down the middle to make a special point, as in illustration, KEEPING OUR COMMUNITY IN GOOD CONDITION. This display, featuring an urban renewal project, offers a kind of before-and-after presentation. The left half suggests a squalid, poorly planned, unattractive neighborhhod in disrepair. In sharp contrast is the right half, covering exactly the same area, but appealingly rehabilitated, and consequently much more desirable.

To achieve the effect shown the teacher cuts two of every symbolic item intended for inclusion, affixing one of each in hodgepodge fashion to the section on the left, as indicated. These are in evidence for a day or two before the discussion begins, to stir youthful interest and curiosity. Accordingly, when the lesson is introduced, the children are eager to participate. The opposite side of the Board is then decorated, with the teacher questioning the students during the lesson as to how they think the neighborhood might be better arranged. As the teacher receives constructive suggestions from the youngsters, she attaches the duplicate pieces in the places designated, winding up with an obviously improved design.

There are times when real objects may be combined effectively on Bulletin Boards with flat cutouts or drawn work (See illustration, AMERICA, AMERICA). Here a turkey feather represents a quill pen, while a miniature American flag enhances the three-dimensional appeal. The Capitol's dome is drawn, the stars and caption letters are cut from paper, and the background derives from colored construction paper.

Teachers who are constantly plagued by lost articles may solve the problem by cleverly fashioning a lost-and-found "tree," and displaying the items in question. (See illustration, LOST AND FOUND TREE). In practically no time at all the articles will be restored to their rightful owners, and taken home.

Shapes, forms and color patterns in themselves sometimes create interesting designs. To cite two examples: illustration, THE 7 BASIC FOODS, and illustration, OUR NEW VOCABULARY WORDS.

Communication through display is often expedited through presentation of familiar things. For instance, a Bulletin Board devoted to music might have as part of the design a board of piano keys, indicating a black and white color scheme. (See illustration, HEMIDEMISEMIQUAVER: A 64TH NOTE). Or the design might include a simply shaped instrument, or many instruments simplified and arranged either in a border at one or two sides, or in strips sandwiched between blocks of information. The color of the instruments—brass or silver tone—would determine the color scheme selected.

A springtime Bulletin Board centering on the circus can appropriately demonstrate the different jobs involved in circus life. As the children learn the diversified occupations they may arrange illustrative figues in or near the tent—for example, performers forming a pyramid. (See illustration, CIRCUS WORKERS; illustration, HERE COMES THE CIRCUS, and illustration, IT'S CIRCUS TIME). Or they might concentrate on the animals, vehicles and performers on parade. Thus, instead of scattering figures haphazardly here and there, the children would point up groups in working position. Accordingly, both the artists and others in the classroom would benefit from the improved design, suggesting sequence and continuity.

If a class is studying a particular country, the teacher might initiate a background based on the native costumes, buildings typical of the area, or famous landmarks. The art forms could be simple and used effectively, repeating the design pattern. Photographs, cutouts, or students' papers related to the topic under study, could be superimposed on the shapes shown. Some teachers have used to good purpose an overall pattern repeated to cover the entire board, on which large cutouts are then mounted. On occasion the motif is taken from fabric. (See illustration, AFRICA; illustration, WE VISIT A DAIRY FARM, and illustration, WE PLANT OUR GARDEN).

Now and then striking display results may be obtained through generous use of repeat patterns involving letters, words, or cutouts. (See illustration, WE WORK AND PLAY TOGETHER, and illustration, NIGHT AND DAY).

For the most part, teachers and librarians will devise their own methods and mechanics for exhibiting students' work. But cited herewith are a few examples that may offer some guidelines: WRITING LETTERS, and PRACTICE GOOD WRITING, showing how students' letters and stories may be presented; also, ANIMALS, FLOWERS AND BIRDS, showing how cutout shapes in an overall repeat pattern can hold together a Bulletin Board of children's nature designs done in art class.

Note how illustration, THE GREAT OUTDOORS, places all sizes of children's work together, and shows dimension.

Another good example is ANIMALS WE DESIGNED. This portrays students' cutout animals of various sizes in a forest setting. First the simple cutouts of trees made of corrugated brown boxes were put into position. Then the animals, only partially in view, were placed so they seem to be walking in the woods, some behind the trees, others in front. The foliage and flowers in the foreground are large in proportion to the remaining elements, to indicate perspective and give the illusion of depth. This arrangement is more intriguing than projecting the whole animal in each case.

Occasionally reproductions of the following may be "borrowed" for Bulletin Board implementation: children's book illustrations; billboard illustrations; magazine illustrations and advertisements; book jackets; maps; illustrations from cereal boxes; calendar art; greeting cards; natural history illustrations. However, when the items in question are protected by copyright, permission in writing must be obtained in advance from the copyright holders, if there is any possibility that a photograph of the display may be published.

The choice of lettering style should set the tone for the Bulletin Board's content. As mentioned earlier, caption letters for Bulletin Boards must always be worked in as part of the design, not as an afterthought. Lively and appealing, they should serve both as introduction and integral part of the display. Placement should be varied, with some Bulletin Board captions in command position at the top, others strategically located elsewhere.

Obviously with lettering, as with other display elements, engaging variety is desirable. Large, heavy letters, for example, are appropriate for displays concerning industry, construction, mining and similar weighty subjects. On the other hand thinner, lighter letters are more suitable for lessons related to poetry, literature, fine arts and additional subjects in "lighter" vein. A display referring to the wilds of Africa would naturally feature bold lettering and vivid, "wild" colors, while in an exhibit centering on graceful Grecian architecture the more subdued colors would predominate, with perhaps touches of brightness for contrast.

Irregular, up-and-down placement of letters denotes humor (See illustration, SAFE PLAY). The same lettering style in conventional straight arrangement is serious in feeling (See other illustration, SAFE PLAY). At times letters and/or numbers, if large and decorative, may comprise the entire display on the Bulletin Board (See illustration, CAN YOU SORT THESE? and illustration, FUN WITH NUMBERS). These may sometimes be cut in the shape of animals or objects. (See illustration, BIN STRIPS). In the event the teacher decides to make his own caption letters, a pattern of the style favored, in the proper size, should first be outlined on cardboard just thick enough to cut easily with scissors, sharp knife or razor blade. These can then be used as a guide to trace around.

Three-dimensional cardboard, strawboard or paper letters in assorted styles and colors may be purchased from commercial suppliers of display materials (consult Appendix). Or letters may be drawn and cut from newspapers, magazines, thin cardboard, fabric, construction paper, wallpaper, wrapping paper, blotters, burlap or felt. If the school has a workshop, heavier letters may be produced from wallboard, or even wood or metal, for special effect. The size and style are optional, depending on proportional suitability to space at hand and subject matter treated. Letters available for purchase come in numerous sizes, styles and thicknesses, and may be pasted, pinned, or otherwise neatly affixed. Each display merits its own interesting style, but when dismantled, the letters should be saved for future use.

In addition to the Roman and other familiar lettering types, teachers and librarians may wish to add interest occasionally with captions that are "different." For variety's sake, to help carry out a particular theme, decorative letters may be made in unusual forms, simulating Chinese, Hebrew or other foreign language characters, old English calligraphy, or an alphabet style reminiscent of the "gay nineties" (See illustration, LETTERING). A pattern of the style and size desired should be cut from cardboard with scissors, knife or razor blade, then used as a guide to trace around as needed.

As indicated previously, letters may derive from any materials that are cutable: Newspapers (either headlines or body pages); discarded magazines (these give good color, and a full page may be alloted to each letter, as in illustration, EAT and illustration, LOVE); wrapping papers; fabrics; cardboard; blotting paper; burlap; corrugated paper; felt. Letters may also be formed with rope, cord, yarn and ribbon (See illustration, LET'S NOT LITTER). For holiday captions, letters may be coated with glue and dusted with glitter, sand, spices, miniature flowers, or "snowflakes" cut from white paper doilies.

Students may not always understand the reasons for a specific lettering style, but they will nevertheless instinctively enjoy the end result if the style is compatible with, and enhances the design. For just as do their elders, many youngsters possess natural good taste, and instantly recognize display elements that somehow seem right for a particular Bulletin Board.

In a majority of cases, caption letters should be evenly aligned and words equidistant from each other. (For more detailed information about lettering see EFFECTIVE LIBRARY EXHIBITS and POSTER IDEAS AND BULLETIN BOARD TECHNIQUES). Display workers would do well to observe the spacing in newspaper headlines, book jackets and magazines, done by professionals, and follow their example.

To supplement the caption clear, simply-worded explanatory notes, attractively hand-lettered or neatly typed, should accompany single items or groups of items wherever necessary. Ideally, the comprehensive design must be such that the eye will proceed progressively from one area to the other, until the entire Bulletin Board is covered, and its content readily understood and mentally digested.

ILLUSTRATIONS

MATERIALS:
Photographic cutouts and maps from discarded magazines, construction paper, colored cellophane, wool yarn, fabric, pins.

COLORS:
White, black, green, red, purple, orange, pink, multicolor magazine photographs and maps.

METHOD:
1. Line Board with white paper.
2. Based on pattern in this book, prepare figure from construction paper, cut apart and rearrange in position similar to that shown in illustration.
3. Dress the figure with apparel cut from brightly colored magazine pages. Pin on.
4. Add a round face of white construction paper, boots, mittens, cone-shaped hat with pom-pom on top.
5. Cut silhouette of skyline and pin to bottom of Board area.
6. Cut circles in various sizes for caption letters and magazine photographs and maps of places around the world to be studied. Pin them above figure. In order that the circles will simulate balloons, attach strings of wool yarn beyond the lower curves, pulling down to figure's hands, and pin into position.
7. With marking pen draw eyes and smile on face, and pin fabric scarf around neck.
8. Cover some of the circle balloons with colored cellophane.

WORLD TRAVEL

WORLD TRAVEL WITH BOOKS

MATERIALS:
Cardboard box, dowel stick, straw hat, globe, marking pen, construction paper, upholstery tacks, glue.

COLORS:
White, black, green, multicolor globe, multicolor straw hat.

METHOD:
1. Line Board with white paper.
2. Turn bottom section of large, fairly shallow cardboard box upside down. Draw on page lines with marking pen, so that the box will simulate a book.
3. Add a list of travel titles to book spine, slit page lines and insert a piece of construction paper cut to resemble a bookmark.
4. Attach box to Board by means of upholstery tacks, using as many as needed to hold it firmly in place.
5. Set globe on the book, add hat and dowel stick with paper caption flag (same shape as bookmark) lettered with marking pen, glued on.
6. Add a white construction paper smiling mouth to world globe.

NOTE: This display adapts well to both classroom and library use.

FRANCE

MATERIALS:
Heavy construction paper, single and double masking tape, pins.

COLORS:
Black, red, blue, white.

METHOD:
1. Roll a large, full sheet of heavy black construction paper to form kiosk, fastening the ends where they meet with masking tape.
2. Cut strip for top of the roll from red paper, trimming the sides so that the bottom fits the roll and the top flares out slightly.
3. Tape on the dome-shaped piece of black construction paper.
4. Using a thin, lightweight dowell stick, add the miniature French flag (made from small strips of red, white and blue paper) to the top.
5. Place informational notices, posters, photographs, students' work, or other selected items, on the kiosk with double masking tape. Pin to the Bulletin Board, or set on a table in front of the Board.

ALTERNATE SUGGESTION:
Stand kiosk before a painted French street scene done by students, or arrange a series of decorated kiosks in a row. This type of free-standing display is adaptable to year-round presentation of classroom or art work. Change often. Rolled corrugated board is also suitable for kiosk construction, and the exhibit materials may be attached in the same way. Recommended particularly for library case or table display featuring books about France.

PICTURES MADE OF WOOL

MATERIALS:
Construction paper, students' art work, thin cardboard, wool yarn, marking pen, pins, glue.

COLORS:
Black, white, magenta, orange.

METHOD:
1. Line Board with white paper.
2. Cut a piece of thin cardboard into a spool shape by trimming away a portion of both sides, leaving the top and bottom edges as seen in photograph.
3. Wind orange and magenta strands of wool yarn around the spool, and attach ends to a narrow, tapered strip of cardboard with a hole at the wider end, simulating a threaded needle. Pin to Board, lower right.
4. About midway on the white paper, slightly toward the left, pencil in the main caption, "Pictures."
5. Apply glue to the pencil lines and cover with the magenta and orange wool yarn, with the pieces extending from the final letter to the needle's eye. Then with marking pen add the phrase "made of wool" under the word, "Pictures."
6. Place one vertical and two horizontal panels of black construction paper in position, as shown in illustration. Use these as mats for student art work done in class.

MAKE SPRINGTIME SAFE PLAY TIME

MATERIALS:
Construction paper, large paper bag, pins, glue.

COLORS:
White, black, dark blue, pink, yellow, orange, green, brown.

METHOD:
1. Pin on white paper background.
2. Attach band of green construction paper at bottom, for grass.
3. Affix a large paper bag to Board, with small wheels and a handle cut from black construction paper and pinned away from the backdrop, to give the feeling of a cart (garden or golf).
4. Add simple flowers and sports equipment shapes, tucked into bag opening.
5. Pin bat and ball away from the background, for dimension, and golf balls—one on tee, the other on grass.
6. Caption letters are cut from white construction paper and glued to bag. Their irregular, up-and-down arrangement adds a spring-like quality to the Board.

ALTERNATIVE TITLE:
SPRING SPORTS

ALTERNATIVE SUGGESTIONS:
Sports equipment may be drawings, such as the tennis racket seen here, or lightweight plastic toys easy to affix to the backdrop. Many students would probably enjoy cutting out the flowers and sports equipment. These could be changed from time to time, in order that all students' art work might be displayed. If space is available, several carts could be arranged in a row, with a variety of decorations, messages and papers on view.

WINTER FUN

MATERIALS:
Construction paper, corrugated board from a discarded box, styrofoam ball, posters or magazine photographs of wintery scenes, mat knife, pins, glue.

COLORS:
Black, white, tan.

METHOD:
1. Line Board with black paper.
2. Based on pattern given in this book, draw mitten on corrugated board, and cut upper and lower sections, with mat knife.
3. Mount pictures on upper section of mitten.
4. Attach mitten to Bulletin Board at slight angle (this adds to the fun theme, improves attention-getting value, and provides variation for the mounted items), leaving sufficient space between upper and lower parts for caption letters.
5. Cut wide strips of white construction paper and fit together to form the caption.
6. Cut styrofoam ball in half and pin or glue above mitten thumb.

ALTERNATE TITLES:
WINTER WANDERINGS
WE WRITE ABOUT WINTER

NOTE:
A series of such mittens and snowballs would be effective in extensive Bulletin Board areas devoted to a WINTER IS FUN theme. Works produced in art class, or compositions covering some phase of winter activity could be superimposed on the mittens. Pictures or writings should be changed frequently, to sustain interest, and at the same time avoid crowding. The simplicity of this type Board intensifies the stark wintery feeling.

THE MOODS OF THE SEASONS

MATERIALS:
Construction paper, magazine photographs, students' art work, marking pen, pins.

COLORS:
White, black, yellow, blue, green, red.

METHOD:
1. Line Board with white paper.
2. Cut four construction paper circles (blue, green, yellow, red), using one-quarter of each to form a special circle, leaving just a little white space between the segments.
3. Cut four strips of construction paper in corresponding colors.
4. Cut out two sets of black construction paper numerals, 1 through 4, affixing 1 set to the circle, the other to the strips.
5. Pin on strips, with circle in-between, as shown in illustration.
6. Cut auxiliary caption letters from black construction paper and place on the strips, coordinating the circle colors with the strip colors.
7. Add magazine photographs and students' art work of the four seasons to circle segments.
8. The main caption, running across the top of the display, consists of script letters cut from black construction paper.

NOTE:
This design is adaptable to almost any topic. The colored strips and circle quarters require little art work. As a result workers obtain maximum design quality through bright colors and simplicity of style.

A VISIT TO A MUSEUM

MATERIALS:
Construction paper, marking pen, posters and pictures of great art, cutouts from discarded magazines, patterned magazine page, poster paint, pins.

COLORS:
White, dark blue, yellow-green, dark green, purple, red, multicolor pictures.

METHOD:
1. Line Board with white paper.
2. Using full sheets of blue construction paper, cut the center away so that each will resemble an arched doorway.
3. Place in a row the arches and their centers, sometimes alternating, sometimes not, as seen in illustration. Leave space for columns.
4. Place full sheets of construction paper behind some arches and parts of sheets for others, as mats for the various pieces of art to be featured.
5. Cut columns from purple construction paper, slightly tapered at tops and bases, and add marking pen lines to represent grooves.
6. The bottom portion of the Board is decorated with curly lines of white poster paint done with a brush, to give the feeling of a marble floor.
7. The potted palm near the left column is cut from light yellow-green and dark green construction paper, then glued to a pot cut from a magazine page with allover pattern.
8. The caption letters, done in Roman style, are cut from dark blue construction paper and placed at center bottom of the display area. The whole arrangement tends to enhance the "museum mood."

NOTE:
If preferred, this Bulletin Board could be executed before the visit to the museum, except for the art reproductions. After the visit the teacher and students might discuss famous paintings viewed, and prints could then be assembled for mounting in the designated areas. It is advisable to change the pictures at intervals, to sustain classroom interest.

OUR FOREST FRIENDS

MATERIALS:
Fabric, sheet, bamboo stick, ribbon, construction paper, raw cotton, marking pens, pins, glue.

COLORS:
White, black, orange, yellow, green, pink, multicolor fabric.

METHOD:
1. With large, heavy pins attach a bamboo pole to the Bulletin Board, and onto it fasten an old sheet, which may also be used as a prop for a school play.
2. Youngsters may cut and pin on discarded items they have brought from home (fabric, ribbon, raw cotton, etc.) creating the forest setting.
3. Caption letters are cut out and glued to a sheet of construction paper, then pinned into the position of being held by the calico cat, as illustrated.
4. All representations of animals, birds, flowers, insects and sun have faces drawn on with marking pens. The faces are then cut out, and children put their own faces in the holes for purposes of the lesson. Afterward the drawn faces are pinned back into proper position. (This is a good way to involve even the shyest students, who might not otherwise participate actively in the proceedings. Stepping "behind stage" and speaking through the animals in a discussion about animal habits, habitats and conservation, would probably have wide juvenile acceptance. Studying ecology could thus prove practically painless, even fun, for participants as well as the audience in a classroom.

A VISIT TO A MUSEUM

Our Forest Friends

A VISIT TO ARIZONA

MATERIALS:
Tissue paper, corrugated board, construction paper, pins.

COLORS:
White, dark blue, purple, dark tan, red, turquoise.

METHOD:
1. Line Board with white paper.
2. Cut sheets of shaded tissue paper or several different shades of tissue paper into wavy shapes, the larger ones for the upper display area, and the thinner ones for the lower section. (Two people are required to hold the tissue, while another cuts).
3. Pin tissue to Board as seen in illustration, leaving the top white space for the cutout construction paper caption letters to follow the contour of the wavy sky shape. The white space below the multicolored sky serves as a mat area for photographs and drawings related to the subject, while the bottom white space remains blank. (A strip of white paper immediately to the left of the display cuts the colored tissue rendition in a clean, straight line, while on the opposite side the tissue extends to the end of the Board, creating the feeling that viewers are moving on or travelling through Arizona).
4. From dark tan corrugated board cut the simple cactus plant and two branches, then pin to backdrop with branch at right behind main portion, and the one at left in front, for dimension.

NOTE:
The ribs of the corrugated board offer sharp contrast in texture to the flat treatment of the rest of the design. Colors in question were selected to represent the beautiful Arizona sky. Such an exhibit encourages a youngster to share with his fellow students the experience of a summer trip to another part of the United States, or perhaps to a foreign land, largely through photographs he has taken. The teacher might include the student cameraman's name in the presentation, thereby stimulating pride in his accomplishment and inspiring others to submit pictures of their own journeys and adventures. In this particular case the cactus, symbol of the desert, is immediately recognized, and the message quickly conveyed. Similar success may be achieved when featuring other areas, if typical symbols are employed.

MERRY CHRISTMAS

MATERIALS: Construction paper, wide wrapping ribbon, thick wool yarn, marking pen, pins.

COLORS: Black, white, magenta, orange, turquoise and olive green.

METHOD:
1. Line Board with black paper.
2. Pin large sheet of construction paper to Board, piecing as necessary to get the largest possible "box" in proportion to the backdrop.
3. Arrange gay ribbon bow and streamers with cut ends.
4. On the holiday tag cut from construction paper, write the message with marking pen.

NOTE:
Side by side, such oversized boxes on several bulletin boards offer an effective and festive display, with a minimum of time, money and labor. The choice of Christmas colors slightly off the beaten track—magenta, orange, turquoise and olive green—gives the impression of the traditional treatment of the season, yet creates more excitement. In fact, this simple Bulletin Board depends on its dynamic color arrangement for its appeal.

BUON NATALE, GLADELIG JUL, JOYEUX NOEL

MATERIALS: Construction paper, gold metallic wrapping paper, pins.

COLORS: White, black, gold, hot pink, orange, red-orange.

METHOD:
1. Line Board with white construction paper.
2. Draw and cut out three horns.
3. Place three sheets of black paper on display area, leaving white between and below the black papers.
4. Pin on the horns, and from each hang a banner of colored construction paper, as shown in illustration.
5. "Tie" banners on with crisscross strips of paper, picking up colors of Board's design.
6. Add stars made from paper (similar to crisscross strips, but larger) in-between black panels.
7. The caption letters are cut from black construction paper, and fastened below the black panels in the manner of fringe complementing the banners.

NOTE:
Discarded magazine pictures and drawings, or information about Christmas in other lands, may be pinned onto the banners. Related reading lists may also be used to decorate the banners, or appropriate designs done by students, illustrating Christmas observances in foreign countries.

ALTERNATE IDEAS:
The same type of display might herald the advent of a library story hour, with the banners bearing information indicating the time and place. Or the banners could yield information concerning ancient historic happenings.

HAPPY HOLIDAY!

MATERIALS:
Construction paper, wool yarn, magazine photographs, glue, glitter, pins.

COLORS:
Black, white, hot pink, orange, multicolor magazine photographs.

METHOD:
1. Line Board with black paper.
2. Cut circles of different sizes from pages of discarded magazines, using the gayest and brightest colored pages available. They need not be Christmas pictures. As shown here a chandelier, festive table settings turned sideways, flowers, jewels, fabric patterns, may be transformed into ornaments.
3. To some balls add decorative tops and ends.
4. From heavy wool yarn make bows and strings for hanging the balls, attaching with pins. After balls are in place add strings, then bows.
5. For an extra festive feature, put a little glue on some of the balls before they are attached to the Board, and sprinkle on glitter.

WAS YOUR BREAKFAST GOOD AND HEALTHY?

MATERIALS:
Construction paper, fabric, marking pens, chalk, magazine cutouts of food, pins.

COLORS:
Black, white, light and dark orange, brown, blue, yellow, green.

METHOD:
1. Line Board with white paper.
2. Leaving a wide border at top of display area and a narrow one at bottom, place a band of yellow construction paper, as seen in illustration.
3. Pin oversized cutouts from discarded magazines, or students' drawings of various breakfast foods as pictured: one whole, one-quarter orange; a slice of toast; an egg cup; bacon; milk in glass and pitcher; fabric place mat with place setting and finally, at extreme right, some gay daisies in a glass pitcher, all adding up to a bright, sunny, breakfast table.
4. The caption is done with marking pen in big, bold, casual lettering style, starting at the upper left margin and finishing at the lower right, to carry the eye from one end of the Board to the other.
5. Add a tag on the flowers reading, Don't Eat the Daisies.

NOTE:
The entire Board suggests healthful nutrition in a light, appealing manner, which is a good way to introduce this important subject.

SOME BLACK AMERICANS–

HOW MANY DO YOU KNOW?

MATERIALS:
Construction paper, cardboard, photographs, striped wrapping paper, students' written information, pins.

COLORS:
Black, white, red, blue, khaki, gray.

METHOD:
1. Line Board with white paper so that its edges may serve as a border for the entire design.
2. On the left side of the display area pin a sheet of gray construction paper, and a larger sheet of khaki cardboard on the right (the front of a tan carton may be used for the latter purpose, if desired), pinned away from the backdrop to give dimension.
3. Cut and attach a large construction paper silhouette as shown, to represent Black Americans, and to set the tone for the Board.
4. Place rectangles of striped wrapping paper behind the silhouette on the gray area, and in front, on the khaki area.
5. A strip of white construction paper with marking pen lettering is pinned to the gray paper, lined up with the khaki side of the Board. The caption continues above the striped paper on the khaki side, in the same way, only reduced in size.
6. Students' written work, photographs and music associated with achieving Blacks, are featured in the display, some on mats, and others placed directly on the background, as illustrated. Add stars cut from construction paper and some blank sheets of construction paper the same size as the pictorial items, for color coordination.

NOTE:
As more Blacks are studied and discussed, students may change the photographs. This is a quick and easy format to use for numerous topics, with proper substitution of pictorial material, patterned paper, decorations and captions.

SOME BLACK AMERICAN AUTHORS

MATERIALS:
Books cut from an advertisement, construction paper, wrapping paper, cardboard, cellophane, photographs (or drawings) of authors, commercial letters, pins, glue.

COLORS:
Black, white, red, yellow, blue.

METHOD:
1. Line Board with white paper.
2. The caption, composed of black commercial letters or cutout construction paper letters, is glued to a strip of white cardboard and pinned toward bottom of Board to represent a shelf.
3. On the "shelf" place a group of books cut from a large advertisement. Cover the spines with strips of construction or wrapping paper. To book spines add names and photographs (or drawings) of authors being discussed.
4. Add a pair of cutout black paper bookends (silhouettes) and ink bottle with red paper quill pen seen at right. (The pen symbolizes the writing instrument.)

NOTE:
A table of correlative library books would be a valuable addition to the display.

DO YOU BRUSH AFTER EVERY MEAL?

MATERIALS:
Patterned wallpaper, construction paper, marking pen, glue, pins.

COLORS:
Light and dark brown, yellow, red-orange, turquoise, black, white.

METHOD:
1. Line Board with small-figured wallpaper.
2. Cut two large construction paper mugs, trimming off just enough from the sides of the paper sheets to form the shapes, and pin mugs to Board.
3. Add cutout handles, eyes and a big, bright smile to each mug; also, pin an oversized paper toothpaste tube to one, and an oversized toothbrush to the other.
4. The caption lettering is done with marking pen on white paper rectangles, which are glued to mats of construction paper cut comic-strip balloon fashion, to indicate conversation between the bathroom mugs.

NOTE:
Depending on space available, many pairs of mugs might be employed to stress other aspects of dental care, with one mug asking the question, and the other providing the answer.

PAINT WITH STRING

MATERIALS:
Lightweight cardboard, string, paint, glue.

COLORS:
Black, gray, red.

METHOD:
1. Glue cutout red cardboard or commercial letters to right side of lightweight sheet of gray cardboard.
2. Punch holes here and there through the cardboard, and run string over and around the letters, to look as if they had been tied together.
3. Cut away excess cardboard, leaving only the portion bearing the letters.
4. Use this as the caption for a display of students' art work done with string dipped into paint to form designs. (Here the sign is pinned to a Bulletin Board lined with gray paper, on which two black panels bearing children's string paintings are mounted).

NOTE:
This idea derives from a magazine, with the caption changed to suit the current need. Alert, perceptive teachers and librarians may frequently adapt magazine presentations to their own purposes.

LET'S NOT LITTER

MATERIALS:
One-half of plastic waste basket, assorted pieces of colorful trash, satin gift-wrap ribbons, mat knife, large and small pins, needlenose pliers.

COLORS:
White, turquoise, green, purple, orange, pink, black.

METHOD:
1. Line Board with white paper.
2. Cut plastic waste basket in half with mat knife.
3. Pin above to Bulletin Board with large pins, using needlenose pliers.
4. Fill the basket with colorful trash (printed paper napkins, tissue paper, shiny ribbons, cutout flowers, straws, empty milk carton, paper bags, brightly decorated paper cups).
5. Draw ribbons from basket and form the caption with them, after lightly writing in message first with pencil, then following pencil lines with ribbons and pinning into place with small pins.
6. Add extra pieces of trash to background and a message tied to the basket about the importance of depositing trash in proper receptacles.

THE GREAT OUTDOORS

MATERIALS:
Construction paper, green marking pens, pins.

COLORS:
White, brown, green, yellow-green, tan, pink, orange, golden yellow, purple, dark blue.

METHOD:
1. Line Board with white paper.
2. Help students place vari-sized nature cutouts and drawings together, mural fashion, on a big Bulletin Board, with the large items in the foreground and smaller ones in the background, to indicate depth.
3. After students have pinned on all pieces, unite the mural with marking-pen lines (hit and miss, in several areas) of various greens to give the illusion of land going from one side to the other.
4. Add orange paper sun at top, and caption letters done with marking pen, following contour of the design.

NOTE:
This is a workable mural for all grades. When older children are involved, their art work, understandably, will be more sophisticated.

6TH GRADE EXHIBITION

MATERIALS:
Construction paper, cardboard, marking pen, students' art work.

COLORS:
Black, white, varied colors of children's art work.

METHOD:
1. Line Board with white paper.
2. Cut out A shapes as seen in illustration, adding extra crossbars to form artists' easels.
3. Place a neatly lettered cardboard sign with caption on first easel, simulating announcement of an exhibition.
4. Place students' paintings on other easels, lined up slightly to the right, but higher than the first easel, as if they were behind it. Add student's nameplate with each painting, as would be done in a museum or gallery.

NOTE:
Use as many easels as available space can accommodate. If space is limited, use three easels as shown, and change paintings often.

ALTERNATE IDEA:
Prints of famous paintings may be arranged in this manner, to acquaint students with fine art. The easels might remain through the school year, with the pictures changing frequently. A display such as this would also make an appropriate backdrop for a library display of books devoted to great painters, or books setting forth painting techniques.

IT'S FALL AGAIN

MATERIALS:
Construction paper, magazine pictures, lightweight cardboard, glue.

COLORS:
Brown, black, white, various fall shades.

METHOD:
1. Line the Board with brown paper.
2. Using the pattern of a stylized leaf, cut from construction paper or lightweight cardboard an oversized leaf big enough to occupy most of the display area.
3. Glue onto leaf shape a collage of colorful autumn scenes collected by the students from discarded magazines, extending them beyond the leaf edges.
4. Turn over and cut away excess portions of pictures, following the shape of the leaf.
5. Caption (and any other information desired) is superimposed on collage, in black on white, so that the message may be read at a glance, despite the bright background colors.

NOTES:
Students will enjoy doing large leaves. If many are turned out and arranged around the room, they will add a cheerful, decorative touch to the classroom during some of autumn's dull days. Substituting bright green and other spring colors, along with a spring theme, post-winter displays may be handled in the same way.

NIGHT..
..AND
DAY..
NIGHT..AND..DAY...

MATERIALS:
Construction paper, blue cellophane, marking pen, commercial letters, pins.

COLORS:
White, blue, dark green, light green, brown, yellow, orange, black.

METHOD:
1. Line Board with white paper.
2. Using the worker's own arm and hand as a guide, from brown paper cut four free-form tree shapes, to comprise a repeat pattern, as shown.
3. From green paper cut free-form foliage for each tree.
4. Divide the display area into four panels, placing tree trunk and foliage on each.
5. Following the illustration, decorate each panel with duplicate small cat and flower shapes cut from construction paper. (To expedite matters, all similar shapes are cut at the same time. Also, cut two suns for day-time renditions, and two quarter-moons for their evening counterparts.)
6. Cover the two night panels with blue cellophane, for sharp contrast with the daytime panels.
7. Pin on the caption letters, with small green separation circles in-between the words, indicating the never-ending sequence of time.
8. Add to the white panels a student's original poem devoted to the theme, lettered neatly on white paper.

NOTE:
Repeat as many night and day panels as the classroom space permits. It is a good way to impress upon the students the essential truth of time, and at the same time is appealingly decorative. Observe the stratagem of having the cat awake by day, and asleep by night —which may amuse onlookers.

BIRTHDAY CAKE

MATERIALS:
Three graduated boxes without lids, masking tape, upholstery tacks, crepe paper, magazine pictures of icing on cakes, short pencils, construction paper, glue, glitter (if desired), pins, paper doilies.

COLORS:
All pastels.

METHOD:
1. Stack graduated boxes (open-ended at bottom), tape together with masking tape to form solid structure.
2. Cover with pastel crepe paper, secure with pins. Glue onto boxes the cutouts of icing (as many different pictures as can be obtained). Some of the crepe paper may show.
3. Glue doilies around bottom of the cake.
4. Poke as many holes as there are to be "candles" in top box.
5. Dip pencil bottoms into glue and place in holes.
6. Cut appropriate color paper for "flames" and glue to each pencil point.
7. If preferred, the cake may be sprayed with glue, and a sprinkling of glitter added.

NOTE:
Parents often bring cupcakes to school to celebrate a child's birthday. This stacked box idea provides a good cake cover to protect the sweets until party time. Gay horns, blowers, hats or ribbons arranged around the cake, add a festive air. If it is not to serve as a cover, the paper cake can be pinned to the Bulletin Board with upholstery tacks. Use as many tacks as are necessary to fasten the cake properly. Obviously, a large cake would require more tacks than a smaller one.

LET'S BE PROUD OF OUR HOMES

MATERIALS:
Chalk, construction paper, marking pen, wool yarn, print fabric, glue, pins.

COLORS:
Pink, orange, white, purple, yellow, black, magenta, khaki.

METHOD:
1. Line Board with deep pink paper.
2. Draw chalk lines to indicate brick pattern.
3. Frame the window by using side of the white chalk to make wide lines.
4. Cover lower window area with a large sheet of dark construction paper to simulate interior of home.
5. Use bright color construction paper for window shade.
6. Pin a window box on sill and glue on flowers cut from print fabrics.
7. The caption is lettered on the shade. (Or cutout letters may be glued on.)
8. Glue fabric flowers to left center of caption and just below the last word.
9. Draw broken line with marking pen across bottom of shade, to represent stitching, and add a pull make of wool yarn.

NOTE:
A line of such windows arranged on a large Bulletin Board, with different messages lettered on the shades, is a bright and attractive way to communicate with a class about urban renewal projects, and to create a feeling of pride in one's own home or neighborhood.

CAN YOU SORT THESE?

MATERIALS:
Construction paper, cardboard, chalk, pins.

COLORS:
Black, white, apple green, orange, golden yellow.

METHOD:
1. Line Board with black paper. (This display is done in two parts, to be used together or separately, as needed).
2. Cut caption letters and marionette figure from white construction paper and pin onto left side, as shown. The puppet strings are drawn with white chalk.
3. The right side features numerals cut from black construction paper and glued to pieces of brightly-colored cardboard, arranged by students in various number patterns.

NOTES:
Both sections may be used for youngsters in the lower grades, to add a fun element to a math lesson. The right-hand portion, with its bright and decorative number arrangement, would project the same lighthearted appeal to somewhat older groups. In the latter case, the caption letters may be borrowed from the marionette panel, and attached to a black strip that would fit over the numbers.

A whole series of numbers and alphabet letters cut from gay cardboard could be saved, and used again and again. Requiring little or no additional illustration, they are decorative enough to stand alone in the implementation of favorable design.

PEACE＊PEACE＊PEACE

JOY＊JOY＊JOY

PEACE ON EARTH

MATERIALS:
White lace paper doilies, construction paper, gold foil paper, ribbon, marking pens, pins.

COLORS:
Black, white, gold, magenta, turquoise.

METHOD:
1. Line classroom Bulletin Board with black paper.
2. Use pattern contained in this book to cut out as many angels as needed to form a repetitive design around the room.
3. Rearrange arms and legs to simulate flying position, dress in cutout paper doilies and pin to backdrop.
4. Letter caption on strips of white construction paper.
5. Using gold paper for "lining," place the strips ribbon fashion, with cut ends, as if they constituted a flying pennant (see illustration).
6. Add a doily halo and magenta ribbon stick to each unit.
7. Decorate pennant, stockings and top of stick with turquoise stars (drawn with marking pen).
8. Add an appealing, wide-eyed expression on face, and a wisp of magenta hair (with marking pens).

NOTE:
The repeat pattern of the design, its simplicity and message, make this Bulletin Board fun to do. The angel's white doily dress and bright colors against the black background help convey the crisp feeling of the season.

ALTERNATE IDEA:
The angel pictured, if alternated around the room with the horn and banner on illustration, A PROGRAM OF CHRISTMAS MUSIC, would also comprise a striking group display. The caption could be changed, if desired, as indicated, or eliminated.

MERRY CHRISTMAS, HAPPY CHANUKAH

MATERIALS:
Construction paper, marking pens, string, pins.

COLORS:
Black, white, yellow, blue, orange, green.

METHOD:
1. Line Board with black paper.
2. Pin on boxes (full sheets of construction paper) one above the other, the bottom one a little below center, the other edged slightly toward the left.
3. To fashion construction paper ribbons, cut construction paper circle, then trim off outer edges and tie into bows. The circular strips will twist and coil with little or no effort on the worker's part, making festive decorations.
4. Add tags with gay marking-pen borders in colors appropriate to each holiday (strings pulled through holes of tags)—gold, white, blue and green for the Christmas package, and orange, white and blue for the Chanukah package. Blue is the coordinating color for both.

HOLIDAY FUN

MATERIALS:
Construction paper, lightweight white paper, raw cotton, pins, glue.

COLORS:
Gray, brown, white, blue, orange, red, green.

METHOD:
1. Line Board with gray paper.
2. Cover lower half with lightweight white paper and allow to ripple, for snowy effect.
3. Draw, cut out and pin on the two houses, side by side, and two trees.
4. Place a picture window on each house, one decorated for Christmas, the other for Chanukah.
5. First draw, then cut caption letters from construction paper. The word FUN predominates, with raw cotton glued to the face of each letter, representing snow.
6. Add raw cotton snowflakes on gray sky—to give cold, outdoor look, while houses appear cozy and warm.

NOTE:
Here the traditional colors are used for each holiday—red and green for Christmas, and blue and orange for the Chanukah lights. The message of the display is readily apparent—that basically people are much the same, even though their customs and cultures may differ.

HAVE A HAPPY NEW YEAR

MATERIAL:
Colored paper, black paper, colored confetti, narrow, gay holiday ribbons, pins, glue.

COLORS:
Red, golden yellow, dark blue, light blue, red-orange, magenta, green, black, white.

METHOD:
1. Line Board with white paper.
2. Use black construction paper to make each letter as large and bold as display space allows.
3. Cut brightly colored paper to fit into open areas of letters.
4. Place the letters word by word, evenly aligned on the left, and filling up most of the display area.
5. Pin on holiday ribbons and confetti at lower right.

NOTE:
This is a striking example of how a Bulletin Board may be adapted from a magazine. For the minimum time invested in its preparation, one achieves maximum effect, due to the arresting colors and oversized letters.

HOLIDAY COOKERY

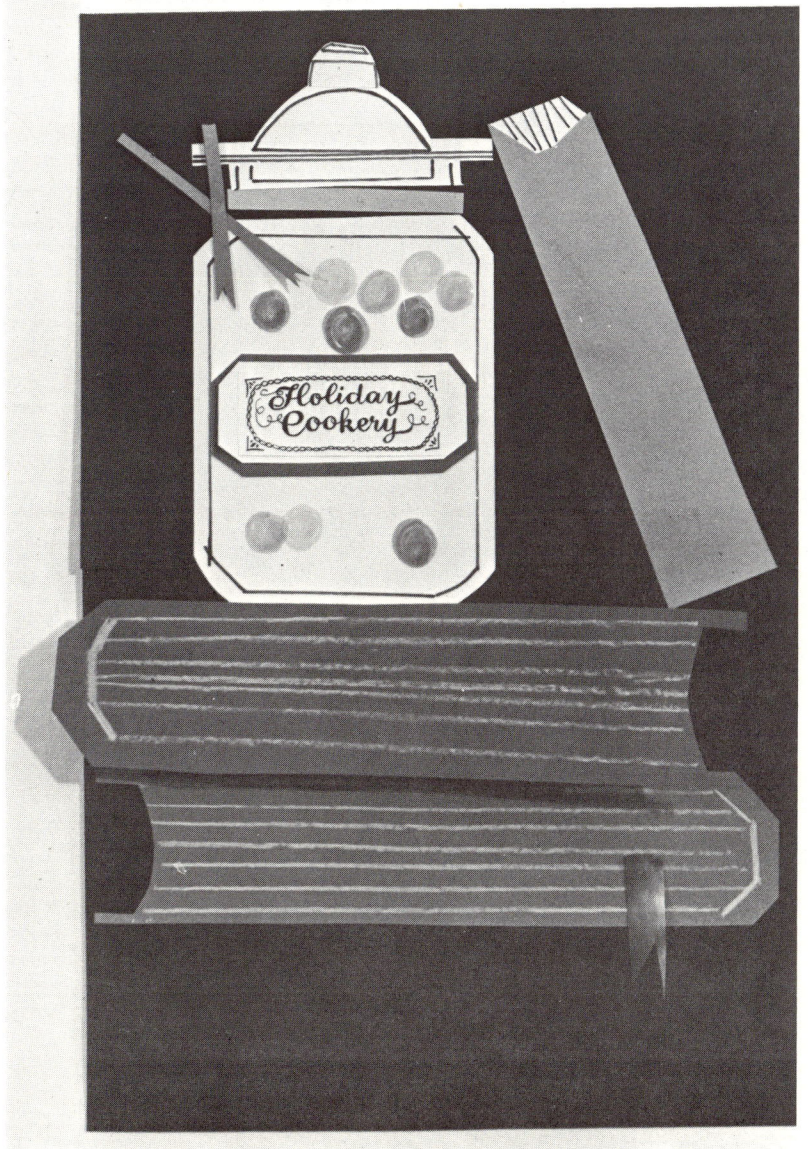

MATERIALS:
Construction paper, colored tissue paper, ribbon, marking pen, chalk, pins.

COLORS:
Black, white, orange, blue, green, yellow-green, yellow, purple.

METHOD:
1. Line Board with black paper.
2. Cut a large apothecary jar shape (see pattern section) from white paper and add small circles of colored tissue paper to simulate candy.
3. With marking pen draw black lines near edges of jar and lid to indicate thickness of glass.
4. Cut two books from construction paper and attach them to lower section of the Board, the bottom fore edge up against the backdrop, and the one above it pinned away from the background for dimension. (See books in pattern section.)
5. Affix the apothecary jar as if it were resting on the upper book's front cover, and lean another construction paper book against the jar lid, its spine showing. This book's page lines are drawn with marking pen on white paper and inserted behind the spine, the top of which is cut into a form of V shape, to indicate depth. Page lines on the books below the jar are done with white chalk.
6. Add narrow ribbon around neck of jar, and bookmark to bottom book; also, label on jar's center front, bearing the caption handwritten with marking pen. The display unit conveys a festive holiday mood.

NOTE:
This type of exhibit is recommended for library use with cookbooks. A school library might adapt the idea at holiday time, showing cookbooks for children.

ALTERNATE TITLE:
  HOLIDAY TREATS.

HAPPY VALENTINE'S DAY

MATERIALS:
Construction paper, round white paper doilies, ribbon, raw cotton, pencil, pastry bag, paper plates, thick poster paint and brush, crepe paper, glue, pins.

COLORS:
Pink, dark brown, white, yellow-orange, magenta.

METHOD:
1. Line Board with white paper.
2. Cover bottom half with pastel crepe paper, to simulate a party table.
3. Based on pattern in this book, cut an apothecary jar.
4. Next cut a footed cake plate from construction paper and doilies, similar to that shown here.
5. Wide bands of dark brown construction paper form the cake's chocolate sides, while two pieces of white construction paper cut at an angle form the inner cake wedge space.
6. To make the frothy party icing, pull and swirl raw cotton, then cover the cake top with it.
7. Pin cake on footed dish, and add a decorative heart glued to a pencil which projects from the icing.
8. Fasten small cutout hearts in bright colors to icing and cutout cake area, as well as to the apothecary jar (the latter simulating candy gumdrops).
9. Attach gay narrow party ribbons to both the jar and footed dish.
10. Pin a triangular piece of white paper and a small brown piece, to represent the cake wedge, on a paper plate decorated with a doily. Add icing, and a cutout or plastic fork to plate.
11. Cut out a hand from brown paper, and lace doily cuff, as seen in upper right. Put a real pastry bag in the hand, pinning to backdrop with fingers in position illustrated, to provide a touch of realism.
12. The caption (after being lightly pencilled in) is done with a wide brush dipped into thick, rich brown paint, in the manner of icing. (To be sure the paint does not run over the Board, the caption might first be executed on construction paper laid on a flat surface).

NOTE:
This idea derives from a gumdrop cake recipe. If the teacher chooses, she may obtain such a recipe, mimeograph copies (unless prohibited by copyright), then have students fold them into heart-shaped doilies to take home as gifts for their mothers on Valentine's Day.

WITCH

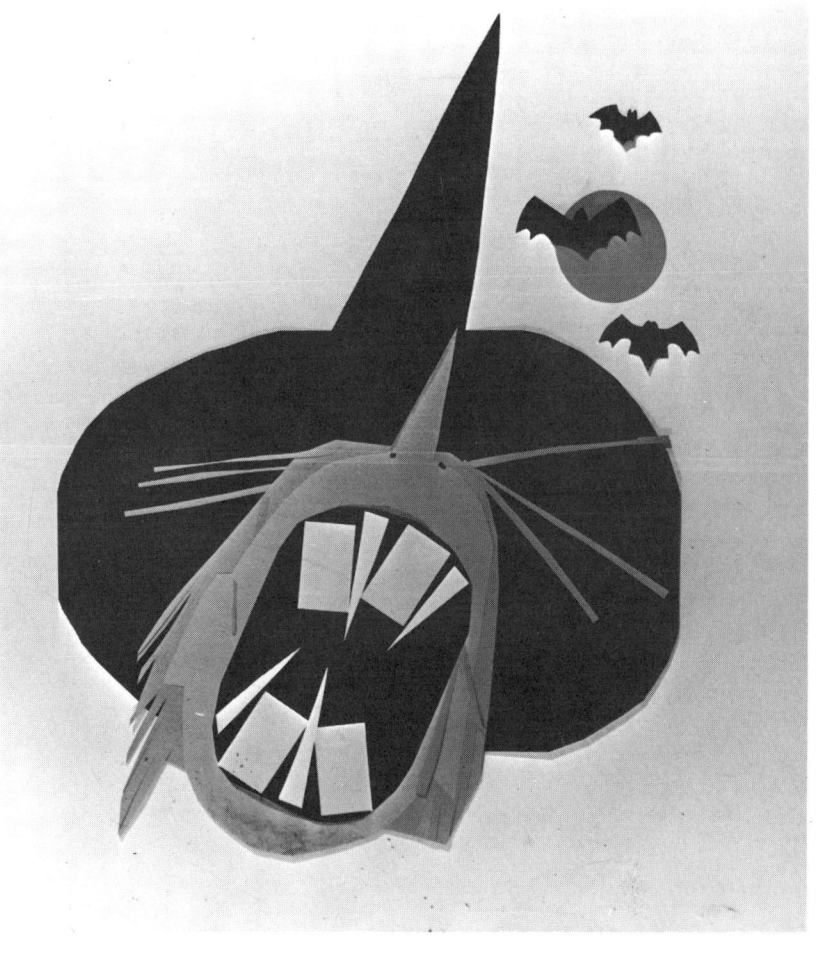

MATERIALS:
Construction paper, students' work, pins.

COLORS:
Black, white, orange, pink, gray.

METHOD:
1. Cut a wide, black vertical oval for witch's open mouth large enough to accommodate a selection of students' written papers.
2. Cut a larger gray oval for witch's face, adding a pointed nose.
3. Cut an orange oval to represent the hair, fringing irregularly, and adding stray "hairs," as shown.
4. Cut a large black horizontal oval for the hat, adding the center point bigger, but same shape as the nose.
5. Starting with the hat, lay one oval over the other—black, orange, gray, ending with the open mouth.
6. Add some pointed white paper teeth, tiny black paper eyes, and students' poems or stories about Halloween.
7. Pin a small pink moon and some miniature cutout bats to background, to create feeling of distance and further the Halloween idea.

NOTE:
The students might like to create their individual witches. These may then be displayed around the room, providing exhibition space for numerous stories and poems. Should only one witch be used, change the papers often. Like some others adapted to school and library purposes, this design stems from a magazine advertisement.

HEARTS AND FLOWERS

MATERIALS:
Square white paper doilies, cellophane, red wrapping paper, construction paper, pins.

COLORS:
White, red, orange, purple, pink, light and dark tan, yellow-green, dark green, olive green, khaki.

METHOD:
1. Line Board with white paper.
2. Extend an arm horizontally left to right across the Board, almost to the end, about one-third from bottom. To fashion the arm as shown, use: red wrapping paper for the forearm; light and dark tan construction paper for hand, so that it will appear to have the fingers bent in holding position; square paper doily cut to resemble sleeve cuff. All are pinned on.
3. Cut heart-shaped flowers and their petals from construction paper, wrapping paper, and doilies, with cellophane hearts superimposed on the latter. Fasten to backdrop.
4. Attach stems of construction paper to flowers and insert behind hand.
5. The bunch of flowers is tied together with a strip of wrapping paper clipped at ends to resemble ribbon. The ribbon is pinned at stems and tips, the remainder left to ripple free, catching the light and adding dimension.
6. Caption lettering is done in stylized script across top of Board, parallel with position of the arm. Its khaki color blends with the green and yellow-green of stems and flowers.
7. Add a decorative heart bracelet to wrist, picking up both design and color.

NOTE:
Save this arm for repeated use later on. The hand could hold different items for other display ideas: flags for United Nations Week, or Flag Week; cutouts of brooms, mops, paint brushes and flowers suggesting helping mother about the house, or for CLEAN UP, PAINT UP WEEK.

MR. TURKEY

MATERIALS:
Construction paper, marking pens, poster paint and brush, patterned wrapping paper, pins.

COLORS:
Yellow, green, yellow-green, brown, dark red, orange, black.

METHOD:
1. Line Board with yellow paper.
2. Cover the entire background with oversized chicken wire design, using green and black marking pens.
3. To make the turkey cut a large circle of suitable patterned wrapping paper (based on pattern in this book) or construction paper decorated with a stylized feather design repeated all around the circle with marking pens in shades of green, dark red, yellow-green and orange.
4. For neck of the turkey cut a triangular shape (in proportion to the circle body) of construction paper decorated with horizontal stripes of dark red and orange (using marking pens) from top of triangle to feathered areas, as seen in photograph.
5. Add feathers at bottom of neck area and a small circle for the head, as shown.
6. Make the construction paper tail, with its stylized feathers. Add a smaller shape of same design for wing, as illustrated.
7. Pin tail, body, head and neck sections away from backdrop, for dimension, and tuck wing under neck section.
8. Add a round eye, bill, and dark red caruncle.
9. MR. TURKEY, done in dark red poster paint over the chicken wire, follows the curve of the fowl's component parts. If preferred, the caption letters may be cut from the dark red construction paper, then pinned on.

NOTE:
Several of each of the three basic shapes comprising this turkey could be cut, and a group of the birds clustered together on the Bulletin Board, or lined up in a row against the chicken wire, to simulate a turkey farm.

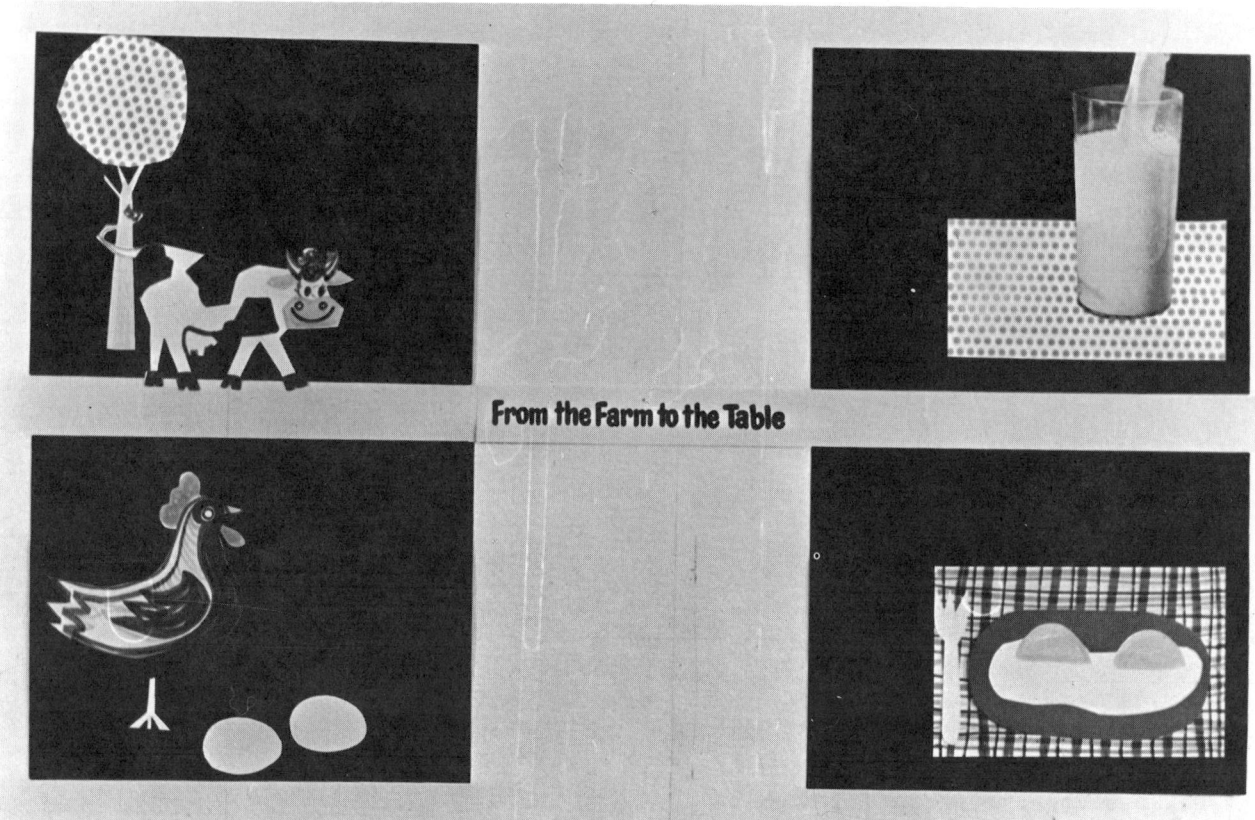

FROM THE FARM TO THE TABLE

MATERIALS:
Construction paper, discarded magazines, lightweight cardboard, patterned wrapping paper, marking pens, pins.

COLORS:
White, black, brown, multicolor magazine pictures.

METHOD:
1. Line Board with white paper, or, if the condition of the Board permits, leave as it is.
2. Place large sheets of black construction paper at right and left, as shown, to serve as backdrops for the pictorial art.
3. From discarded magazines remove pictures of farm life representations, pointing up topics in the study plan.
4. Glue these onto thin cardboard and cut out.
5. Cut out and affix patterned paper rectangles, and tree with its brown construction paper trunk.
6. Mount farm representations away from background, for dimension.
7. With marking pen, in script letters, place the caption on a strip of white construction paper and pin onto the center, linking the two sides of the Bulletin Board into one cohesive unit.

GOOD FOOD BUILDS STRONG BODIES

MATERIALS:
Construction paper, magazine cutouts, fabric, string, marking pen, pins.

COLORS:
Black, white, orange, green, multicolor magazine photographs.

METHOD:
1. Line Board with black paper.
2. Pin on sheets of white construction paper, one next to the other, to form this figure, to stand at an angle, as shown in accompanying illustration. The head is a complete circle, placed on a square sheet of construction paper, for the neck. The lifted left arm is a construction paper rectangle with corner trimmed off to form the hand. The same is true of the right arm (and hand), in down position.
3. Add two small paper triangles for thumbs, and pin away from backdrop, to hold items.
4. Pin on shoes, made by cutting paper triangles and placing one point under trouser bottoms, then snipping out small wedges from shoe bottoms to separate heels and soles.
5. Use the figure for mounting appropriate magazine pictures brought to class by students. The caption letters, cut from construction paper, fit into the body design, as do the food pictures, relating to the message quickly and easily.
6. Add a few marking pen lines to indicate hair and ear, as well as cutout paper for closed eyelids and happy, open mouth.
7. A construction paper cutout of a fork is inserted under the thumb of extended hand. From the fork to the mouth attach a thin strip of construction paper to represent food being eaten.
8. The right hand holds a fish on a string (a food page from a magazine cut into fish shape).
9. Add shoelaces of string and a fabric checked napkin around the figure's neck.
10. The circles of construction paper with black marking pen lines around them are decorative notes to make the body seem full of illustrations. If desired, food pictures may be substituted.

NOTE:
This idea was sparked by a television commercial. Some teachers may want to start out with an undecorated figure, and fill in good food representations as they are studied by students in the classroom. A series of such figures around the room, stressing healthful foods, would be striking and colorful, fun to do and see.

THE 7 BASIC FOODS

MATERIALS:
Construction paper, students' food drawings or cutouts from discarded magazines, chalk, marking pen, glue, pins.

COLORS:
Purple, gray, lavender, deep pink, brown, maroon, light blue, blue-green.

METHOD:
1. Line Board with white paper.
2. Pin on nine sheets of colored construction paper equidistant from each other, three to a row, and separated only by narrow white backdrop border.
3. With chalk and marking pen, students may draw onto seven of the sheets representations of the seven basic foods (or the food items could be cut from old magazines and glued to the construction paper).
4. Cut a figure 7 from light blue construction paper, the full height of the sheet, and pin onto the purple rectangle at lower left. The 7 is preceded by the article, The, lettered with marking pen on a short white strip of paper, and followed in the next block of color (deep pink) by the words, BASIC FOODS, on a longer strip.

NOTE:
This Board could be linked to a nearby table showing the actual seven basic food groups. (If fewer than seven basic food groups are featured, the number of display blocks will be reduced accordingly, and the corresponding numeral substituted.)

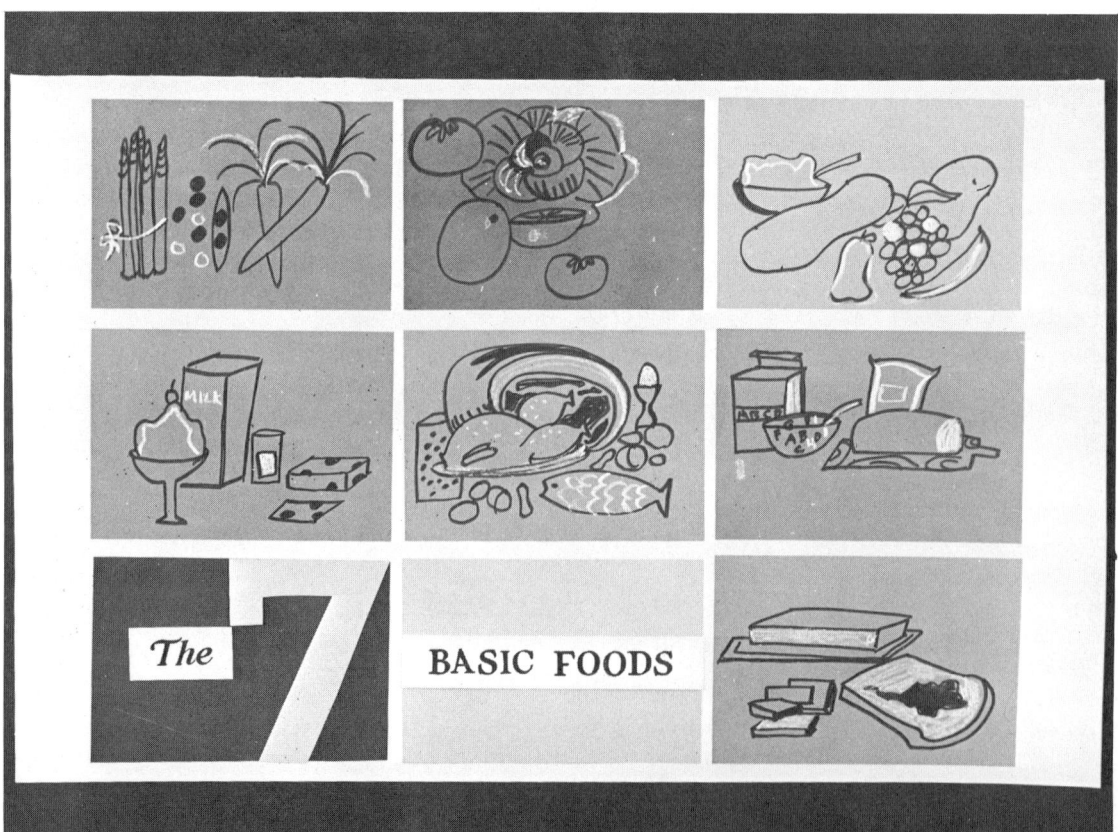

WE VISIT A DAIRY FARM

MATERIALS:
Fabric, lightweight cardboard, construction paper (heavy), pins.

COLORS:
Black, white, blue, tan, yellow.

METHOD:
1. Line the Board with a black-and-white checked fabric (or black and white squares of construction paper will give the same effect).
2. Pin on large cardboard or heavy construction paper cutouts of the various dairy products studied, done by pupils. (Shown here are just a few examples, but any number of items could be used. Representations should be changed as often as necessary, to indicate the variety of products included in the unit of study).
3. The cutout letters are bold, with those on the sun denoting freshness.
4. The simple decorations on the containers for the dairy products suggest a set of dishes, and give unity to the design.

NOTE:
The check pattern to many is reminiscent of country and farm life, setting the mood at a glance. The oversized quality of the products attracts immediate attention.

CAN YOU SOLVE THESE MEASURING PROBLEMS?

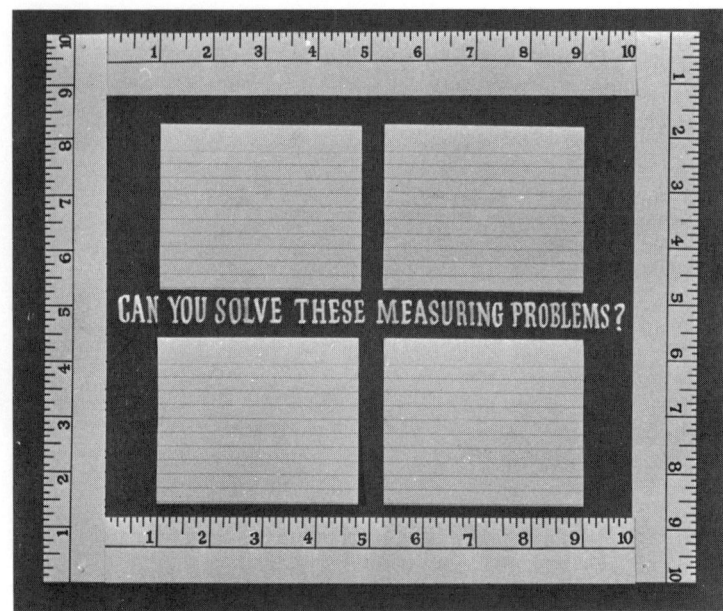

MATERIALS:
Construction paper, lined paper, marking pens, pins.

COLORS:
Black, white, red, blue.

METHOD:
1. Line Board with blue construction paper.
2. With strips of white construction paper and marking pen, prepare oversized replicas of rulers and pin onto backdrop in picture frame fashion.
3. Using the paper rulers as a border design, place written problems on Board as seen in illustration, and a center line of white paper cutout caption letters.

ALTERNATE SUGGESTION:
When students have completed the assignment in question, replace the problems with the students' correct solutions, done in class as a form of written work.

ROMAN NUMERALS

MATERIALS:
Construction paper, strip of wood, poster paint, staples, curtain hooks, glue, pins.

COLORS:
Black, gray.

METHOD:
1. Cut a sheet of gray construction paper to represent a Roman wall hanging, and staple onto stick which has been painted black.
2. The Roman numerals and corresponding date are cut from black paper and glued onto gray paper in any way suitable for the lesson.
3. Hang the panel from curtain hooks, attaching the display to whatever backdrop is conveniently available.

NOTE:
This exhibit, because of its simplicity, is easy to prepare and creates a favorable class atmosphere for discussing Roman numerals. The banner idea will come in handy at other times, too, especially where conventional Bulletin Board space is lacking.

ENJOY NUMBERS: THEY GROW ON YOU

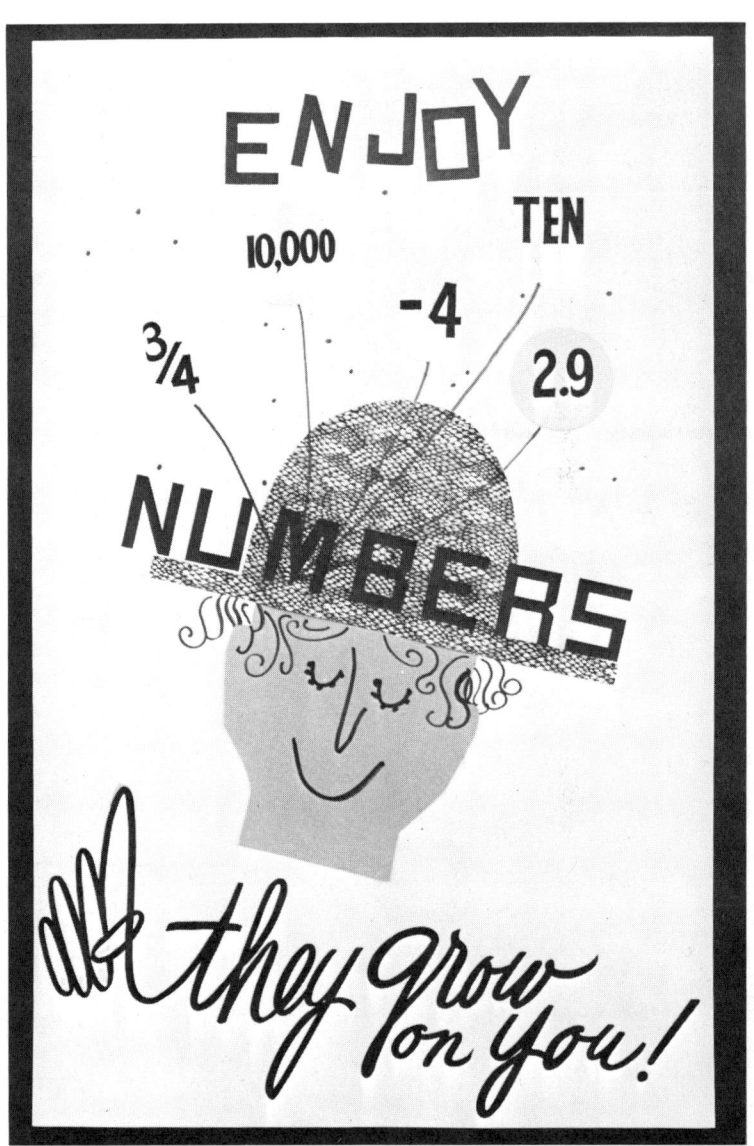

MATERIALS:
Construction paper, marking pens, wrapping paper, glue or pins.

COLORS:
White, light blue, navy blue, yellow, orange, brown, black, multicolor wrapping paper.

METHOD:
1. Line Board with white paper.
2. Using largest piece of construction paper the Board will accommodate, cut oversize head and neck shape, and pin or glue to backdrop.
3. With marking pens decorate with amusing facial expression and hair, as shown in illustration.
4. Cut hat with brim from patterned wrapping paper and fasten above hair.
5. At varying points above hat place construction paper circles bearing types of numbers to be studied (fractions, whole numbers, decimals, etc.) and around each draw a scalloped larger circle with marking pen, to simulate flower petals. Then draw stem lines converging to a point on hat brim at left.
6. Upper caption letters are cut from construction paper and bottom caption letters are done in oversized script style, with marking pen. ENJOY runs across top, while NUMBERS appears on hat brim. The initial letter near bottom edge is attached to first finger of the hand near lower left corner, adding to the humorous quality, treating the subject of numbers as fun.

BALANCE THIS SCALE

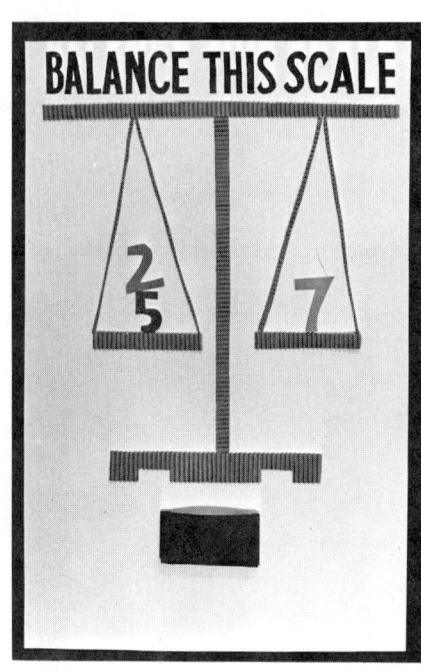

MATERIALS:
Corrugated board, cardboard, construction paper, pins.

COLORS:
Brown, white, red, blue.

METHOD:
1. Line Board with white paper.
2. Cut corrugated board into the shape of a scale, using narrow and wider strips, and pin onto Board, as seen in photograph.
3. Make a cardboard pocket to hold construction paper cutout numbers in bright colors, and attach under scale.
4. Have students arrange numbers as they are discussed during the lesson, using both units of the scale to achieve proper value balance.

NATURE NOTES

MATERIALS:
Construction paper, marking pens.

COLORS:
Green, brown, white, yellow, orange, pink, black, light blue, red.

METHOD:
1. After checking an actual clip board, make an oversized replica by cutting brown construction paper into clip shape and ring handle, then drawing lines near outer edges of both, to lend touches of realism.
2. Pin the clip to a base deriving from a full sheet of green construction paper, on which the corners have been rounded.
3. Cut a smaller piece of white "notebook" paper, and round its edges.
4. Looking at an actual piece of notebook paper, with a light blue thin marking pen and ruler draw lines across the "page." Then draw a vertical red line down the left side of the paper, and black circles to represent the marginal holes.
5. Attach display notes, photographs, informational papers to the clip board.
6. Add caption. In this case Nature Notes was lettered over a decorative tissue paper flower done in art class. Augmenting the flavor of the theme is the construction paper butterfly perched on the ring holder.

NOTE:
This is a competent device for year-round communication. Teachers moving from room to room may wish to use a sturdy cardboard base instead of the construction paper.

WE USE OUR LIBRARY

MATERIALS:
Construction paper, marking pen, pins.

COLORS:
White, blue, black.

METHOD:
1. Line Board with white paper.
2. Using a large sheet of construction paper, write and cut out the word, "We," to occupy the upper half. Pin to Board.
3. Draw and cut out the book cover, open flat.
4. Use a marking pen for lines indicating pages.
5. Draw and cut caption letters, and affix to area below book.
6. Fill in faces of W with marking pen.

NOTE:
Since the appeal of this design depends largely on the effectiveness of the caption letters, a student with a talent for calligraphy would do well with the assignment.

DO YOU KNOW THESE FAMOUS PEOPLE?

MATERIALS:
Construction paper, photographs, pins.

COLORS:
White, black, red.

METHOD:
1. Line Board with white paper.
2. Pin photographs of famous people in a line, with construction paper mats to set them off and produce a simple, striking design. Each picture is mounted on red paper, allowing only a thin edge of red to show. Then all are mounted on a sheet of black construction paper, trimming away until only a narrow border is seen at the sides to link the photographs together.
3. The caption is done on white paper with black marking pen. To add a decorative note to an otherwise plain presentation, a large construction paper question mark is pinned onto the right margin, next to the caption.

ALTERNATE SUGGESTION:
Trim off the corners of the pictures, place in the same format seen in illustration, and use as a filmstrip idea (adaptable to any subject, with suitable caption change). Libraries could display pictures bearing on books made into motion pictures, with the heading, WE SAW IT AT THE MOVIES or, FROM BOOKS TO FILMS. Of course, in this case an oversize exclamation point would supplant the question mark.

REACH THE SKI LODGE

MATERIALS:
Construction paper, photograph of a ski lodge, marking pen, chalk, pins.

COLORS:
Dark blue, deep pink, white.

METHOD:
1. Line Board with blue paper.
2. Cut a sheet of white construction paper into a jagged mountain shape and place on the left side of Board to form a snowy setting for a mountain ski lodge.
3. Beyond ski lodge roof add some pine trees done with marking pen lines, and at bottom of the panel pin on a blue construction paper rectangle suggesting a winter reading list.
4. Cut additional sheets of white construction paper into mountain peaks extending downward from the ski lodge at left to lower right section.
5. Place three miniature skiing figures on peaks as if they were going up the mountain to achieve their goal of reaching the ski lodge.
6. The caption, lettered on the blue sky in white chalk, completes the design.

NOTE:
The incentive for reaching any goal could be treated in the same way. Libraries might adapt this idea for a reading game, with the mountain peaks representing certain reading plateaus or titles. It might also be applicable to certain phases of PTA activities or fund collections.

HOW TO GIVE A PARTY

MATERIALS:
Construction paper, styrofoam ball, thumbtacks, party hat, tissue paper, lace paper doily, large tin coffee can, pins, table.

COLORS:
Red, white, multicolor party hat, black, orange, gold.

METHOD:
1. Decorate styrofoam ball with thumbtack eyes, pin on construction paper mouth, tissue hair, and party hat.
2. Place head in large, doily-covered coffee can, on table.
3. Stand book with caption lettered on cover in front of coffee can and surround it with a group of party books.

NOTE:
Headdress, book title, and accompanying books may be changed for different display themes.

SAFE PLAY

MATERIALS:
Wrapping paper, construction paper, American flag, black shiny paper, cutout of baseball player, pins.

COLORS:
Red, white, blue, black.

METHOD:
1. Line Board with wrapping paper.
2. Cut large caption letters from black construction paper and place at bottom of the central display area.
3. Above the caption, at left, attach a cutout from a discarded magazine, or a student's drawing, of a baseball player in action, pinning away from backdrop, for dimension.
4. Cut a large baseball on which the worker has simulated autographs of prominent major league players, affix to upper right of the display, pinning away from background, for dimension.
5. Edge Board with strips of black paper.
6. Pin on miniature American flag at upper left.

NOTE:
Both the flag and the color scheme contribute to the all-American flavor. A timely display for early spring, when reminders about observing safety rules and good sportsmanship are in order.

SAFE PLAY

MATERIALS:
Construction paper, fabric, rope, paper lace doilies, pins.

COLORS:
White, brown, tan, black, orange.

METHOD:
1. Line Board with white paper.
2. Based on pattern given in this book, draw and cut out figure of girl, arranged to falling position.
3. Cut out a dress of fabric and edge bottom and sleeves with lace doilies.
4. Pin figure onto backdrop, with head and one leg away from Board, for dimension.
5. Cut out a shape of hair, draw on chalk lines for appearance of dimension, curl ends, tuck under head and fasten to dress.
6. Pin on jump rope from hand to hand, and small circles below feet, for roller skate wheels.
7. Cut out and attach oversized, bold caption letters.

DON'T LEAVE TOYS ON THE STEPS

MATERIALS:
Wallpaper, fabric, rubber ball, blue cardboard, box, rug remnant, toys, jump rope, potted plant, masking tape, small display table, desk or stand, pins.

COLORS:
White, light blue, dark blue, tan, black, orange.

METHOD:
1. Line Board with wallpaper.
2. Cut a piece of thin cardboard to simulate stair steps, pinning away from backdrop.
3. Draw boy (based on figure pattern in this book) on construction paper, cut apart and put together again with arms and legs in positions illustrated.
4. Dress boy in cutout fabric suit.
5. Wrap rope around boy's waist.
6. Attach rope handles to backdrop by pinning through rope, making use of double masking tape on back of handles.
7. Pin cutout cardboard toys to background.
8. Cut rubber ball in half and with large pins through edges attach to Bulletin Board.
9. Pin the sign onto the wall, in the manner of hanging a picture.
10. The lettering on the sign may be done with a black marking pen.
11. Place the rug remnant on the display table, desk or stand, then line a box with calico print, and lean it against the steps. Set the potted plant next to the box, and scatter toys all around.

COWBOYS...TALES & TRAILS

MATERIALS:
Construction paper, wool, wooden bead or ball with hole through it, chalk, gold medallion (leftover Christmas decoration), pins, symbolic silhouettes representative of the West—horse and cattle heads, cactus, a rifle, etc.

COLORS:
White, black, red, orange, purple, blue, yellow, brown.

METHOD:
1. Using a child's cowboy hat as a guide, cut a shape from construction paper, or with poster paints create a hat almost as large as the Bulletin Board.
2. Place the symbols on pieces of colored construction paper, fitting them side by side to form the hatband.
3. Pin on the gold medallion and several strands of wool yarn pulled through the wooden bead.
4. The caption follows the shape of the hat, and the cutout letters seem part of the overall design.

ALTERNATE SUGGESTION:
Information about the subject concerned, typed or neatly handwritten, may be fitted into the hatband along with the picture symbols. Drawings of the hat and symbols are likely to be a class project of special interest to boys.
This type Bulletin Board would go well in a school or public library display featuring cowboy stories and Western history. The larger-than-life quality captures juvenile attention and imagination.

YOUR FLAG AND MINE

MATERIALS:
Construction paper, American flag, large paper box top, pins.

COLORS:
Black, red, white, blue.

METHOD:
1. Using a large, flat paper box for the display area, divide vertically down the center, covering the right half with black construction paper and the left half with white construction paper. Pin to Bulletin Board.
2. Cut two large figures (one black, the other white, duplicating pattern in this book), and using half of each, place the black one on the white paper with left arm extended, and the white one on the black paper with right arm extended.
3. Pin American flag to center section, its vertical edges meeting both extended arms.
4. On black-and-white strip just above Old Glory put white and black cutout letters spelling out YOUR FLAG. On same type strip below the banner, in similar letters, spell out AND MINE.

NOTE:
Where there is little Bulletin Board space this exhibit, with an easel back or propped against the wall, would make an ideal table display, and because of its light weight could easily be moved from room to room.

INDIAN STORIES

MATERIALS:
Construction paper, patterned wrapping paper, students' written or drawn work, pins.

COLORS:
White, deep pink, brown, black.

METHOD:
1. Line Board with white paper.
2. Use three full sheets of construction paper for mounting students' written or drawn work, and place in a row across the Board.
3. Cut a head and feet for each, and pin to backdrop, as shown in illustration.
4. Cut out strips of brown paper to resemble twigs. Fit and glue the pieces together to form the caption, and pin each letter away from Board, for dimension.
5. Each headdress is cut from two different patterns of wrapping paper.

ALTERNATE SUGGESTION:
If space permits, seven more Indians may be added to the three in question, and the caption might read, 10 LITTLE INDIAN STORIES. Though the stories and pictures should be changed frequently, the basic arrangement could remain intact.

NOTE:
Considerable information about American Indians, for pupils ranging from kindergarten through sixth grade, could be handled in this way. The simple figures, quick and easy to do, set the stage, make an interesting repeat pattern, and provide a place to pin up student work in cartoon fashion, appealing to all ages.

UNDERSTANDING EACH OTHER

MATERIALS:
Construction paper, fabric, heavy cardboard, marking pen, pins.

COLORS:
Black, white, light blue, dark blue, red.

METHOD:
1. To create a Bulletin Board where none exists, attach a piece of heavy cardboard to the wall (in this case, light blue).
2. Center a sheet of deeper blue construction paper toward the bottom of the cardboard, and pin on, then add two smaller sheets of paper—black to the left, and white to the right.
3. A large, cutout figure (see pattern section)—half white, half black—is pinned to the center, its red, white and blue hat made of fabric and construction paper, as shown in illustration. Cutout paper stars decorate the hatband.
4. The caption letters are done with marking pen on strips of paper extending from the figure's arms to Board's edges, resting on the smaller sheets of construction paper. The latter may serve as mats for sociological information, current events, or students' writings.

NOTE:
This Bulletin Board symbolizing equality, responsibility, understanding, the need for people to work in harmony—may remain in the classroom throughout the school year, with its information or papers changed frequently. Should no wall space for such a project be available, the same exhibit can be reinforced with an easel support on the back, and made to stand on a table or desk.

MATERIALS:
Carpet remnant, raw cotton, toy airplane, thin cardboard, pins.

COLORS:
Blue, white, black, multicolored toy airplane.

METHOD:
1. Line Bulletin Board with one or more pieces of carpet. Let the carpet determine the size of the display area, leaving the remainder blank. (In this way attention is concentrated on the message, with the surrounding space free.)
2. Set two raw cotton clouds in place by pinning into the rug fabric.
3. Using the wing area of the plane as a guide, trace shape onto a piece of white, lightweight cardboard.
4. Letter caption on the above and superimpose on wings.
5. Fasten toy plane to sky on a slant between the cloud formations.

NOTE:
If additional information is to be imparted other planes, with their respective messages, may be affixed to backdrop. Another device for creating more space for captions or information would be a paper streamer attached to the plane's tail, simulating a flying advertisement. This display demonstrates how only a portion of a Bulletin Board may be used to good advantage.

CLIMB INTO THE SKY

RAINY DAY FUN TABLE

MATERIALS:
Patterned wrapping paper, chalk, cutout or commercial letters, construction paper, marking pen, pins.

COLORS:
Dark green, white, light and dark pink.

METHOD:
1. Line Board with dark green paper.
2. Cut an umbrella shape out of patterned paper (for this illustration paper with umbrella design, ideal for the purpose, was used) and pin away from Board, to give impression of depth.
3. Draw chalk lines to simulate falling rain everywhere except in area protected by the umbrella.
4. Beneath the umbrella handle pin cutout or commercial letters in jump style for caption. For the sake of variety, the second line of the caption is done by tracing around commercial letters on a strip of white paper, then filling in with colored marking pen.

NOTE:
This Board should be prepared in conjunction with a table of books and games set out for indoor recess, during inclement weather.

TOWARD A BETTER TOMORROW, TOGETHER

MATERIALS:
Construction paper, glue, pins.

COLORS:
Black, off-white, bright blue, white.

METHOD:
1. Line Board with bright blue paper.
2. Using pattern in this book as a guide, cut two black and two off-white oversize hands to fit the display area, and pin on.
3. Black and off-white construction paper rectangles will form the arms, or sleeves.
4. The caption letters, cut from white construction paper, are glued to strips of black paper and pinned into the positions seen in photograph.

NOTE:
The large, construction paper sleeves could serve as mats for mounting information about the subject projected, or for students' creative writing. Since hands are so expressive, save these for future use.

ALTERNATE SUGGESTION:
Make watchbands from strips of construction paper and add large circles with watch faces done with marking pen, for a lesson teaching youngsters how to tell time. Also, such a display could have the title, TIME FOR _____ (teacher fits in any wording desired), to be used with reading or other programs.

IT'S CIRCUS TIME

MATERIALS:
Construction paper, ribbon, paper doily, marking pens, miniature paper umbrellas, thumbtacks, pins.

COLORS:
Yellow, blue, green, black, red, white, red-orange.

METHOD:
1. Line slightly more than two-thirds of the display area with white paper, the remainder toward the bottom with black.
2. Based on pattern in this book, cut four construction paper elephants. Add ears and shawl-like wrappings over elephants' backs, decorated with marking-pen lines.
3. Attach the elephants atop each other to the Board, using black thumbtacks for eyes, which also secure heads to backdrop. Pin tail ends away from Board, to create dimension.
4. Punch small holes in elephant trunks and insert umbrella handles, then secure all with pins.
5. Using figure from pattern section, cut out and rearrange acrobat in balancing position on highest elephant, after dressing her in performer's costume with paper, doily and ribbon.
6. Add umbrella to acrobat's hand, and fasten as in Step 4.

NOTE:
The elephants' construction paper wrappers or harnesses afford space for related information or numbers. Also, the elephants may be used in connection with a counting lesson, stacking as many as desired, adding or taking away. The balancing act adds to the fun idea.

ALTERNATE SUGGESTION:
Students may stack up titles of books read during the school year, or librarians may employ this technique to display new spring reading.

51

CIRCLES ARE EVERYWHERE

MATERIALS:
Cardboard, construction paper, magazine photographs, glue, pins.

COLORS:
Gray, white, light blue, multicolor magazine photographs.

METHOD:
1. Line Board with gray paper.
2. Cut caption letters from blue construction paper, glue on strip of white cardboard, then pin onto Board slightly below center, extending from extreme left, about two-thirds to the right.
3. Cut out vari-sized white construction paper circles, as well as circles from magazine illustrations of everyday things and mount on the right half of the display area as pictured, (reinforcing the point of the message with little effort).

ALTERNATE SUGGESTION:
It might be interesting to vary the treatment from time to time, featuring triangles, squares, rectangles and others in turn (including the pictures of familiar objects). Or, if sufficient space is available, the above arrangement might be presented on several Boards at one time, implying that shapes are, indeed, everywhere, in great diversity. Instead of magazine illustrations, some students might choose to bring suitably shaped photographs from home, or substitute their own drawings.

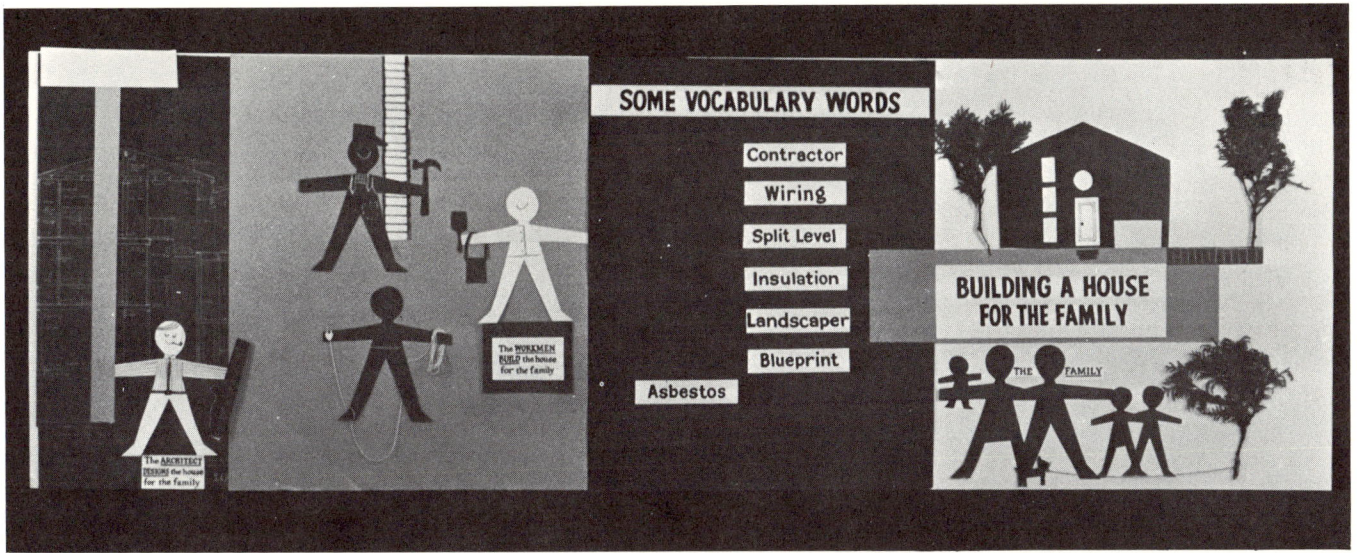

BUILDING A HOUSE FOR THE FAMILY

MATERIALS:
Construction paper, lightweight cardboard, blueprint, tree branches or twigs, cord, chalk, marking pen, pins.

COLORS:
White, dark blue, light gray-green (putty color).

METHOD:
1. Line Board with white paper.
2. Divide display area into four sections of disparate widths, as seen in illustration: *a blueprint adjoining narrow white edge at left for the first section; putty (gray-green) construction paper for the second panel; paper the same shade as the blueprint for the third panel and finally, the white background comprises the fourth panel. (*The white edge to left of blueprint helps tie the design together. If no blueprint is available, simulate one by drawing straight lines on blue paper with white chalk).
3. PANEL I: Add an oversized T square, cut from the putty and white paper. Cut the figure of an architect from white construction paper, using figure pattern in this book. Dress him appropriately with marking-pen striped shirt and tie, stand him on a block of construction paper, on which his title and job description are neatly lettered with marking pen.
4. PANEL II: Cut out workmen as for Panel I. Dress as shown, adding hammer and ladder with carpenter figure, paint pail and brush to painter, and a wire wrapped around the right arm of the electrician with plug in hand. The latter stands on a piece of construction paper bearing information about the group, their designations and how they contribute to the home building project.
5. PANEL III: Use this panel for the heading, SOME VOCABULARY WORDS, and change or add new vocabulary words as necessary, lettered with marking pen on strips of construction paper or lightweight cardboard. (Pin strips on, so that they are easy to put up or take down.)
6. PANEL IV: Show shape of house cut from blue construction paper. Let putty colored paper (extended onto adjacent blue panel to help unify design) indicate the street as well as serving as a mat for the main caption, which has been lettered in dark blue on white cardboard or paper with marking pen (cutout letters may be substituted, if desired). Add cutouts of bottom figures representing members of the family and household pet to lower portion of this panel. Label them, in the manner employed in the preceding panels. Pin on tree branches or twigs to give a touch of realism (evergreens will retain their color for the duration of the display), cord leash for dog fastened to tree, and perch baby on mother's arm.

NOTE:
Obviously, the blue and white color scheme ties in with the blueprint, which sets the tone for the entire Board. The putty color goes well with the combination, suggesting an association with architecture, concrete and general building construction. Although Bulletin Board viewers are not always consciously aware of such color concepts, they nevertheless instinctively find them pleasing. Accordingly, the display's message registers more easily, and the overall impression for both viewers and worker is favorable and fun.

GATHER NEW WORDS

MATERIALS:
Construction paper, narrow wooden molding, cardboard, stapler, poster paints, stippling brush, masking tape, pins.

COLORS:
White, black, orange, puple, yellow-green, pink, tan, blue-gray, green.

METHOD:
1. Line the Board with white construction paper.
2. Cut large paper circles, using a trash can lid or other large round object as a guide, and trim away just enough of each to form the flower petals.
3. Cut smaller paper circles for the flower centers, and staple the two together.
4. Attach stem made of wooden molding to each flower with masking tape, and gather the group into a bouquet. Each should be fastened to Board at the flower.
5. Letter the vocabulary words pertaining to flower and growth onto circles of cardboard smaller than the flower centers and colored with yellow-green poster paints applied with a stippling brush. (These may be changed as new words are introduced.) Pin to flower centers.
6. A rectangle cut from cardboard becomes the container to hold the flowers.
7. Caption letters fit the shape of the container.
8. Pin on a sheet of construction paper and two handles as shown in illustration, then pin lettered container away from Board, to give three-dimensional effect.
9. Cut butterfly from paper, fold, and pin away from Board, for dimension.

NOTE:
This idea is particularly suited to the spring season, but can be adapted to any series of words at other times of the year, with the color scheme changing accordingly. If preferred, the Board can omit any display of words until such time as they are learned, then added one by one.

THE TREE

MATERIALS:
Construction paper, marking pen, pins.

COLORS:
Blue, green, olive green, dark green, yellow-green, purple, black, white.

METHOD:
1. Line Board with white paper.
2. Place three large sheets of construction paper in a row, vertically on right, to represent houses, and one sheet horizontally, to represent land on which they stand.
3. Add roofs, windows and doors, to indicate urban area.
4. Cut tree shapes (based on tree pattern in this book) in three or four different sizes, and colors of the houses, pinning them to narrow strip of construction paper on the left, as a reminder of the country.
5. Add a tree to city portion of the display.
6. The center caption toward the top is done in dark green cutout construction paper letters. The supplementary caption letters at the bottom, designed to draw the eye across the Board from one side to the other, are black cutout letters glued to a white strip of paper and fastened to backdrop. Location notes ("In the City" and "In the Country") appearing under the contrasting environments, are done with marking pen in large script.

NOTE:
Cited here is an example of how a Bulletin Board can be decorated by balancing one side against the other, using uniform color schemes, and leaving adequate white space around the display units. Further contrast might be obtained by including the figures of children appropriately garbed for city and country living.

FAMILY LIFE TOGETHER

MATERIALS:
Construction paper, discarded magazine photographs, lightweight cardboard, screening, plastic tomato carton, button, glue, pins.

COLORS:
Black, white, blue, red, khaki, green, purple, pink, multicolor photographs.

METHOD:
1. Line Board with white construction paper.
2. Cut and pin on band of green construction paper for grassy, lower section of display area.
3. Place rectangle of khaki construction paper on grass, to simulate house.
4. At left and slightly behind house, pin on chimney, made up of red, purple and pink rectangles of construction paper.
5. Add a blue construction paper triangle indicating roof, and on its face mount picture cutouts of items likely to be found in an attic.
6. Pin on black construction paper door, with house number and button doorknob in position. Also, the front steps, made by folding construction paper or thin cardboard and pinning the top tread just under the door, allowing remaining treads to stand away from background, for dimension.
7. A porch scene cut from a magazine and covered with metal mesh is affixed to the side of the house for the screened-in porch. The latter has a scalloped awning of red construction paper, and a safety railing made from a plastic tomato carton.
8. To the right of the door place cutout photographs of rooms illustrating family life. In this case four pictures were used, but a larger house, if space is available, would accommodate more.
9. Add strips of white paper to simulate window frame (at the same time these serve to mat the photographs).
10. At left of the entrance appears a typical living room as seen through a bay window. To achieve this effect, glue the picture cutout to a piece of lightweight cardboard. While it is still damp roll slightly to give rounded look, and pin edges to backdrop, with center protruding. Add strips of white paper for window frame, overhang above, and window box below.
11. Fasten caption—done in large, bold, cutout letters on white cardboard or paper strip—above door and window area.

NOTE:
This particular display may be adapted to numerous home-oriented subjects (READING AT HOME, PLAYING AT HOME, SCIENCE AT HOME, SAFETY AT HOME), stressing the home in relation to life's diversified activities and manifestations.

WE WORK AND PLAY TOGETHER

MATERIALS:
Foreign language newspapers, construction paper, colored cellophane, ribbon, black ink or poster paint, pen or brush, pins.

COLORS:
Black, white, purple, green, yellow.

METHOD:
1. Line Bulletin Board with black paper.
2. Use figure pattern in this book to cut paper dolls from newspapers deriving from different countries.
3. Group three figures on the left, as shown, adding eyes and mouths.
4. On a wide strip of white paper letter the large caption, TOGETHER, in black ink or poster paint, then align the bottom of the strip with feet of the trio.
5. Use strip as platform for two additional figures.
6. Cut out circles of white paper for balloons.
7. Cover balloons, clothing and mouths of all figures with colored cellophane.
8. Pin ribbon from balloons to hands.
9. Cut triangular shapes of white construction paper for pennants to bear introductory phrases for the caption, also done in black ink or poster paint.
10. Narrow strips of colored construction paper may serve as pennant sticks.
11. Set newspaper hats on children's heads and pin all pieces in place.

NOTE:
Students of foreign origin or descent, particularly in the large metropolitan areas, may have access to foreign newspapers for the doll figures. Save the latter for repeated future use. Captions may be changed to fit the topic (see illustration, WE READ AND LEARN ABOUT EACH OTHER).

HAVE A HOBBY

MATERIALS:
Construction paper, a butterfly collection, butterfly net, picture frame, dried flowers, ribbon, box top, pins, hammer, picture hook, marking pen.

COLORS:
White, green, red, yellow, blue, black.

METHOD:
1. Line approximately upper two-thirds of Board with white paper, and the remaining lower portion with black.
2. On a sheet of construction paper fastened to a shallow box top, pin student's collection of butterflies with descriptive labels. (Pin with great care, as insects are brittle.)
3. Pin the box top arrangement to backdrop.
4. Hammer a picture hook into Bulletin Board and hang frame around the box top, picture fashion.
5. Put a label on the picture, bearing the student's name. This will give him deserved recognition.
6. Pin a butterfly onto the extreme left side of the black section, as if it were on a table. Over this pin a butterfly net.
7. To the right of the net pin another butterfly from the collection onto a brightly colored piece of construction paper, and identify it.
8. Toward the right add cutout construction paper books (one flat, three upright), with more butterflies decorating the spines.
9. The main caption across the top of the Board is spelled out with commercial letters. The supplementary small sign, "What do you collect?", lettered with marking pen on construction paper in the worker's own hand, is the same size as the construction paper mat for the butterfly on the table.
10. To increase the "collector's" atmosphere, add a cutout paper vase, and pin behind it a bunch of dried flowers tied together with a ribbon. Book titles about collecting may be lettered on the book spines.

NOTE:
This type of one-man show may inspire the exhibitor's classmates to organize and share their own hobby collections.

CIRCUS WORKERS

MATERIALS:
Construction paper, marking pens, pins.

COLORS:
Gray, dark blue, light brown, white, red.

METHOD:
1. Line Board with gray paper.
2. Cut and pin on simple, bold, large shapes of construction paper to form the policeman (figure should occupy most of display area).
3. Add marking pen mouth (smiling), white buttons and hat shield.
4. The worker's own hand may serve as the hand pattern, enlarging and cutting from construction paper, squaring off the fingers to coordinate with the other elements. (Observe that the hand is much larger in proportion than the policeman's head, for special emphasis.)
5. The caption letters, cut from construction paper, read STOP (red on the white hand) and OBEY LIGHTS (white on gray backdrop); they fit well into the overall design.

NOTE:
This Bulletin Board offers a striking example of how a large display area may stress one thought, rather than crowd in many ideas which might escape attention. The larger the design, the better, because the Bulletin Board depends on the oversized, commanding shapes to get the message across with simplicity and directness.

MATERIALS:
Construction paper, cardboard, paper doilies, fabric, shiny paper, stars, chalk, felt marking pen, pins.

COLORS:
Gray, white, black, blue, red, orange, green.

METHOD:
1. Line Board with gray paper.
2. Pattern the pyramid figures to left and right after figure drawing presented in this book, and pin on.
3. Using fabric, paper and doilies, fashion appropriate costumes to depict the various types of circus performers.
4. Leave space between the construction paper tent top and bottom for the caption lettering, done with chalk.
5. The fat lady, partly visible in the doorway, also may be based on a pattern in the book, but cut wider, to appear weighty. (The left portion of the tent is left free from the background, to allow insertion of the fat lady, and give her the illusion of movement).
6. Each worker stands on his own job label, lettered with marking pen. The only exception is the fat lady. Her descriptive term appears in pennant shape, to harmonize with pennants atop the tent.

STOP-OBEY LIGHTS

HERE COMES THE CIRCUS

MATERIALS:
Construction paper, marking pens, paper lace doilies, children's drawings or cutouts of animals, pins.

COLORS:
White, black, red, blue, yellow, red-orange, pink.

METHOD:
1. Line Board with white paper.
2. Using clown pattern in this book or a cutout from a discarded magazine, cut out three paper clowns.
3. Cut and pin on three animal cages, each consisting of: top (a strip of a large, black sheet of construction paper folded in center, and trimmed into shape seen in photograph. Any wavy shape will do, because center folding makes both sides exactly alike); bottom (a band of black construction paper on which is superimposed a small white replica of the top, for the animal's generic name); black construction paper circles for the wheels, and narrow black paper strips for the cage edges.
4. Sheets of bright yellow construction paper are pinned on to serve as backdrops for the animal cutouts. Add more narrow black vertical strips over the animals, to represent cage bars, if they can be arranged so as not to obstruct the view of the animals.
5. Add strips of black paper from tops of cages to top of display area, and red triangular paper pennants.
6. After the cages, animals and flags are attached, dress clowns in white lace doily collars, add marking pen facial features and hair, and smiling lips of construction paper. Also add marking pen dots to the clowns' costumes and a pom-pom to the top of each hat.
7. Cut caption letters from black construction paper and place in the clowns' hands, as shown in illustration.
8. For a final and festive touch scatter marking pen confetti on the bottom of the display, picking up all the bright colors in the design (or real confetti may be used, if preferred).

NOTE:
Change picture cutouts of animals from time to time, or use the cage space for information or stories about the circus, written by students. The train of cages may be as long as classroom Bulletin Boards allow.

ANIMALS WE DESIGNED

MATERIALS:
Construction paper, crepe paper, corrugated board, mat knife or scissors, poster paint and roller, cardboard, animal cutouts, marking pens, pins.

COLORS:
Olive green, brown, bright green, dark green, yellow-green, light pink, hot pink, orange, tangerine, white.

METHOD:
1. Cover the cardboard intended as the background for the forest scene with olive green poster paint, using a roller, and spreading the paint thickly at times, allowing the texture of the roller to show.
2. As seen in the illustration, pin on assortment of tree trunks and branches cut from brown corrugated board, with some of the smaller trees toward the rear, suggesting distance. For greater realism, roll the wider trunks slightly. (Corrugated board is easy to handle, and can be cut with a mat knife or scissors. When rolled it gives the impression of dimension.)
3. Fasten some leaves to the trees.
4. Attach crepe paper to bottom section of the display —bunched, rather than smooth—to resemble the grass of a dense forest, and add floral groups in bright colors.
5. Print caption on white cardboard rectangle and affix to tree trunk.
6. Position vari-sized cardboard or construction paper animal cutouts done by students on grass and among trees, to create natural, jungle-like atmosphere. (Some of the animal and insect features may be drawn with marking pens or poster paint.)

AMERICA, AMERICA

MATERIALS:
Construction paper, lightweight cardboard, American flag, facsimile of Declaration of Independence, turkey or chicken feather, blue marking pen, glue, pins, symbols of freedom (stars, eagle and shield, students' drawing of Capitol dome and adjoining area, Washington Monument cutout).

COLORS:
Red, white, blue, gold.

METHOD:
1. Line Board with white paper.
2. Cut irregular strips of red and blue construction paper, placing the red at top and bottom, with blue in the center, as seen in illustration.
3. Glue student's drawings of Capitol dome and Washington Monument on light cardboard, cut out, and pin away from board to give dimension.
4. Roll facsimile document slightly and pin upper left and lower right corners under red strips, as shown.
5. Glue and pin on feather quill pen, then attach flag, eagle and shield, and stars.
6. Cut out large white construction paper letters in graduated size conforming to strip shapes, thus adding to Board's simplicity and casual treatment.
7. With marking pen put smaller letters of caption on Capitol building section below dome.

NOTE:
Here is an example of how even serious subjects may be treated in an unpretentious manner, with pleasing results for both worker and viewers. Reducing the display's components to their simplest form, easily handled by children; leaving sizable areas of free space; making use of big, bold areas of color, oversized letters and effective historic representation—all these combine to convey the desired message.

ALTERNATE SUGGESTION:
Pin two bands of white construction paper at right and left of the display, for students' compositions about democracy, mounted on sheets of red and blue paper.

HAVE A SAFE VACATION

MATERIALS:
Construction paper, cardboard, large and small towels, straw hat, ball fringe, print fabric, tan chalk, marking pen, cellophane, ribbon, wool yarn, coloring book, cutouts, pins.

COLORS:
White, blue, dark green, bright green, yellow-green, red, orange, tan, magenta.

METHOD:
1. Line Board with white construction paper.
2. Using tan chalk, rub the broad side of the chalk across the paper to give the look of sand. (The texture of the construction paper will add to the realistic effect.)
3. Pin on a towel as large as needed for the area (two were used here).
4. The girl is the basic figure found in the pattern section, and rearranged for the position indicated.
5. Cut bathing suit from print fabric. Add wool for hair, cardboard circles with lenses of cellophane for sunglasses, and tuck small towel under girl's arm.
6. The umbrella is cut from lightweight cardboard, rolled slightly. Decorate with polka dots of construction paper and glue ball fringe onto edge.
7. Pin umbrella away from background, for dimension.
8. Add stick handle of cardboard and perch a bird at the top (bird, sun, bucket and ball were taken from a child's coloring book).
9. Pin on a real beach hat from the dime store, and tie a gay ribbon around it for added decoration.
10. With a wide marking pen create a line framing the whole Board, and make ripples for the water.
11. The caption letters are first drawn on construction paper, then cut out. They are bold, easy to read, and easy to do.

READ BEFORE YOU SKI

MATERIALS:
White glossy paper, color aid paper or construction paper, cardboard, paper doilies, cotton, green marking pen, glitter if desired, white liquid adhesive, pins.

COLORS:
Black, white, two shades of hot pink, green, khaki.

METHOD:
1. Line the Bulletin Board with white glossy paper.
2. Cut one arm, legs at angles shown, add boot shapes.
3. Pin on skis—one away from Bulletin Board, to give dimension.
4. Also, pin one side of book away from background, and with green marking pen add lines to simulate pages.
5. Caption lettering in the form of stylized handwriting fits into the general design.
6. Pin a mound of cotton snow to bottom and cut small circular units from doilies, for snowflakes.
7. Dot cotton with Elmer's or other white liquid adhesive. (If a frosty look is desired, sprinkle on glitter).

ALTERNATE TITLES:
READING FOR FUN
DO YOU KNOW THE SAFETY RULES?
PLAY WITH CARE—EVERYWHERE!

NOTE:
The idea for this Bulletin Board was sparked by a cartoon advertisement seen in a magazine, a good springboard for one's own imagination. The bright colors, and the black boots, skis and caption letters, seem crisp and wintry against the white backdrop.

SPRING RAIN BRINGS FLOWERS

MATERIALS:
Umbrella, raincoat, mitten, blue cellophane, construction paper, glue, pins.

COLORS:
White, red, yellow, blue, green, orange, black.

METHOD:
1. Line Board with white paper.
2. Pin an old, discarded yellow raincoat to backdrop.
3. Cut out black paper boot shapes, using a newspaper advertisement as a guide, and decorate with yellow strips of paper to match the raincoat.
4. Attach one real black mitten and one flat construction paper mitten the same size.
5. Cut raindrop from blue cellophane and glue to Board above paper mitten.
6. Cut free-form puddle of blue cellophane and glue over right boot, putting glue around edge of cellophane shape so that the edges will not roll.
7. Add more shapes for water below cellophane puddle cut from scraps of construction paper by the students, and as many flowers as the space will accommodate.
8. Using the tab on the umbrella that holds it closed, pin umbrella to top of display area, and pin the handle loop to real mitten, securing with as many pins as necessary to keep the umbrella stable.
9. Cut the large caption word, "Rain," from black construction paper and pin onto backdrop. The remaining portions of the message are lettered on strips of white paper with marking pen, and pinned above and below the large letters.

NOTE:
This is a good way to construct a figure without drawing. If there is room for a series of such umbrella arrangements, students may be able to bring in needed clothing from home.

ALTERNATE IDEAS FOR SPORTS DISPLAYS:
1. For the figure use a tennis sweater, real racket and construction paper head with real tennis hat, and pin to Board.
2. Pin on a baseball shirt, a construction paper head with baseball cap, and have a real bat leaning against the Board.

OCEANS AND CONTINENTS

MATERIALS:
Cardboard, boat cutout, white poster paint and brush, white plastic glue, colored tissue paper.

COLORS:
White, black, purple, blue.

METHOD:
1. Cut a long, not too narrow strip of cardboard. Cover this first with white plastic glue, then with tissue paper strips of blue tones shading into purple.
2. Letter the caption onto the strip with white poster paint.
3. While the cardboard and tissue paper are still moist, shape them into ripples so that the strip, curving in and out and giving the watery, wavy feeling, will stand free. The lettering takes on an interesting "sea" look as it curves with the cardboard.
4. Add a cutout of a ship sailing at a distance on the ocean.
5. The tissue paper colors make the foreground simulate water, while off in the distance and behind the boat, the deep purple resembles land.

NOTE:
Books centering on the display's theme should be shown with the strip. The latter could also be tacked onto a Bulletin Board as the heading for a display presenting students' written or art work.

PUZZLED? ASK QUESTIONS

MATERIALS:
Glossy colored paper, brown wrapping paper, glue or pins.

COLORS:
Black, white, turquoise, green, blue, orange, red-orange, pink.

METHOD:
1. Line Board with black paper.
2. Draw puzzle on brown wrapping paper, to use as a pattern.
3. Lay pattern over colored paper and cut apart, then assemble pieces in proper position, as shown, attaching with glue or pins.
4. Cut out caption letters and attach at top and bottom, to fit into overall design.

NOTE:
If preferred, caption may be made with commercial letters, which are available in various sizes and styles. Maps may also be presented in puzzle-fashion. Since this Bulletin Board's design depends for its impact mostly on color, use the brightest colors obtainable. Vivid shades against black are always a standout.

GET READY FOR WINTER

MATERIALS:
Tissue paper, construction paper, corrugated board, marking pen, pins.

COLORS:
Olive green, orange, gold, tan, blue-green, mauve, black, white.

METHOD:
1. Line Board with tissue paper cut into strips of different fall colors (in this case olive green, orange, gold, etc.), or use multicolored tissue paper.
2. Cut an oversized acorn from corrugated board, with the rib running horizontally for the top, or cap portion, and vertically for the bottom.
3. Decorate the acorn with crisscross lines on the upper area, and draw a marking pen smile on lower section, adding two orange circle eyes. Pin onto left side of tissue paper backdrop.
4. The caption, emanating from the acorn head, is lettered on a strip of white construction paper, starting relatively small at the point of origin at left, and growing larger as the message stretches out toward the right. The word, WINTER, rendered in black, stands out in tone as well as size.
5. Outline the acorn with black marking pen.

NOTE:
Since the caption is such a significant part of the design, it should be done with style, by a person skilled in hand-lettering. If this is not possible, commercial cutout letters in varying sizes may be purchased, to achieve the necessary graduated effect.

READ ABOUT YOUR HOBBY

MATERIALS:
Construction paper, cellophane, cardboard, marking pens, chalk.

COLORS:
Black, white, turquoise, blue, light purple, light green, yellow, magenta.

METHOD:
1. Line Board with black paper.
2. Attach a strip of turquoise cardboard toward the bottom, away from the backdrop, leaving some of the black color exposed below, and extending beyond the sides somewhat, in the manner of a shelf.
3. To form the spines of the books at right and left, as well as the volumes' decorations and bookmarks, cut strips of construction paper freehand.
4. Cut shape of paper resembling bottle, and with marking pen draw outline to denote bottle's thickness; also draw (or cutout) a sailboat on its face, and add paper cork.
5. Cover the bottle with cellophane, simulating glass.
6. Caption letters, done with white chalk on the black cardboard, are evenly aligned on the left just above the bottle. They help guide viewers' eyes to the other display elements, and as a result caption and cutouts blend effectively, quickly conveying the desired message.

HOLD ON TO YOUR HAT

MATERIALS:
Straw place mat, construction paper, feather, small stuffed bird, calendar, marking pen, pins.

COLORS:
White, turquoise, green, two shades of purple, tan (natural straw), black.

METHOD:
1. Line display area with full sheet of cardboard.
2. Cut a discarded natural straw place mat into shape of a hat, and pin onto cardboard.
3. Place the March page from an oversized calendar just below the hat.
4. Using the hand pattern in this book, or the worker's own hand as a guide, cut out two construction paper purple (different shades) hands and attach to Bulletin Board as if they were holding the hat (see illustration).
5. Circle important dates on the March calendar, pin feather and stuffed bird to hat crown.
6. The caption decorates the white hatband (the larger letters being cut from construction paper, while the small ones are done with matching color marking pen).

WRITING

LETTERS

MATERIALS:
Wallpaper, construction paper, wide-tipped marking pen, pins.

COLORS:
White, green, pink.

METHOD:
1. Line Board with white construction paper.
2. Using an ordinary envelope as a guide, cut green paper rectangle for the body and two triangular shapes for the flaps—pink for bottom and patterned wallpaper with narrow construction paper border at top.
3. Place a full sheet of green construction paper next to the enlarged envelope.
4. Cut and pin border of patterned wallpaper to the top of the "writing paper." Thus an area is provided for mounting students' letters composed during a class assignment. The caption lettering, done with a green marking pen, conforms in space and style to the worker's handwriting.

ALTERNATE SUGGESTIONS:
While the color scheme presented seems appropriate for spring, other wallpaper designs and colors could tie in with other seasons. Teachers who encourage their students to communicate with pen pals might employ this type of display. A foreign motif could be introduced, with the youngsters creating their own stationery designs. For example, if the correspondents are Dutch, the envelope flaps and writing paper could be decorated with drawings of tulips, windmills or wooden shoes.

NOTE:
Simplicity is one of the charms of this type of Bulletin Board. The exhibit area should feature relatively few of the students' contributions at one time, to avoid crowding, but these should be changed frequently to allow widespread representation.

COMMUNICATION

MATERIALS:
Construction paper, pins, gummed stars, numerals, punctuation marks, Christmas package decorations, bits of wrapping paper, art work, cutouts from discarded magazines, children's games and commercial illustrations from cereal and soap boxes.

COLORS:
White, brown, plus any others desired for brightness and contrast among available items listed above.

METHOD:
1. Silhouette heads of the boy and girl serving as the Bulletin Board's basic background, were patterned after full-page photographs appearing in a popular magazine. Each was cut from a full sheet of brown construction paper and attached right and left, facing each other, on the blue backdrop.
2. The various other items were pinned onto the head shapes, with the caption cutout letters placed between the mouths of the two children.

NOTE:
With the proper caption changes, this treatment could apply to many different subjects.

THE AMERICAN INDIAN

MATERIALS:
Construction paper, pins.

COLORS:
Orange, yellow, brown, white.

METHOD:
1. Line display area with orange construction paper which has been fringed on edges, in the manner of a rug.
2. Place a sheet of brown construction paper in center, and add Indian design to right and left sides, with captions between the design elements, top and bottom. The central empty section may be decorated with photographs or information pertaining to the topic.

NOTE:
A series of such displays, done by students and featuring related pictures, information, objects of interest, book jackets and pamphlets, would add considerably to study of the classroom Indian unit.

ALTERNATE IDEA:
The same format, with appropriate designs and captions, might be adapted to the study of foreign countries.

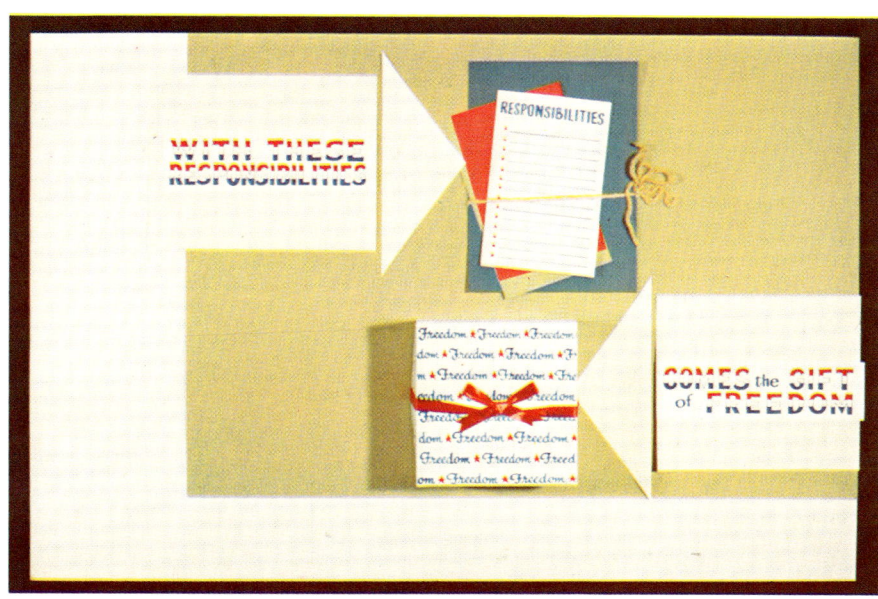

WITH THESE RESPONSIBILITIES COMES THE GIFT OF FREEDOM

MATERIALS:
Construction paper, wool yarn, marking pens, ribbon, shallow box, pins.

COLORS:
Khaki, red, white, blue, off-white.

METHOD:
1. Line Board with khaki paper.
2. Pin full sheets of off-white construction paper with matching triangles onto upper left and lower right sections of Board, to form the arrows.
3. On a rectangle of white construction paper letter a list of responsibilities of American citizenship, previously discussed in class.
4. At point of top arrow pin pieces of blue, khaki, red and the white lettered construction paper at angles, so that all colors may be seen. Then tie together with a piece of wool yarn.
5. Decorate a box top with a construction paper allover pattern of the word, "Freedom," done with a marking pen, and tied with ribbon in the manner of a gift. First pin box bottom securely into position on backdrop, then slip on the decorated box top.
6. The caption lettering is done on white construction paper with red and blue marking pens, and attached to the off-white arrows.

COME TO STORY HOUR

MATERIALS:
Heavy cardboard, construction paper, poster paint and brush, glue, pins.

COLORS:
Blue, orange, white, black, turquoise.

METHOD:
1. Using figure pattern in this book, make woman as large as necessary (the one shown here is lifesize, and can be free-standing with easel support on the back, or propped against a door or wall).
2. With marking pen and a few well-placed lines, the figure can become a peasant woman.
3. Arrange hair into topknot, by means of white paint with black accents.
4. Paint in apron area, stockings, shoes and smiling mouth (these could also be cut from construction paper and glued on).
5. Pin or glue to thumbs folded sheets of construction paper representing books, with marking pen page lines.
6. The caption lettering may be done with paint or marking pen (neatly but not too professionally to simulate juvenile printing) in the story lady's apron section.

NOTE:
While in this instance the story figure is pinned to the Bulletin Board against a sheet of blue cardboard, the same figure may also stand (propped up) against the entrance to the library's children's room, to welcome youngsters to story hour. Any storybook character could be handled in the same way.

FATHER

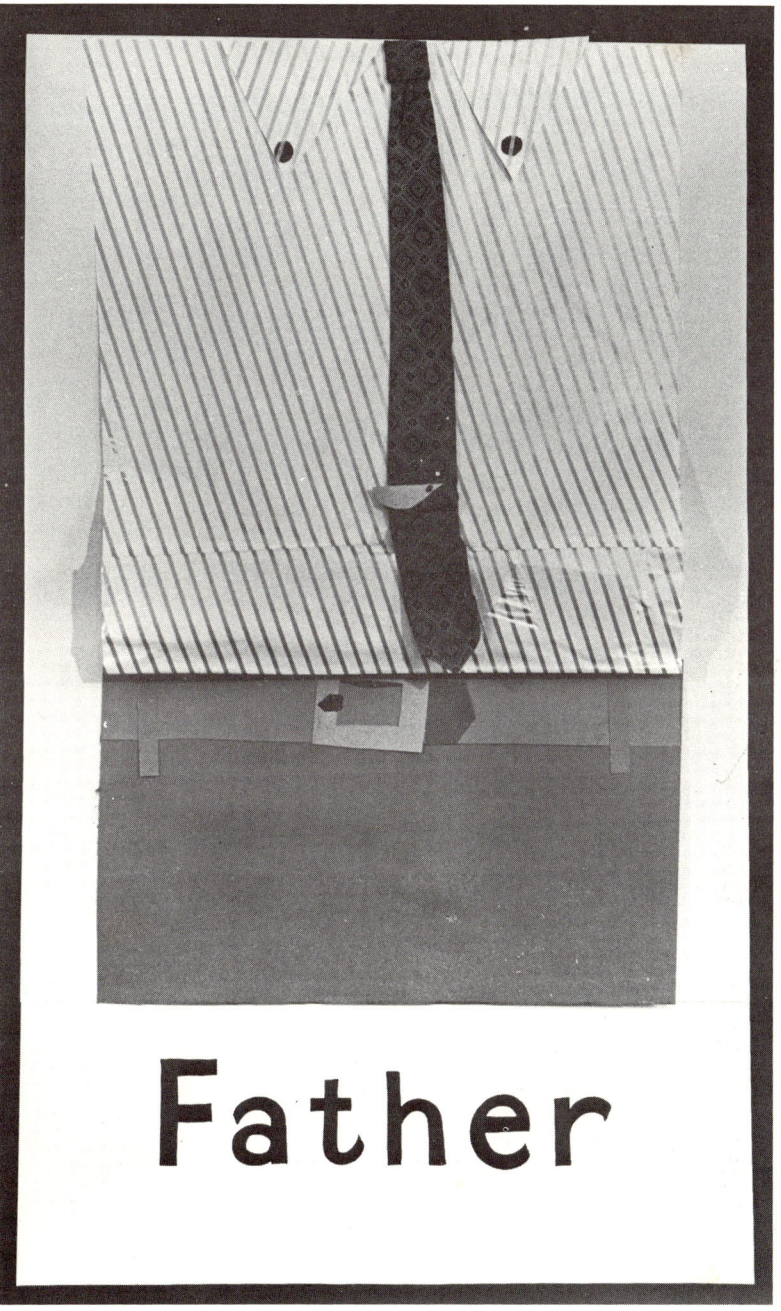

MATERIALS:
Striped wrapping paper, cardboard, a real tie, construction paper, marking pen, pins.

COLORS:
Gray, white, brown, blue, orange.

METHOD:
1. Pin on white cardboard for background.
2. Striped wrapping paper represents the shirt, with two triangular shapes at the top indicating the collar, marking pen buttons, real tie, and orange construction paper tie clasp.
3. A full sheet of brown construction paper suggests the trousers. The belt is formed by means of a strip of blue construction paper, with orange paper loops and gray paper buckle.
4. Cut large, bold caption letters from black construction paper, glue onto a strip of white construction paper, and pin toward bottom of display area.

SEE NOTE FOLLOWING BABY ILLUSTRATION

MOTHER

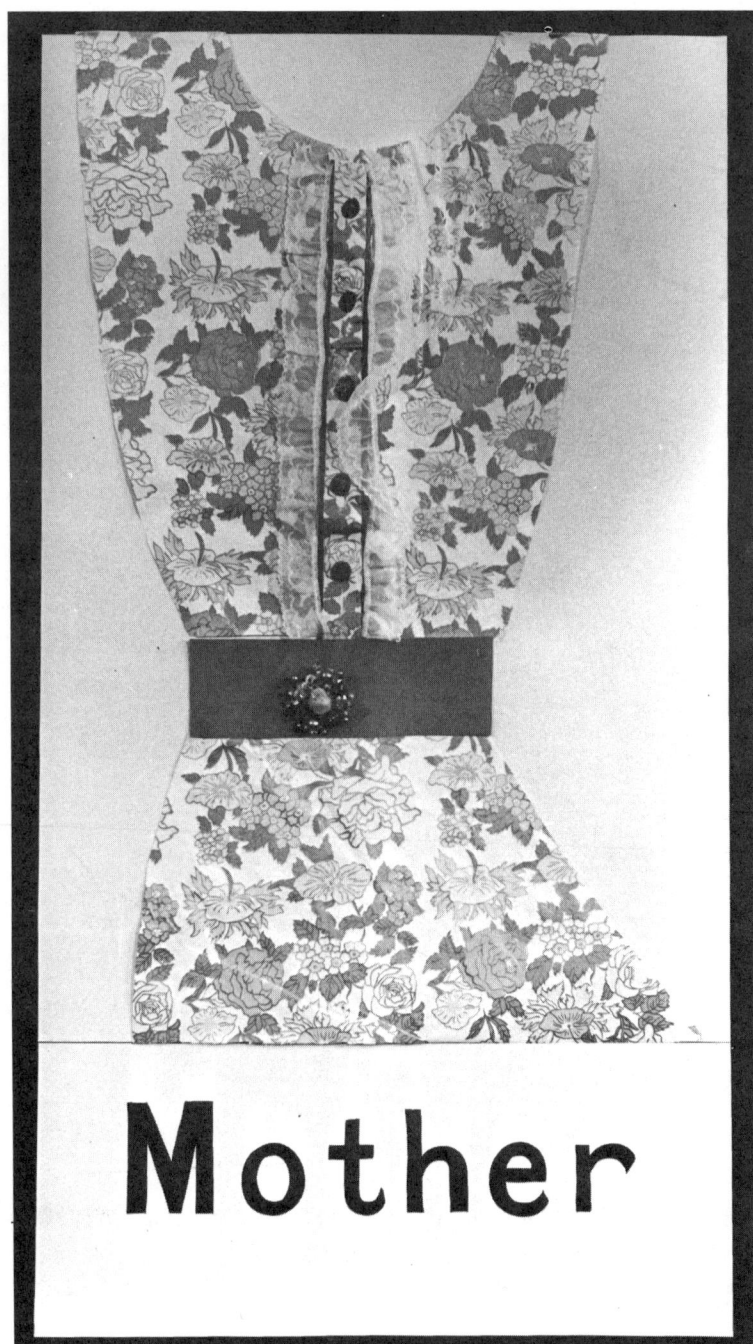

MATERIALS:
Cardboard, floral print wrapping paper, dime-store "gold" pin, or a pin from discarded costume jewelry, construction paper, ruffled trimming, marking pen, glue, pins.

COLORS:
White, blue, black, multicolor patterned wrapping paper.

METHODS:
1. Pin on white cardboard for background.
2. Cut dress portions from two sheets of patterned wrapping paper (tapering at waistline to indicate feminine figure), add real ruffling down center front and marking pen buttons. Then pin on construction paper belt with fancy pin fastener (dime-store pin, or piece of discarded costume jewelry).
3. Cut large bold caption letters from black construction paper, glue onto strip of white construction paper, and pin toward bottom of display area.

SEE NOTE FOLLOWING BABY ILLUSTRATION

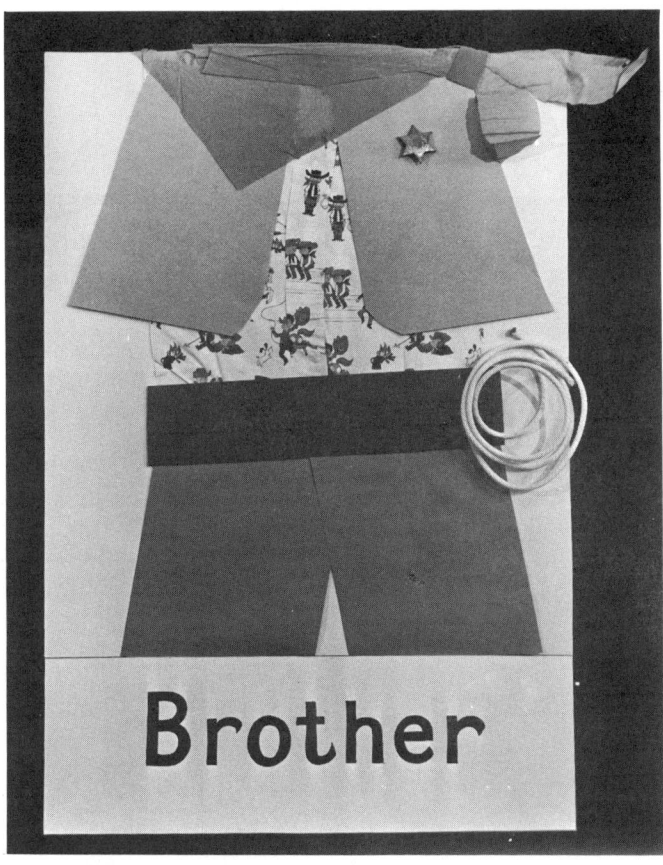

BROTHER

MATERIALS:
Cardboard, construction paper, patterned cowboy wrapping paper, toy sheriff's badge, rope, crepe paper, glue, pins.

COLORS:
White, green, orange, turquoise, black.

METHOD:
1. Pin on white cardboard for background.
2. Cowboy print wrapping paper forms the shirt.
3. The vest is made with two sheets of orange construction paper rounded off at the lower inner corners.
4. Two sheets of blue construction paper overlapping at the waist form the short pants.
5. The belt is a strip of black construction paper with rope "lariat" pinned at the right.
6. Add green crepe paper neckerchief and toy sheriff's badge.
7. Cut large, bold caption letters from black construction paper, glue onto a strip of white construction paper, and pin toward bottom of display area.

SEE NOTE FOLLOWING BABY ILLUSTRATION.

SISTER

MATERIALS:
Cardboard, patterned wrapping paper, construction paper, ball fringe, eyelet trimming, marking pen, glue, pins.

COLORS:
Red, green, white, black.

METHOD:
1. Pin on white cardboard for background.
2. One sheet of wrapping paper forms the dress, with sides tapered upward, feminine fashion.
3. Add eyelet trimming and ball fringe at hemline.
4. Pin on pocket with white and red construction paper flowers, and black marking pen leaves and stems.
5. Also pin on two pieces of black construction paper for girl's legs, one straight, the other at an angle.
6. Cut large, bold caption letters from black construction paper, glue onto a strip of white construction paper, and pin toward bottom of display area.

SEE NOTE FOLLOWING BABY ILLUSTRATION

75

BABY

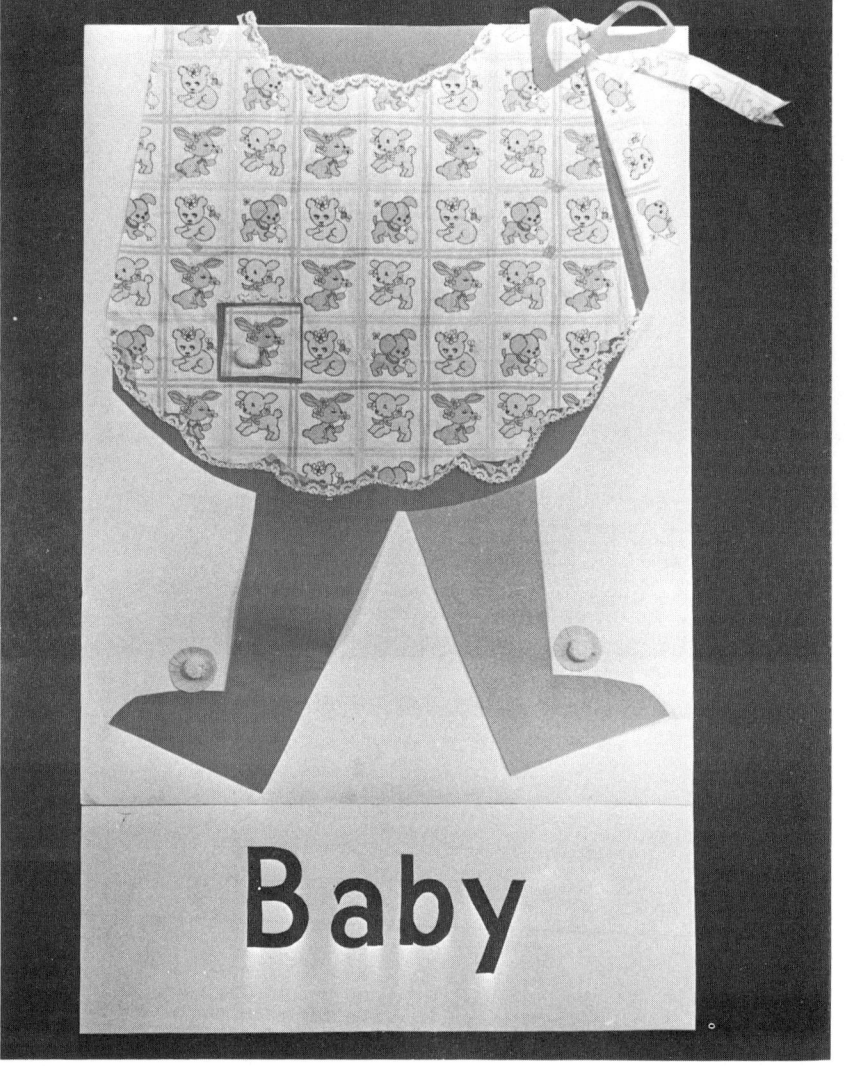

MATERIALS:
Cardboard, patterned animal wrapping paper, construction paper, pom-poms, glue, pins.

COLORS:
Blue, pink, green, multicolor wrapping paper.

METHOD:
1. Pin on white cardboard for background.
2. Cut patterned animal wrapping paper into a scalloped bib shape, and glue onto green construction paper following bib shape, without scallops.
3. Add bows of patterned paper and construction paper to upper right, and patterned pocket toward bib's lower left.
4. Pin on two construction paper legs—one blue, the other pink, and add pom-poms on feet.
5. Cut large, bold caption letters from black construction paper, glue onto a strip of white construction paper, and pin toward bottom of display area.

NOTE:
The foregoing family group figures are constructed individually for more diversified classroom use. Instead of attaching them to the Bulletin Board, students could hold up the figure displays in front of them, as if manipulating scenery. (Just one more example of possible student involvement in exhibits enterprises). In addition to representations of family members, students might enjoy turning out other types of figures for classroom discussion on animals, storybook characters, prominent athletes, and others. The oversized quality of such partial representations as are shown, and the simplicity of their shapes, make for pleasant viewing, while requiring scant expenditures of time and money.

THE SEASON'S BEST

MATERIALS:
Students' work, cutout or real Christmas ornaments, marking pens, construction paper, pins.

COLORS:
Black, white, magenta, orange, turquoise, green, purple, gold.

METHOD:
1. Line Board with black construction paper.
2. Place a large black triangle in center of Board as guide for pinning on students' best papers and Christmas ornaments, in the shape of a Christmas tree.
3. Add tree trunk, set in decorated pot, resting on construction paper rug, decorated with marking pen fringe and other lines. The caption appears in the rug's central section.

NOTE:
The size of this design on the Board is obviously determined by the quantity of student work to be displayed. Should Bulletin Board space permit, a number of such exhibits would enable many papers to be shown simultaneously.

BOOKS ON CHILD CARE

MATERIALS:
Construction paper, printed fabric, marking pen, thumbtacks, beaded bracelet, staple gun, pins.

COLORS:
Yellow, black, white, gray, red-orange, blue, pink.

METHOD:
1. Line Board with yellow paper.
2. Cut figure's head and neck from white construction paper, or a child's head from a discarded magazine.
3. Add a construction paper child's hat bent slightly at brim for three-dimensional effect.
4. The arms are cut from printed fabric and turned up at cuffs for a bit of realism. Add a cutout fabric collar with thumbtacks. (The latter not only serve as buttons, but also secure fabric pieces to Board).
5. Using the hand pattern in this book as a guide, cut the child's hands from gray paper, and the adult's larger hand from white paper. The latter—its wrist projecting beyond the Board—is decorated with fingernail polish and real bracelet.
6. Several folded sheets of paper stapled together form the three-dimensional book pinned to child's left hand.
7. The bold caption letters are cut from black construction paper. The large word, BOOKS, balances the remainder, done in smaller letters and lined up on the right to carry the eye from the beginning to the end of the visual message quickly and easily.

NOTE:
The theme for this display was inspired by the print fabric—faces and hats. Enhancing the humor of the Board are the decoration on the youngster's hat, and the suggestion that he is reading a book on child care.

ALTERNATE IDEA:
The same objective could be achieved by using a child's hand reaching up for an adult hand (symbolic guidance), while a third hand holds the book.

BE A MOTHER'S HELPER

MATERIALS:
Construction paper, wooden spoons, a bunch of dried flowers, apron, pins.

COLORS:
White, red, blue, green, yellow, multicolor apron.

METHOD:
1. Line Board with white paper.
2. Pin on real apron.
3. Fasten wooden items and flowers in pocket, by using large steel pins. (With needlenose pliers, push pins way into Board, at the side of each implement, then bend over to hold securely in place).
4. Add cutout caption letters to follow movement of apron ties.

INSIDE FUN FOR A RAINY DAY

MATERIALS:
Construction paper, marking pen, paper doilies, fabrics, chalk, pins, wool yarn.

COLORS:
Blue, yellow, white, black, green, pink, orange, brown.

METHOD:
1. Line Board with blue construction paper.
2. Draw diagonal lines with white chalk to indicate rain.
3. From a sheet of white paper representing body of the house, cut a horizontal rectangle to simulate open window, then pin on and add white lace doily curtains.
4. Place a white paper triangle above the left portion of the house, for the gabled roof, and the flat roof area to the right, on which part of the caption has been lettered.
5. The remainder of the caption, done with black marking pen on a strip of yellow paper, appears as the foundation of the house.
6. Add window boxes at right (two short, horizontal strips of white paper, each holding a flower), and tree with birdhouse and bird at left. For a touch of humor the birdhouse is a virtual replica of the people's house. Embellish tree with marking pen lines, as seen in illustration.
7. Place in their various positions the individuals busy with inside fun: mother coming down the stairs to serve refreshments, youngsters at play, and their small friend with raincoat and umbrella preparing to join the group indoors. (All figures are based on figure pattern in this book, cut and rearranged into their respective pursuits. Fabric constitutes the clothing within the house, and wool yarn ornaments the head of the girl at right).

HOLLAND

MATERIALS:
Construction paper, wood-grained contact paper, pins.

COLORS:
Blue, orange, white, brown. (Since this Bulletin Board depends primarily for its effect on color, the colors representative of the subject are naturally featured, with brown added for the wooden shoes, a typical symbol of Holland).

METHOD:
1. Line Board with white paper.
2. Sheets of construction paper with the country's name repeated in white on horizontal and vertical caption strips, are mounted as mats for related information, student papers, or appropriate photographs.
3. The tulip is cut from construction paper, and the shoe below it from wood-grained contact paper. (See pattern section). Both are pinned at lower left.

NOTE:
The paper panels may be arranged in different ways, with the various display elements repeated as often as required to fill up available space.

BOOKS ABOUT HOLLAND

MATERIALS:
Construction paper, Netherlands flag, marking pen, cardboard, magazine cutout or drawing of Dutch wooden shoe, pins.

COLORS:
Red, orange, white, blue.

METHOD:
1. Use a large sheet of white cardboard for the book's front cover.
2. Decorate with magazine cutout or drawing of a Dutch wooden shoe, and a miniature Dutch flag, commercial or made with construction paper, pinned away from cardboard, for dimension.
3. Add caption to simulate book title, using colors of Netherlands flag.
4. Cut a piece of white construction paper at a slight angle, place at top of book as shown in illustration, and with marking pen indicate page lines.
5. Add a dark blue spine of construction paper, angled in at top where it meets pages and front cover, for appearance of dimension.
6. Insert a fringed bookmark between pages, for a touch of realism.
7. This oversized book can be pinned to Bulletin Board or, if a back support is added, will stand free on a table display of books about Holland.

NOTE:
If the book is to stand alone on the floor, use two large sheets of cardboard stapled together, and stand at an angle. Construction paper pages cut at an angle and attached to the back cardboard, will give dimension. Similar displays featuring other countries may be arranged, with the symbols and cover titles appropriately changed. The book may also present a plain white cardboard front, onto which can be pinned various book jackets devoted to any given subject under discussion.

ARMCHAIR TRAVEL

MATERIALS:
Construction paper, fabric, paper lace doily, map, marking pen, glue, pins.

COLORS:
White, brown, red, blue, green, gray, multicolor fabric.

METHOD:
1. Line Board with white paper.
2. Using a picture of a chair as a guide, enlarge to size necessary by block method explained in this book, and cut out.
3. Place chair on a sheet of construction paper simulating a rug, and pin or glue fringe to rug's left edge.
4. Add lamp, doily (antimacassar) on arm of chair, a plant, a pipe, and a folded piece of construction paper to which a map has been glued, representing a book of road maps.
5. With marking pen draw a stream of curly smoke emitted from pipe.
6. Spell out caption in ornamental letters with curly serifs.

NOTE:
This design may be employed effectively as a library display, implying that readers who are not able to travel may relax at home with good travel books. To actual travellers it may also suggest reading in advance about places to be visited. Whenever home reading is presented as a display theme, it is important to project it as a pleasant, comfortable, enjoyable experience.

ONE WORLD

MATERIALS:
Construction paper, chalk, flags, marking pens, pins.

COLORS:
White, blue, orange, yellow, pink, purple, black, multicolor flags.

METHOD:
1. Line Board with white paper.
2. Cut a paper circle world and draw chalk lines, simulating longitude and latitude.
3. Cut paper caption letters and superimpose on world, as shown.
4. Pin onto Board.
5. Based on figure pattern in this book, cut out five paper children, arms extended, with costumes as indicated in photograph. (Use marking pen and chalk lines where necessary). Pin the youngsters around the sides and top of the world, leaving bottom free.
6. At the extreme left pin on a row of miniature flags representing the countries illustrated by the children. Or the flags may be pinned into the hands of the children by students during class discussion.

NOTE:
If numerous countries are to be studied, or read about, the figures could be added individually, starting with the country first introduced, and placing its representative at left of the globe. As the lessons progress, the other children are fastened in their respective positions, one by one. Should the display expand to other Bulletin Boards and tables, each could duplicate one of the figures, with related reading matter close by. If a Book Fair featuring books about other lands is contemplated, the tables with their figures in native garb would be colorful and appealing as attention-getters for the books on view. A Bulletin Board similar to the one shown would help welcome visitors to the Fair.

PARADE OF CHILDREN (UNITED NATIONS)

MATERIALS:
Construction paper, miniature flags of various lands, marking pen, chalk, pins.

COLORS:
Gray, black, white, various flag colors.

METHOD:
1. Using pattern in this book, cut figures from construction paper.
2. With marking pen and paper, dress the youngsters in costumes representing their respective countries.
3. Stand each figure on strip of black construction paper bearing the name of his country in white chalk.
4. Pin figures to Bulletin Board and fasten the flag of each, also with pins, to left hands.

NOTE:
The varied, vivid colors of the flags carry viewers' eyes across the Board parade fashion. The black, white and gray of the costumes contrast sharply with the bright colors, and set them off to advantage. Students may prepare the figures as part of a project featuring lands overseas. As they study additional countries, more figures and flags can join the parade. If preferred, the figures can be used individually, with fairly extensive information about their areas' history, geography, climate, culture, economy, etc. They may be cut any desired size, or combination of sizes. For example, if Japan were the class topic, one large Japanese figure could be cut and suitably dressed, then attached to the Board at one end of the room, to introduce the subject. As more is learned about the country and its people, small figures might be cut out and dressed by students, and placed at the other end of the room. The Board area in-between provides space for information, maps, charts and pictures. Table displays may also be coordinated, using the same type cutouts with easel supports, to stand free as backdrop figures for related books and pamphlets.

INDIA

MATERIALS:
Construction paper, wrapping paper, students' art work, graphs, photographs, written information.

COLORS:
White, black, red, blue, green, gold.

METHOD:
1. Line Board with white paper.
2. Divide Board into colors as shown, covering much of the inner area with Paisley print wrapping paper (attach only a part of this paper, leaving the remainder free to fold over woman's head in the manner customarily seen in India), and a smaller portion at extreme right.
3. Cut large caption letters from the wrapping paper, and place directly under the green section.
4. Use a magazine picture or student's art work for woman's head.
5. Mount information, graphs, photographs, and related students' art works on the Board, being careful not to overcrowd.

NOTE:
The sizeable areas of solid color offset the busy design of the Paisley print. Since the patterned paper is so interesting, little time and effort are required for the balance of the composition, to command attention. The oversized head, the three-dimensional effect of the folded patterned paper and large print letters, combine to present good color balance and a simple, pleasing way to display material devoted to a foreign country. This entire arrangement was sparked by the wrapping paper. Since there are so many excellent designs on the market, it is relatively easy to come up with fresh ideas. Let the motif of the paper set the style and tone of the Board. As in this instance, the color scheme is taken directly from the printed paper.

EXOTIC READING FROM ROMANTIC LANDS

MATERIALS:
Construction paper, marking pens, pins.

COLORS:
White, light orange, dark orange, pink, brown, gold, yellow, blue, green.

METHOD:
1. Line Board with white paper.
2. Cut wide strips of construction paper for the books and group as shown in illustration.
3. Letter first part of caption on upper book spine centers, decorating areas to right and left with magazine cutouts of exotic patterns.
4. With a marking pen draw vertical lines on these books, to indicate end of covers, then add horizontal lines to simulate pages.
5. On third book from top only page lines are in evidence, with a decorative book mark (also cut from an exotic print pattern taken from a discarded magazine) inserted.
6. The bottom shape, bearing the remainder of the caption, is pinned away from the Board, for dimension.
7. To sharpen the exotic effect, construction paper beads done with marking pens in various colors, frame the books.

NOTE:
The worker's own handwriting may be substituted for the caption lettering, using a few curlicues to go along with the mood of the Board. A display such as that offered here might back up a table of books featuring distant lands, fairy tales, or similar themes.

GREECE

MATERIALS:
Construction paper, commercial letters, photographs and maps of Greece, marking pen, pins.

COLORS:
Light blue, dark blue, white, black, multicolor maps and photographs.

METHOD:
1. Line Board with dark blue construction paper.
2. Cut and pin triangular shape of white construction paper to fit upper third of display area.
3. Below the triangle and its narrow blue border space out and attach three strips of white paper representing side and center columns.
4. Again leaving a narrow border of blue, pin a strip of white paper toward the bottom of the Board, to represent the base of the Grecian structure.
5. The main caption, GREECE, is cut from black construction paper, and pinned to the bottom of the triangular roof.
6. Place written information, maps and photographs pointing up Greek culture (ancient and modern) between and upon columns, as seen in illustration.
7. Add marking-pen line of blue around triangular roof, and blue Greek design along top edge of building base.
8. Below the decoration appears the auxiliary caption wording, YESTERDAY and TODAY, done in black commercial letters.

NOTE:
This design may be effectively executed in lightweight cardboard instead of construction paper, and pinned away from the Board for dimension. If sufficient Bulletin Board space is available, a row of buildings similar to the one pictured could trace Greek art and architecture from earliest times, indicating how new developments are often based on the old.

ALTERNATE SUGGESTION:
Rome may be handled in the same way, featuring Roman numerals as part of a math project.

AFRICA

MATERIALS:
Construction paper, fabric, maps, pins, brown corrugated board.

COLORS:
Black, white, brown.

METHOD:
1. Line Board with black paper at left, white paper at right, and zebra patterned fabric in-between.
2. Cut out a black and white figure, arm and foot extended, and use half of each, pinning the white against the black and the black against the white, as pictured. (These represent the two races in Africa).
3. Attach to the fabric backdrop a large sheet of black construction paper on which a map of Africa made by students is displayed.
4. The caption letters, cut from white construction paper and mounted on a strip of black construction paper, are large and bold.
5. A narrow strip of brown corrugated board pinned at the top and bottom of the display area, gives the feeling of a wall hanging.

NOTE:
Information concerning Africa can be added to the Board by mounting black and white construction paper mats on the patterned backdrop, and attaching pamphlets or leaflets to them. Wild animal or exotic floral fabric patterns and prints could also be associated with the subject featured here.

THE HISTORY OF AFRICA

MATERIALS:
Construction paper, photographs.

COLORS:
Black, white.

METHOD:
1. Line Board with black construction paper.
2. Center large caption letters on Board approximately one-third of the way down. Each letter, big and bold, is drawn on and then cut from white construction paper, to resemble block printing. This sets the mood for the subject.
3. Colorful photographs pertaining to Africa are mounted on white paper and attached to the black backdrop. The smaller black letters are cut in the same manner as the large white ones, and mounted on a strip of white paper.
4. Students' drawings, papers or booklets, if desired, may be used along with, or in place of, the photographs. The display as a whole points up balance, impact and good design with a minimum of art work.

NOTE:
Here is an instance of having empty or negative space work well as filled space. The arrangement is concentrated, the bright pictures making a dramatic splash in the center, while the black boldly holds the design together and rests the eye. Altogether, it is a good example of using only part of a given space for the display of visuals, leaving the remainder blank. Thus a relatively small exhibit can be presented effectively.

THE WORLD NEWS

MATERIALS:
Construction paper, maps, tissue paper, rubber cement, marking pen, white shellac, cardboard, news clips, pins or glue.

COLORS:
Navy blue, tan, black, white.

METHOD:
1. Line Board with navy blue paper.
2. Cut map(s) in shape of a rectangle slightly less than half the upper display area, and mount on cardboard with rubber cement.
3. Coat the map(s) with a thin layer of rubber cement.
4. While the above is wet cover with sheet(s) of tan tissue paper, working quickly.
5. Coat the tissue paper with a thin layer of rubber cement. Let dry (the adhesive will remain a bit tacky, even when dry).
6. Cover area with white shellac and let dry.
7. Add cutout of world (circle with proper marking pen lines) and cutout caption letters decorated with arrows instead of serifs, pointing north, east, south and west—implying that world news flows from all directions.
8. Pin or glue to display area, with narrow border of blue at top and on both sides.
9. Affix current events news clips or students' written work to lower section.

NOTE:
If preferred, the process by which the tissue paper is joined to the map(s) may be done with white plastic glue, eliminating the shellac step (see illustration, MOVING AIR). Since the rubber cement tissue paper technique is tricky on occasion, it may be advisable to try it first on scrap paper. But the successful result presents a professional-looking overlay of color which is most satisfactory.

OUR CITY AND HOW IT GROWS

MATERIALS:
Construction paper, newspaper clippings, marking pen, ruler, pins.

COLORS:
Black, white.

METHOD:
1. Line Board with white paper.
2. Cut out bold, white construction paper letters to simulate newspaper headlines, and glue them onto a strip of black construction paper.
3. Pin on toward bottom of display area.
4. Cut large black caption letters and pin above the black strip on the white background.
5. With marking pen and ruler draw vertical lines to represent newspaper columns, and below them place a thin horizontal strip of black construction paper to separate the news section from the lettered base.
6. Use the display as a local current events Board, featuring clippings brought in by students which deal with the development on numerous fronts of their city. The clippings should be attached from bottom to top, in the manner of building construction, giving the appearance from across the room of a skyline.

NOTE:
This Board stems from the illustration EXTRA CREDIT, with the news clips and caption placement reversed. The format is the same, but the proportions changed to fit the space at hand. (A practical example of how one idea may spawn another).

CARING FOR OUR PETS

MATERIALS:
Construction paper, ribbon, students' work, pins.

COLORS:
White, blue-green, orange, black.

METHOD:
1. Line the Board with white paper.
2. A student's large animal head, done in art class, dominates the display at left, with the animal's body made from a large, lightly-trimmed sheet of cardboard or construction paper.
3. Pin on construction paper legs, feeding bowl and rug for animal to stand on (species of animal is indicated on feeding bowl strip).
4. At lower right add two paper cutout figures tugging at a ribbon leash, thereby increasing fun quality of the Board.
5. Cut big, bold caption letters from construction paper, and affix photographs or students' art work about pets and their care.

ANIMAL HOMES

MATERIALS:
Construction paper, photographs or drawings of animals, marking pen, pins.

COLORS:
White, turquoise, yellow, yellow-green, blue, purple, orange.

METHOD:
1. Line Board with white paper.
2. Let the pictures of animals to be exhibited determine the display area. Each animal pictured is placed on a circular mat, which in turn is pinned to a larger mat representing the back of a turtle.
3. Attach head, legs and tail to turtle, keeping the reptile in shades of yellow and yellow-green.
4. Mount the turtle on a sheet of turquoise construction paper, which represents the house.
5. Position purple roof at top and caption letters at bottom in same color, to unify design.
6. The multihued flowers flanking the caption and smoke from the chimney add a decorative touch.

NOTE:
This idea may be useful in introducing the study of animal habits and habitats. Many "home" shapes could be repeated and information, photographs, students' written work or drawings could be attractively and effectively presented, with minimum involvement on the teacher's (or librarian's) part.

ALTERNATE TITLES:
1. **WHERE DO ANIMALS LIVE?**
2. **OUR ANIMAL NEIGHBORS**
3. **LET'S LOOK AT ANIMALS**
4. **GOOD HOMES FOR OUR PETS**

ALTERNATE SUGGESTION:
Using some basic "home" shapes, it might be interesting to arrange a line of houses across the Board, with cutout silhouette figures or magazine cutouts of different things children can do to be helpful around the house. Home shapes should be retained, and adapted to various other display projects throughout the school year.

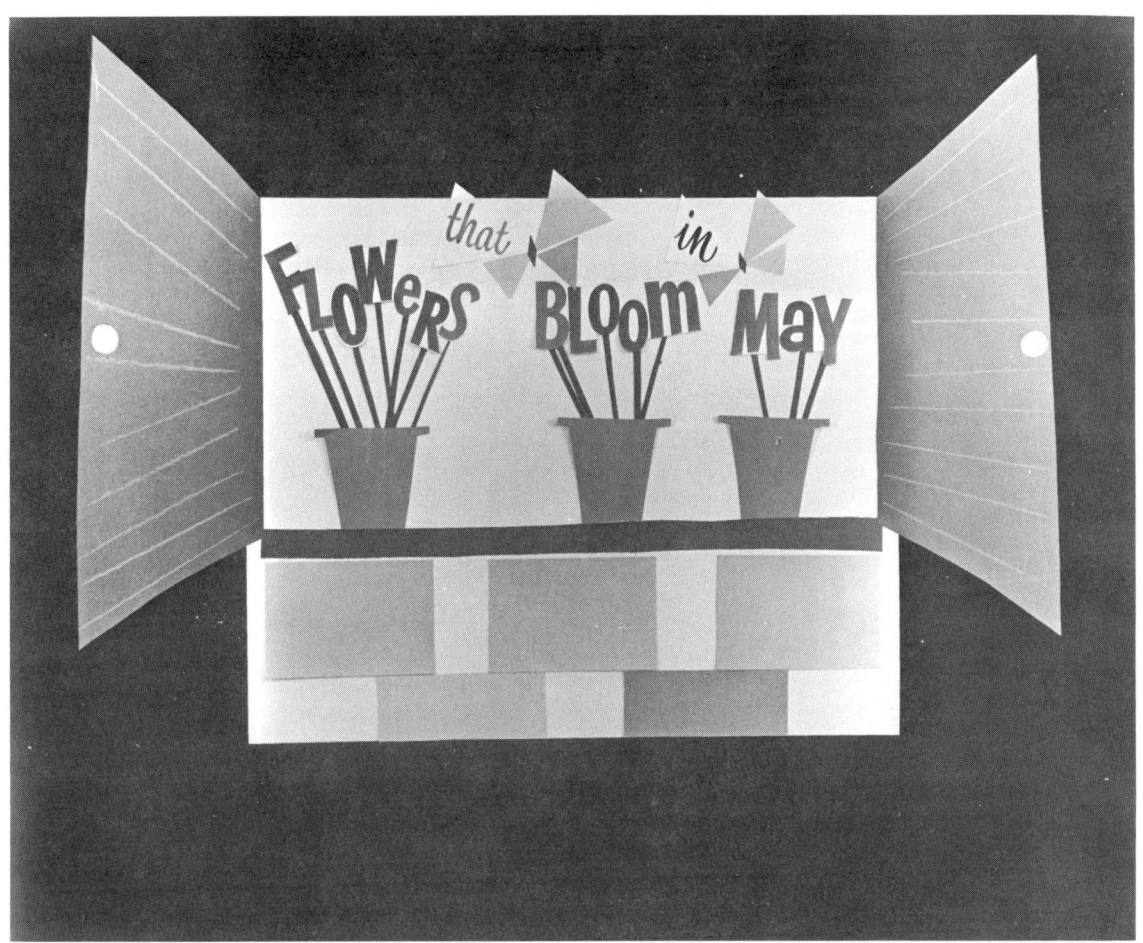

FLOWERS THAT BLOOM IN MAY

MATERIALS:
Construction paper, marking pen, chalk, pins.

COLORS:
Blue, white, orange, red-orange, tan, yellow, green, yellow-green.

METHOD:
1. Line Board with white paper.
2. Cut out letters to form the caption, add construction paper strips for stems and pin behind flowerpot shapes, cut from light orange paper to resemble clay flowerpots.
3. Under the flowerpots pin a strip of blue paper to simulate a window sill.
4. The shutters are two large sheets of construction paper cut at angles, with the smaller ends attached to the window area. Add chalk lines for the louvers and white construction paper knobs.
5. The butterflies are triangular shapes of colored construction paper, with part of the caption lettered on the wings.
6. The larger caption letters (cutouts or commercial) represent the flowers.
7. Pin construction paper rectangles under the window, to give the effect of a brick wall. These will also serve as mats for botanical information, students' papers or floral prints.

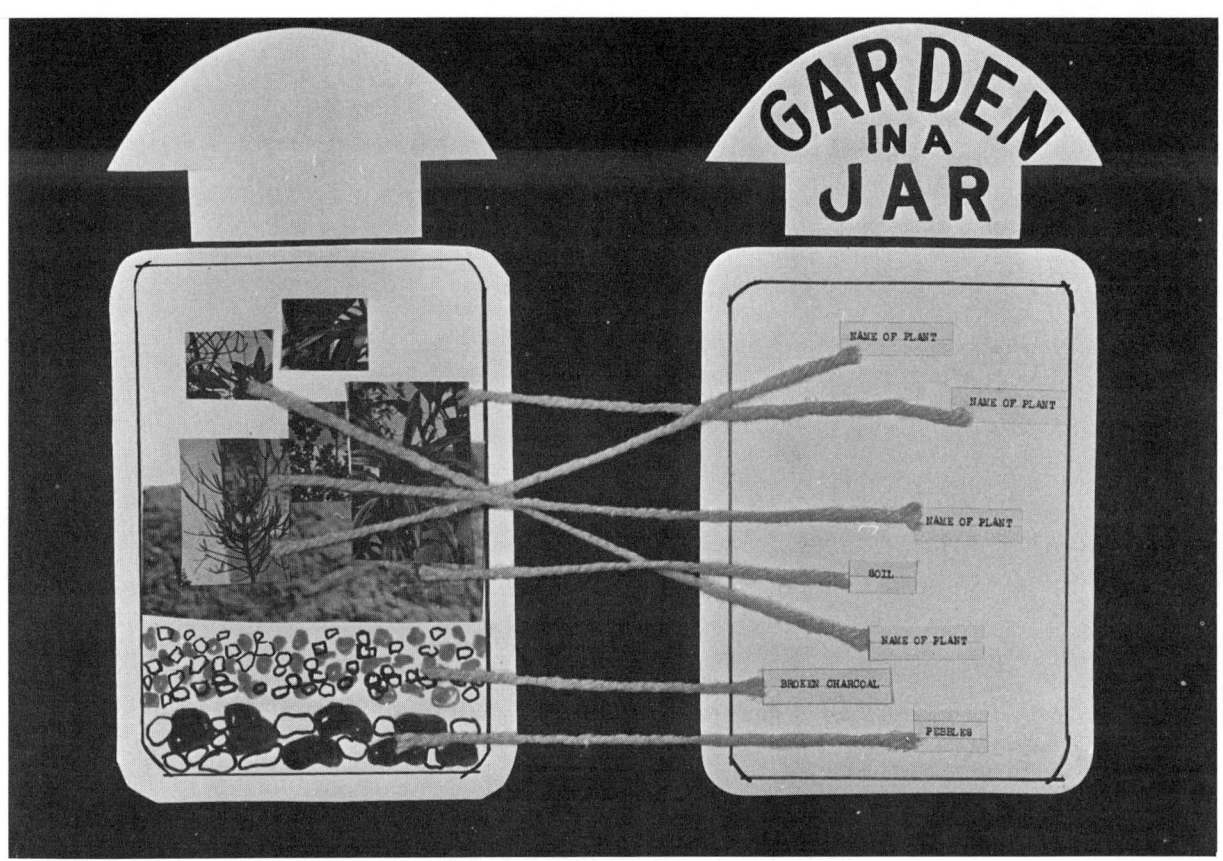

GARDEN IN A JAR

MATERIALS:
Construction paper, magazine pictures, marking pens, wool yarn, pins.

COLORS:
Black, white, orange, brown, tan, green, multicolor magazine photographs, or sketches of plants.

METHOD:
1. Line Board with black paper.
2. Using two full sheets of white construction paper, round off corners and place side by side on Board, in the manner of apothecary jars.
3. Draw a line with black marking pen around the inner edges of jars, to simulate thickness of glass.
4. Cut two lids to fit over jars, using the one at right for the caption lettering, as seen in photograph.
5. The jar at left projects illustrations of terrarium plants, soil and related items, while its counterpart displays the proper nomenclature. Strings of wool yarn connect the two.

NOTE:
If the plan seems feasible, this display could start with the two empty jars, and students might build it up from the bottom to the top, as a real terrarium is developed. As information is gathered, pictures in sketch form, or pertinent magazine photographs are appended to jar at left, while identification labels are added to the companion container. Many other classroom subjects may be treated in the same way, keeping the display simple and bold, as a device for projecting information, and correlating information with art work.

TOUCH AND FEEL

MATERIALS:
Construction paper, assorted items suitable for a tactile chart, glue, pins.

COLORS:
Black, turquoise, white, orange, golden yellow, green, multicolor items on tactile chart.

METHOD:
1. Line Board with black paper.
2. Using the arm-and-hand "tree" pattern shown in the illustration NIGHT . . . AND . . . DAY, cut construction paper shape in turquoise blue.
3. Caption lettering is cut from white construction paper and glued onto arm, which is then pinned horizontally at upper left of display area.
4. Extending outward from the hand toward the right, pin on the various articles students may bring from home for tactile chart.
5. Below the above section add sheets of construction paper in bright colors against the black, for items contributed by the students in line with the headings, SOFT, SMOOTH, ROUGH. The letters may also be cut from paper and glued on, lettered with marking pen, or spelled out with commercial alphabets.

ALTERNATE IDEA:
Use black cardboard for this display, scoring it at the top of colored panels. Bend the upper portion, allowing panels below to rest on a table. The students' articles could then be placed on paper mats.

HEMIDEMISEMIQUAVER: A 64TH NOTE

MATERIALS:
Construction paper, poster paint and brush, pins.

COLORS:
Black, white.

METHOD:
1. Line the display area with white paper.
2. Cut strips of construction paper and attach to form a border of piano keys, top and bottom.
3. Caption is done in script style on a strip of construction paper with poster paint and brush, then pinned onto middle section of the display.

NOTE:
If calligraphy talent on the part of teacher and students is lacking, cutout construction paper letters, or commercial letters, may be substituted.

ALTERNATE SUGGESTION:
In the central section photographs of composers and musicians studied in class might occupy the caption space.

ALTERNATE TITLES:
    SOME FAMOUS MUSIC MAKERS
    GREAT AMERICAN MUSIC
    MUSIC AND MATH (to fit in with the subtitle, A 64TH NOTE)

LISTEN - WHAT DO YOU HEAR?

MATERIALS:
Construction paper, discarded magazine and coloring book cutouts, and/or students' art work illustrating things that make sounds (clocks, vacuum cleaner, steam roller, electric mixer, cat, bell, marching band, musical instruments, whistling tea kettle, truck, crow, train, bird, washing machine, clapping hands, etc.), marking pens, chalk, pins.

COLORS:
Brown, light gray, white, green, blue, yellow-green, multicolor photographs and drawings.

METHOD:
1. Line Board with white paper.
2. Using a large sheet of brown construction paper, cut a large head and neck; add hair, oversized ears, white eyes and mouth, and cut head in half (or substitute newspaper or magazine head for brown paper).
3. Pin halves to right and left edges of display area. Add a blue construction paper pupil to each eye, looking inward.
4. With marking pen draw a sweeping, wavy line simulating a telephone cord from one ear to the other, indicating hearing. Add a construction paper question mark to each ear, to denote listening and questioning.
5. Along the wavy line place blue and green sheets of construction paper, which will serve as mats for the pictures of sound-producing items. Add circles with graph lines of sound done with chalk or marking pen, to intensify atmosphere and color of Board.

BLOW YOUR HORN

MATERIALS:
Construction paper, wide felt-tip pen, pins.

COLORS:
Golden yellow, purple-blue, turquoise, pink, orange.

METHOD:
1. Line Board with golden yellow paper.
2. Cut a large horn from purple-blue construction paper and pin to background, keeping the center of the horn away from the Bulletin Board, to give depth and dimension.
3. Cut and pin on two oval shapes, one inside the other, for the handle of the horn.
4. The message is lettered in a variation of the worker's own handwriting, right on the backdrop, with a wide-tip felt marking pen.
5. Flower decorations are pinned on.

ALTERNATE SUGGESTIONS:
If preferred, the message could be handwritten on strips of construction paper the same color as the outer background area. The center segment might bear the query, "Have You Heard?" with followup information projected on adjacent strips. For those mathematically or musically-minded a numbers or science board, or a staff and musical notes, might be substituted for the flower decorations, and the theme changed accordingly.

NOTE:
Save the horn for repeated future use. While the flowers relate to the spring season, colorful leaves would tie in with autumn, and snowflakes would signify winter.

FINGER PAINTING

MATERIALS:
Construction paper, poster paint, turquoise cellophane, pins.

COLORS:
Black, white, tan, orange, turquoise, yellow, green, purple.

METHOD:
1. Pin black paper to Bulletin Board, as in illustration.
2. From a sheet of tan paper cut away just enough to form the shape of hand indicated, with pointing index finger (see pattern section).
3. Using the same size piece of white construction paper, round off the bottom corners, and trim and taper the top of the jar.
4. Pin jar slightly below the hand.
5. Cut a piece of cellophane somewhat smaller than the jar and pin over forefinger, to give transparent look.
6. In the same manner cut smaller jars for bottom decoration, with strips and smaller rounded rectangles of colored paper to represent the lids and paints.
7. To create the caption the worker's finger is dipped in poster paint, thus achieving the finger paint quality.
8. In the space between upper and lower jars, display finger paintings done by pupils. These should be mounted on colored papers matching those used in the design. Leave some black paper around each piece, to serve as a border.

NOTE:
This type Bulletin Board is particularly advantageous in the school hall, since it remains decorative even while students' works are being changed. Rather than crowd the area, it is better to rotate the paintings. However, if a school is fortunate enough to have several Bulletin Boards in the hallway which are available for the purpose, many paintings can be shown at one time, and the series would be very effective.

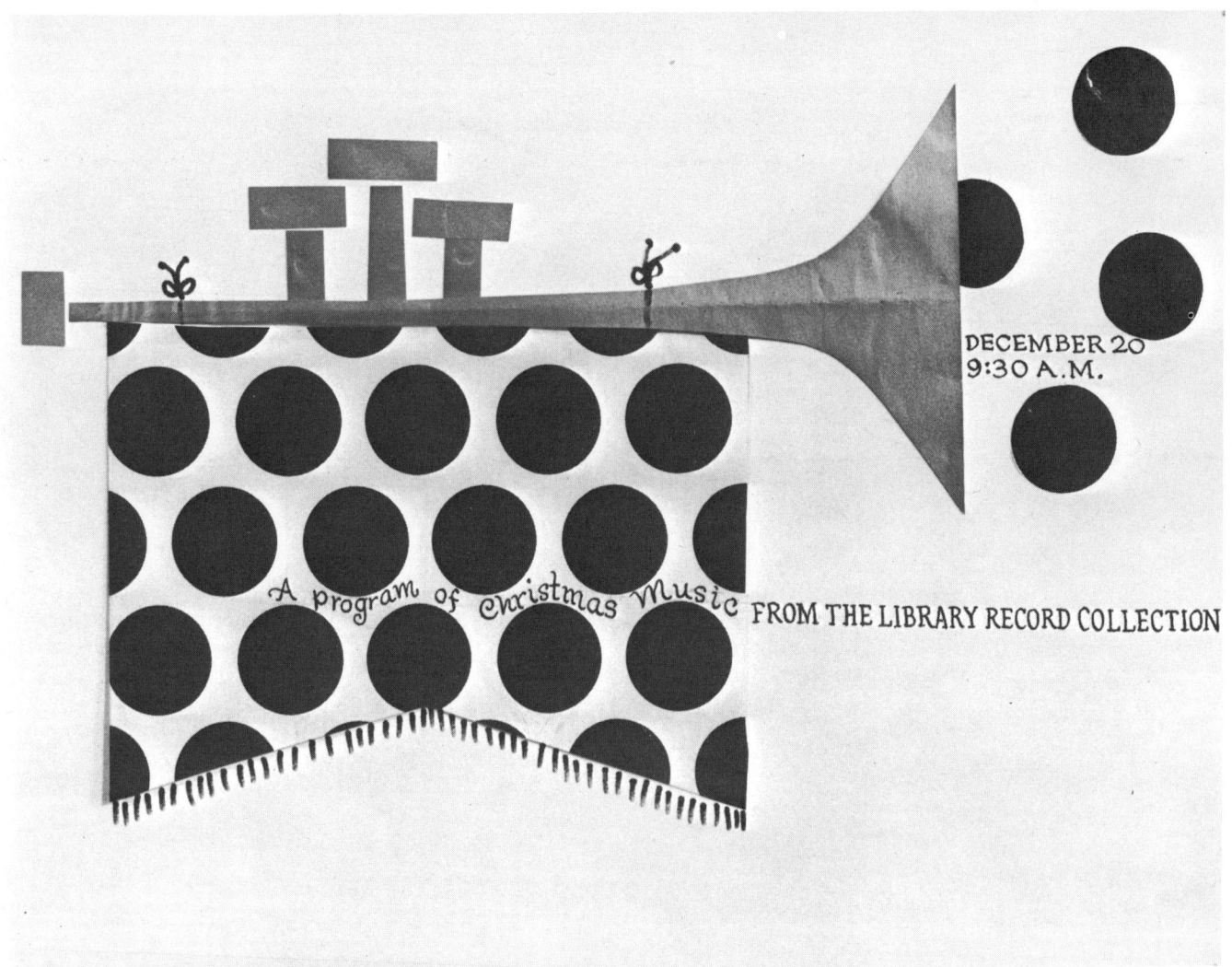

A PROGAM OF CHRISTMAS MUSIC

METHOD:
1. From gold paper cut out a large horn shape (see pattern section) and attach with pins.
2. Hang a banner of polka dot wrapping paper from the instrument.
3. Cut some black dots from a piece of the wrapping paper, and place them as if they were coming from the horn.
4. "Tie" banner with black marking pen bows, and draw fringe at bottom.
5. The caption "dances" around the dots on banner, then continues in a straight line to parallel the horizontal position of the horn.

NOTE:
The polka dots resemble recordings in shape, helping to carry out the overall musical theme.

MATERIALS:
Gold foil paper, black-on-white polka dot patterned wrapping paper, black marking pen, pins.

COLORS:
White, black, gold.

ALTERNATE IDEA:
A general Bulletin Board on music might transform the circles into mats for pictures of well-known composers. Instead of polka dots emanating from the horn, musical notes could be used with the caption, SOME NOTED COMPOSERS.

WE READ AND LEARN ABOUT EACH OTHER

MATERIALS:
Same as WE WORK AND PLAY TOGETHER.

COLORS:
Same as WE WORK AND PLAY TOGETHER.

METHOD:
Same as WE WORK AND PLAY TOGETHER, except for changed caption.

NOTE:
Where sufficient Bulletin Board space is availabe, figures of this type would be effective all along the walls, as a repeat pattern. The Bulletin Board featured offers a pleasing example of how lettering may fit into a display as part of the design, rather than being added as an extra.

NEWS

MATERIALS:
Construction paper, tissue paper, paint, newspaper clippings, glue, pins.

COLORS:
Black, white, gray, green, red, red-orange, purple.

METHOD:
1. Line Board with white paper.
2. Divide the Board into four equal adjoining sections, using four sheets of construction paper the same size—green, red-orange, purple, red—to provide space for news clips pertaining to worldwide current events.
3. The caption, cut from construction paper, combines capital and lowercase letters. The first letter of each word—a black capital glued to a piece of white construction paper—is larger and darker than its lowercase counterparts in North, East, West, South (done in dark gray paint on white paper). After the capitals are glued down, the strip of each is folded away from the rest of the word.
4. Place a rectangle of gray tissue paper over each set of lowercase letters, reducing their impact.
5. Pin the caption onto the Board so that the folds stand away from the backdrop, and the message appears accordion-pleated. Observe that the conspicuous capitals spell out the word, NEWS, easily read from a distance.

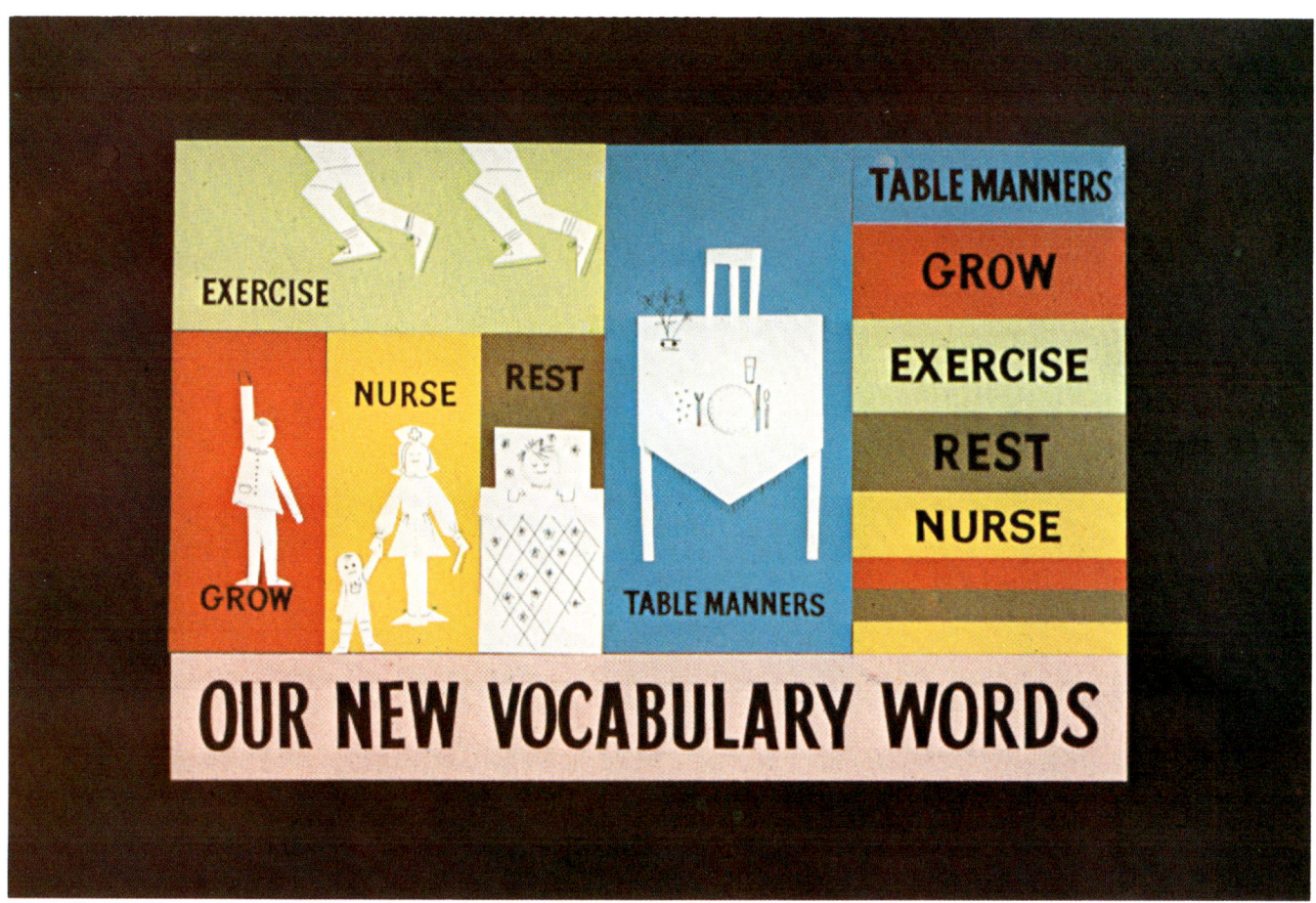

OUR NEW VOCABULARY WORDS

MATERIALS:
Construction paper, marking pens, pins.

COLORS:
Orange, yellow, brown, pink, blue, green, black, white.

METHOD:
1. Line Board with black paper.
2. Cut sheets of construction paper to divide Board into color sections, as illustrated.
3. Place on them construction paper cutouts and drawings interpreting the featured topics, accenting where necessary with marking pen.
4. Auxiliary captions should be done with marking pen, matching the words with related actions.
5. The main caption is spelled out with large, bold commercial letters, running across the bottom of the Board. This lends greater importance to the theme and helps balance the design.

NOTE:
The diversified bright colors, concentrated in the center of a large black area, represent an effective way of decorating an oversized Bulletin Board.

ALTERNATE SUGGESTION:
If preferred, discarded magazine photographs or students' drawings might be used as illustrations instead of those shown. The vocabulary words should be changed often, or added to. By means of pins, the various pieces of construction paper could be easily and quickly attached.

WELCOME TO 5TH GRADE

MATERIALS:
Construction paper, corrugated board, paper lace doilies, magazine photographs of children, or children's art renderings, glue, pins.

COLORS:
Tan, white, pink, blue, and various other hues.

METHOD:
1. Line Board with white paper.
2. Cut a piece of corrugated board to fit proportionately to the display area.
3. Using discarded magazines for photographs of juvenile group, or comparable children's art, glue down cutouts of the children at an angle that makes them appear to be looking through the doorway.
4. Based on pattern in this volume, draw and cut out construction paper teacher figure, rearranging the right arm to wave position, and dress in doily-trimmed, construction paper clothing.
5. The sign over the door bids the youngsters WELCOME TO 5TH GRADE.
6. Glue door to the large, rectangular strip of cardboard and pin strip to Bulletin Board.
7. Glue teacher holding on to door. Since the teacher figure is lightweight, it will stand in position shown.

NOTE:
The door can be placed as desired, and fastened with pins to remain stationary or left free to swing at random. But the strip must be glued tightly to the corrugated door, and then secured to the Bulletin Board.
This is a happy way to welcome pupils back after the long summer vacation, setting the mood for an enjoyable school experience. Save this Board for a farewell display at the close of the school year (see illustration HAVE A GOOD, SAFE SUMMER).

HAVE A GOOD, SAFE SUMMER

MATERIALS:
Same as WELCOME TO 5TH GRADE.

COLORS:
Same as WELCOME TO 5TH GRADE.

METHOD:
Same as WELCOME TO 5TH GRADE, except door tends toward closing position, more in keeping with departure of the children, and different caption.

HOW WE USE MEASURING

MATERIALS:
Madras crepe paper, construction paper, wool yarn, marking pen, pins.

COLORS:
Blue, green, white, yellow, pink, purple.

METHOD:
1. Line Board with madras crepe paper in shades of blue and green.
2. Cut out large sheets of white construction paper to resemble oversized sewing patterns and pin onto Board, lining up with outer edges at the sides.
3. Cut a long, narrow, yellow strip of construction paper; mark off the units with a marking pen to simulate a measuring tape, and attach to Bulletin Board across the lower section. (Join as many strips as necessary to form the tape, done in proper proportion, but oversized).
4. Add construction paper cutouts of simple shapes associated with sewing—a spool with wool yarn wrapped around it to simulate thread, a strawberry pincushion and scissors.
5. The caption, done with a marking pen on strips of white paper, is lettered with an enlarged version of the worker's own handwriting, as shown. Complementing the tape measure, it helps carry viewers' eyes across the Board.
6. With marking pen indicate oversized pins all around the pattern edges, and stick real pins into the strawberry cushion.

NOTE:
Featured here is another way to present math in everyday life, with a familiar scene depicted in oversize shapes. The patterns provide space for information about the topic concerned, or measuring charts.

ALTERNATE IDEA:
Students may devise and execute additional displays related to measuring activities, if more Boards are available.

FUN WITH NUMBERS

MATERIALS:
Construction paper, marking pen, pins.

COLORS:
Black, pink, orange, yellow.

METHOD:
1. Line Board with black paper.
2. Cut and pin on at lower left large construction paper silhouette of head, bubble pipe and hand, along with vari-sized colorful bubbles flowing from pipe, to denote fun.
3. The caption letters are cut from black construction paper and pinned onto largest circle on the right.
4. Math problems on the smaller circles, and mathematical signs on the silhouette head, are done with marking pen.

NOTE:
Use as many number-marked circles as necessary to make a point. The old saying, "the more the merrier," applies here to the bubble decoration.

THE NOVEL
ONE HUNDRED YEARS AGO

MATERIALS:
Construction paper, patterned antique wrapping paper, marking pen, glue, pins.

COLORS:
Red, tan, black, gold.

METHOD:
1. Using the same style numerals as in Illustration JOIN CLUB 100, neatly cut out 100 from the largest available sheet of red construction paper.
2. Then carefully glue taut pieces of patterned wrapping paper printed with old-time advertisements from about a century ago onto the back of the construction paper, facing front, and filling the openings.
3. Cutout letters in gold paper, or gold commerical letters form the two-part caption, glued to a strip of the red paper. Outline letters with black marking pen, and pin the display in place on the Bulletin Board.

NOTE:
Libraries may mark other one hundredth anniversaries in the same way, with appropriate books displayed nearby.

KEEPING OUR COMMUNITY IN GOOD CONDITION

MATERIALS:
Construction paper, corrugated board, cardboard, lace paper doilies, discarded costume jewelry pin, marking pen, mat knife, pins.

COLORS:
Black, white, light green, dark green, brown, dark red, yellow, orange, blue.

METHOD:
1. Cut two rectangles from a corrugated box.
2. Deface one by cutting outer layer of brown paper with mat knife in gashes and tearing pieces away to expose the corrugated ribs. Leave other intact.
3. From construction paper cut two each of roof, chimney, sun, windows with shutters, cat, flowers and trash can.
4. Line Board with white construction paper.
5. Pin on grass sections as shown in illustration.
6. On left, in haphazard fashion, pin on house in disrepair, with one each of the various construction paper items mentioned in Step 3.
7. On right arrange the duplicate pieces in an orderly, constructive way, with jewelry pin for door knocker.
8. Cut and attach fence and steps from cardboard, affixing them improperly to left portion of the display, and properly to the right.
9. Give the cat and sun of the left side a sad expression with marking pen, while those on the right should seem happy and contented.
10. The caption letters are inexpensive commercial ones, arranged across the top of the Bulletin Board. When complete, the overall design contrasts a rundown, poorly-cared-for home with a rehabilitated home, attractive, clean and well-preserved.

110

ANIMALS, FLOWERS AND BIRDS

MATERIALS:
Construction paper, children's cutout figures, commercial letters, pins.

COLORS:
Black, white, yellow, red, green, blue, golden yellow.

METHOD:
1. Line Board with white paper.
2. First cut black triangular shapes from construction paper for top and bottom border decoration, then black circles from the scraps.
3. Place four black rectangles (two shorter, two longer) in the white area between border triangles, the two at right a little higher than those at left. These constitute mats for children's colorful, imaginative art cutouts relating to the subject.
4. Pin commercial letters for caption above panels at left, repeating title below panels at right, in keeping with the repeat pattern of the border design.

WE WRITE ABOUT SPRING

MATERIALS:
Brown wrapping paper, construction paper, marking pen, thin white cardboard, pins.

COLORS:
Pastel pink, various shades of green, purple, lavender, turquoise, white.

METHOD:
1. Line Bulletin Board with white paper.
2. Cover area surrounding the large rectangular center section with wrapping paper, leaving a narrow white border all around.
3. From construction paper and additional pieces of wrapping paper cut large, vari-colored petalled flowers for the upper portion of the main display, and a hill of smaller flowers for the lower section.
4. Pin (or glue) flowers to backdrop.
5. Cut a piece of thin white cardboard for the wagon.
6. Script lettering on wagon, and decorative body and wheel lines, should harmonize in color with the flowers.
7. Using long pins, let the wagon body and wheels stand away from the backdrop, then add the vehicle's handle.
8. The centers of the large flowers provide a base for the students' creative writings about spring.

NOTE:
If new wrapping paper is not available, and the supply budget is low, old gift wrappings from candy boxes and other packages may be pressed into service. Many of the latter are attractive and decorative. A warm iron run over the paper lightly for a few seconds will often reduce creases, and make the paper more presentable. Teachers need not contribute all materials used. Students will want to participate in the project by bringing needed items for effective and exciting Bulletin Boards.

BICYCLE RULES

MATERIALS:
Construction paper, cardboard, marking pen, cellophane, narrow ribbons, wicker basket, straw flowers, upholstery tacks, pins.

COLORS:
White, orange, purple, green, gray, black, yellow, red.

METHOD:
1. Line Board with white paper.
2. Cut two large circles freehand to fit the display area (leaving plenty of white space, as seen in illustration) for the bicycle wheels, and pin to Board.
3. Cut slightly curved shapes for fenders, handlebars, and attach at both ends, leaving center section free, for dimension.
4. Add bar connecting back of bicycle to front, as well as the seat, headlight and pedal.
5. With a marking pen print safety rules for cycling on strips of white cardboard.
6. Attach strips with upholstery tacks at wheel centers, so that they resemble spokes, and can be turned freely.
7. Decorate bicycle basket with straw flowers and pin to handlebars.
8. The balloons are cut from construction paper and cellophane.
9. HAVE FUN is lettered on one balloon, then all are covered with brightly colored cellophane and pinned to back fender by means of gay, narrow ribbons.

NOTES:
All circles and strips (except wheel spokes) are cut freehand, to enhance fun feeling. Since classroom rules and regulations must be frequently introduced, it is generally wise to employ the lighthearted approach, rather than more serious treatment. In this case, and for this subject, the spacious white background gives an airy look. Further, the flying ribbons and balloons, along with the flower-decorated basket, set the mood for fun, yet the important rules are there to read and remember.

LOST AND FOUND TREE

MATERIALS:
Construction paper, tissue paper, bird (paper or stuffed), blue and black marking pens, large pins, pliers, assorted lost and found articles.

COLORS:
Black, white, blue, olive green, turquoise, yellow, orange, multi-color clothing.

METHOD:
1. Line Board with white paper.
2. Cut out tree shape from strips of black paper, putting together as many as required to provide limbs for lost items.
3. Add cutout green tissue leaves to tree, and some drawn with marking pen.
4. Perch brightly-colored, decorative bird at top of tree, with sign in bill (done in black with marking pen on yellow construction paper) reading, "Does anything here belong to you?" (done with blue and black marking pens).
5. With pliers push large, heavy pins into tree and hang wearing apparel, etc., from pinheads.
6. The caption letters form the "pot." Cut from blue and black construction paper, they are glued to a white pot shape (except for the word, *and*, which is inserted with blue marking pen).

NOTE:
The tree arrangement can be seasonal, and kept up through the school year.

THE STORY OF ELECTRICITY

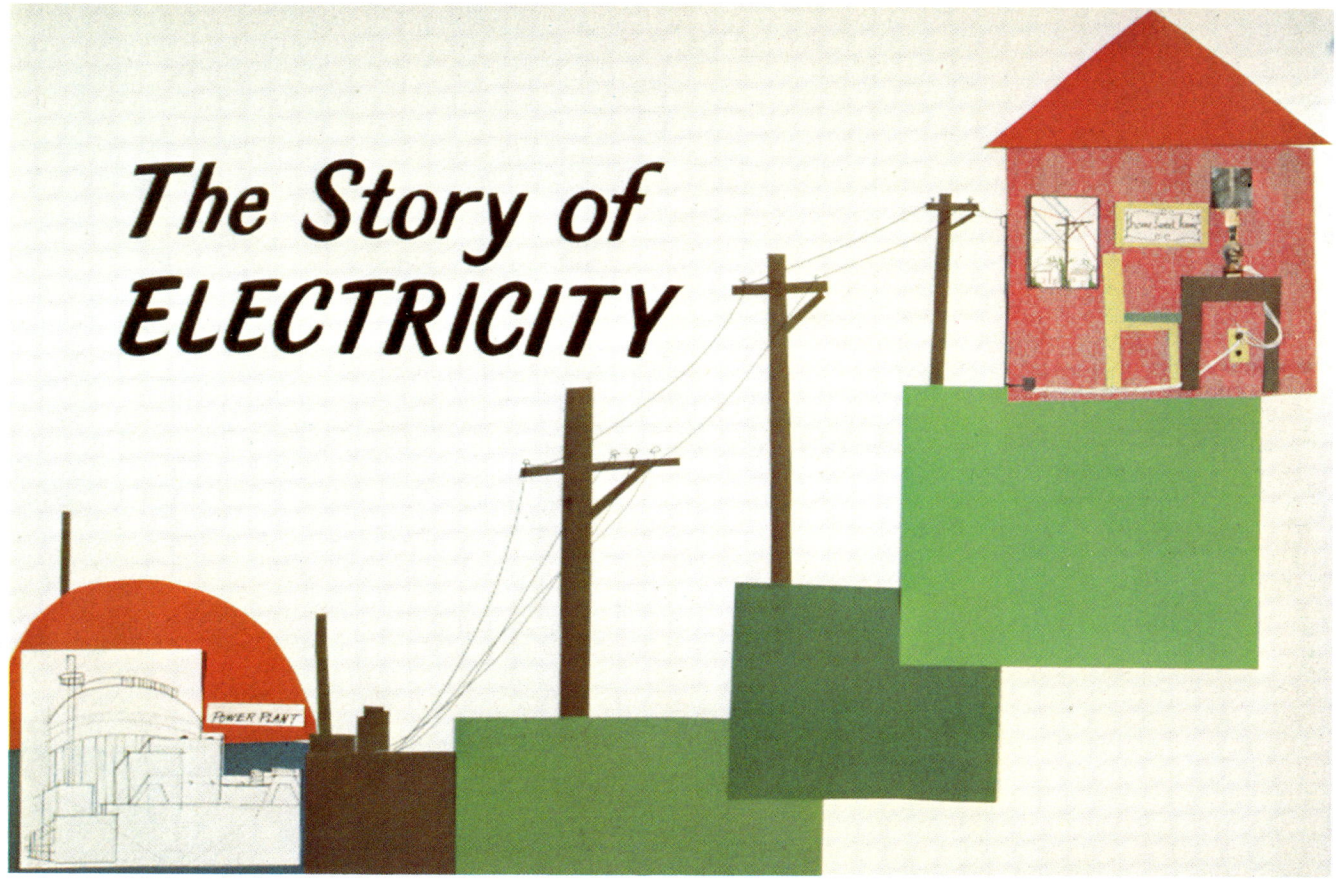

MATERIALS:
Construction paper, string, magazine cutouts, wallpaper, marking pens, glue, pins.

COLORS:
White, red-orange, magenta, blue, brown, olive green, dark green, emerald green, black.

METHOD:
1. Line Board with white paper.
2. Starting at extreme lower left, arrange overlapping sheets of construction paper to progress toward upper right corner (blue and brown on same level, stepping up slightly with olive green, then dark green, emerald green and finally, a rectangle of magenta wallpaper to represent a residence).
3. To the blue paper add a red-orange, construction paper dome, behind which is pinned a thin vertical strip of brown paper, to suggest part of a power plant.
4. Above the brown sheet add a few small pieces of the same color, suggesting the top of a power plant, and to the green rectangles add brown electric poles.
5. To the wallpaper house add a triangular red-orange roof.
6. Glue a magazine cutout or drawing of a power plant, with accompanying descriptive label lettered on white paper with marking pen, onto the blue and red paper at lower left.
7. Add cutout magazine items to the house—a window showing outdoors, with power lines; chair and table; lamp; a wall sampler reading, "Home, Sweet Home," done on a strip of white paper with marking pens, to resemble embroidery in colors relating to the display.
8. Pin a paper electric outlet on wall under table, and run a string to simulate wire from lamp to socket, then to outside and up side of house, over to the electric poles, and down to the brown power plant.
9. Add cutout black caption letters done in slanted bold style.
10. Use the blank sheets of construction paper as mats for information about electricity.

NOTE:
Happily, a few sheets of paper and some string can successfully tell the story of electricity and how it gets from the power station to the home. This display could be arranged by students when the subject is introduced, and they may add information on the mats as study of the unit progresses. Altogether the Board offers convincing evidence that bold, simple shapes, bright color, and plentiful white space can team up to communicate an idea visually.

LIGHT SUMMER READING

MATERIALS:
Construction paper, marking pen, cellophane.

COLORS:
Black, white, pink, purple, yellow, orange.

METHOD:
1. Line Board with black paper.
2. Stack strips of white construction paper with lettered caption on left side of Board to fill up most of the space, creating an oversized picture of books (lettering and decoration on book spines are done with marking pen).
3. Add a large cutout glass shape of white paper, with smaller colored paper shape superimposed, to represent cool liquid in the glass; a lemon slice realistically projecting from glass rim, and a striped drinking straw. Cover glass with cellophane shape slightly larger than liquid contents. A construction paper cherry under the cellophane provides a realistic touch.

NOTE:
This simple treatment conveys the feeling of pleasant summer living, and obliquely suggests quenching not only one's thirst, but also, one's thirst for knowledge. The bright colors and white nicely balance the black space in the display.

ALTERNATE IDEA:
If preferred, two of the book spines may present a list of light summer reading titles, while the caption is condensed to fit the third spine.

WE VISIT A SUPERMARKET

MATERIALS:
Construction paper, cash register tapes, marking pens, plastic wrap, plastic fruit, paper bag, empty grocery and dairy cartons, egg carton, cotton mesh onion bag, tissue paper, cutout paper fruits, double masking tape, pins, glue.

COLORS:
White, brown, yellow, green, blue, turquoise, orange, pink, multicolor packages.

METHOD:
1. Line top half of Board with white paper, and lower half with brown paper.
2. Using a picture or real toy cash register for a guide, enlarge and cut a silhouette side version of the machine from blue construction paper.
3. Also from blue construction paper cut large, bold caption letters and pin onto bottom of white portion of display (to left and right of the cash register), where it meets the brown paper.
4. Glue together cash register tapes as long as necessary and pin onto Board, extending out from top of register, as illustrated, toward caption letters at right, thus drawing the eye from one side of the display to the other. Add a decorative pineapple cutout to top of last three caption letters.
5. Pin all cutout and plastic items to brown portion of Board as shown, in the manner of a counter display:
    a) Watermelon (For this cut a green paper half circle, a smaller white, then still smaller pink circle. Glue them to each other, add black seeds with marking pen, cover the half melon with plastic wrap, and pin to backdrop).
    b) Cut celery from white construction paper, add blue-green lines with marking pens and "leaves" at top of stalks with strips of green tissue paper, pinning to backdrop.
    c) Stuff brown lunch bag with paper, roll top, and pin to Board.
    d) Pin dairy carton to background, then put lid in place.
    e) Pin on cookie box after double masking tape has been put on back to adhere to both the the box and background.
    f) Pin egg carton to Board, then close up.
    g) Cut out a picture of lemons, place in a mesh bag which had held onions, and pin to Board.

NOTE:
The counter could hold an almost endless variety of foods available in supermarkets. Here is one example of how overcrowding an area may be turned to advantage, since the aim is to follow familiar commercial practice.

ALTERNATE SUGGESTION:
After a class visit to a supermarket, the teacher may encourage his pupils to make all items seen there from paper, for the display.

CIRCUS DAYS AND WAYS

MATERIALS:
Construction paper, fabric, marking pen, coloring book cutouts or children's art, pins, glue.

COLORS:
Pink, orange, white, black, purple.

METHOD:
1. Divide the Board horizontally, covering the upper third with polka dot fabric in pink and orange, and larger, lower portion with striped pink and orange fabric.
2. Pin a band of orange paper across the Board where the fabrics meet, thus providing an area for the caption letters. The latter are cut from orange construction paper, glued to strips of white construction paper and fastened to backdrop as shown.
3. Cut a tent shape of white paper with dark purple doorway, and pin into center of Board.
4. Add polka dot fabric entrance curtains, with striped fabric valance.
5. Cut out and pin on circus figures from coloring book, or have students prepare their own circus figures and attach to backdrop in positions corresponding to illustration.
6. Put a book in the circus barker's hand, as well as the fat lady's hand, and stack folded construction paper books, suitably titled, on strong man's head.
7. Add construction paper pennants in colors of the display, to enhance the overall circus atmosphere.

NOTE:
Recommended to libraries wishing to promote circus books, both factual and fictional. Using the white tent is something of a departure from common practice. Since most circus tents are rendered in stripes or other decorative patterns, this is a new way of handling an old idea. The dotted sky adds a festive look, almost conveying the feeling that it is filled with miniature balloons.

HOW TO USE YOUR LIBRARY

MATERIALS:
Construction paper, wood-grained paper, notebook, pencil, large cereal box, pins, glue.

COLORS:
White, brown, red-orange, yellow-orange, blue, lavender, purple, green.

METHOD:
1. Line Board with white paper.
2. Cover lower section with wood-grained paper, to resemble desk or table, then pin on notebook and pencil.
3. Two large sheets of white construction paper pinned to a cut-open cereal box, form the book. The spine is a strip of white construction paper decorated with pieces of orange paper.
4. The caption is lettered with marking pen on a sheet of white construction paper, glued onto the book's front cover.
5. The boy is made by cutting out a large construction paper circle for the head, with added ears, fringed construction paper orange hair, and black cardboard circles for the glasses. Eyelids are done with marking pen.
6. The head is pinned to backdrop, then the book is pinned away from the backdrop, for dimension. Two cutout hands hold the book.
7. Divide the rest of the display area behind the boy as seen in illustration—right side dark brown construction paper and left side white, with rows and rows of books (short strips of colored construction paper, to further the feeling of a library). Add a figure browsing through the books.
8. On the brown panel pin a cutout construction paper figure at filing cabinet, made with rectangular sheets of construction paper.
9. A white caption strip attached to the side of the cabinet, done with marking pen, reads, "Ask for help."

NOTE:
By means of a few sheets of construction paper and very little art work, this Board conveys the impression of a busy, well-stocked library. The large, flat, simple shapes in the foreground, and the smaller shapes done in the same manner, impart perspective and interest quickly and easily. With appropriate caption changes, this idea can be adapted to any subject relating to books.

ALTERNATE SUGGESTION:
Students could create a busy schoolroom scene in much the same way.

BELGIAN CONGO, LAPLAND, SAHARA DESERT

MATERIALS:
Construction paper, white tissue paper, corrugated board, discarded magazine photographs in color, toothpicks, plastic glue, crepe paper, box tops, upholstery tacks, styrofoam ball, wooden stick, paper doilies, cardboard, sandpaper, crayons, marking pen, pins.

COLORS:
Dark green, dark blue, tan, brown, black, orange, white, multicolor magazine photographs.

METHOD:
1. Line Board with white paper.
   (a) CONGO—HOT, WET REGION
      1) Cover section to be used with dark green construction paper.
      2) Cover a box top with green crepe paper and attach with upholstery tacks to Bulletin Board.
      3) Cut a strip of white cardboard to fit front of box top, as seen in illustration, letter on caption, and glue to edge.
      4) On the above, which serves as a platform or stage, place a hut made by students from toothpicks, and a figure cut from construction paper or lightweight cardboard. The figure, based on the one found in the pattern pages of this book, may be dressed in paper clothing characteristic of the featured area. (An easel support on its back enables the figure to stand).
      5) Using an appropriate magazine photograph of flowers cut, glue or pin the piece to background behind toothpick hut, to simulate a dense tropical forest. Insert some flowers in the foreground behind the caption strip, others behind the green construction paper, to left of the tree trunk, to heighten the feeling of depth.
      6) To make the tree trunk, cut and hold a piece of corrugated board so that the ridges are in horizontal position, and pin on; add paper palm tree fronds, each the shape of a quarter-moon, as seen in photograph.
   (b) LAPLAND—COLD REGION
      1) Cover designated section with dark blue construction paper.
      2) Cover box top with white tissue paper and mount on backdrop with upholstery tacks, as in Step 3 of BELGIAN CONGO.
      3) On this platform place an igloo made from half a styrofoam ball. Color doorway open-

ing with black marking pen and place a cutout figure done in the manner of the Congo figure, but dressed for cold weather.
4) Using a magazine photograph of Christmas decoration done with crystals (symbolizing snow and ice) cut in mountain form, glue to white construction paper, and pin to background. Add cut doilies to tissue-paper snow in foreground, onto mountain of snow, and also on dark blue sky. Fasten construction paper flag to wooden stick and secure to box top platform by punching hole and pushing in the lower end of the stick after a little glue has been deposited.

(c) SAHARA DESERT—HOT, DRY REGION
1) Cover section of third display area with tan construction paper.
2) Cover a box top with sandpaper and proceed as in Step 3 of CONGO exhibit, with proper lettering.
3) On this platform place a cardboard tent decorated with brightly colored crayon stripes, and cut out figure in accordance with previous instructions, clothing lightly.
4) From sandpaper cut mounds of sand, and pin or glue to Bulletin Board. Insert some "sand dunes" behind the lettered strip for added realism and depth.
5) Add flag to top of tent, and a bright sun in the sky.

NOTE:
Each display may be used separately, and supplemented with additional material as study about the region progresses. The surrounding area may be used for presenting related information, student papers, or pictures.

BOOKS ON NATURE

MATERIALS:
Construction paper, cardboard, tissue paper, poster paint and brush, marking pen, pins.

COLORS:
Dark green, yellow green, white, pink, orange, yellow-orange.

METHOD:
1. Same procedure for preparing book as for BOOKS ABOUT HOLLAND, except cardboard front cover is wider than it is high.
2. Decorating the cover of this book is a tissue paper flower, done in art class by a student, with three construction paper worms pinned on—one parallel with the flower stem, one between flower petals at left, and the other peering out from the pages of the book.

NOTE:
Another book the same size could be set next to this volume, with a list of recommended nature books on its cover. Or, again, this idea may be adapted as the free-standing central piece of a table display devoted to nature study.

BIRD WATCHING

MATERIALS:
Bird flash cards or bird pictures, construction paper, pins.

COLORS:
Black, white, multicolor bird pictures.

METHOD:
1. Line Board with black paper.
2. Arrange pictures to spell out the word, BIRD, across virtually the entire display area, filling in D with construction paper triangles.
3. Cut out large white construction paper letters to form the rest of the caption, and pin across the Board under bird pictures.

NOTE:
This display is large, decorative, simple and colorful, yet easy to do, requiring relatively little time for preparation and execution.

A CLOSE LOOK AT NATURE

MATERIALS:
Construction paper, cutout or drawing of a bird, chalk, pins, glue.

COLORS:
Black, light blue, lavender, multicolor bird.

METHOD:
1. Line Board with lavender paper, adding black strips to right and left sides.
2. Cut binoculars from black construction paper (eye portion smaller than bottom section), round the edges to give depth. With blue chalk draw curved and vertical lines toward top and bottom, to lend authenticity to the field glass.
3. Pin away from Board.
4. Add center piece as shown in illustration, and on it perch a cutout bird, giving the impression that the bird is watching the bird watcher.
5. The caption letters, cut from light blue paper, are glued to a strip of black paper, and pinned across Board toward the top.
6. A table displaying nature books may be placed below this Board (the bird would seem to be looking at the books, also).

GO SOUTH FOR THE WINTER

MATERIALS:
Construction paper, marking pen, students' drawings of birds, commercial letters, pins.

COLORS:
Black, white, blue, yellow, yellow-orange, red-orange.

METHOD:
1. Line Board with black paper.
2. Cut signpost strips for caption from construction paper, with arrow-shaped ends.
3. The suitcases are sheets of construction paper, with corners clipped.
4. Ornithological specimens on the luggage are represented by students' drawings, or coloring book and magazine cutouts.
5. Paper travel tags provide space for the names of the birds and any additional information needed to introduce the lesson or further the study of bird behavior.

NOTE:
It may be rewarding to start with one bird sitting on a post. Then, as students acquire more information about birds flying to warmer climates in winter, more specimens can be added. Observe the umbrella tucked under the robin's wing, which adds a fun element to the display.

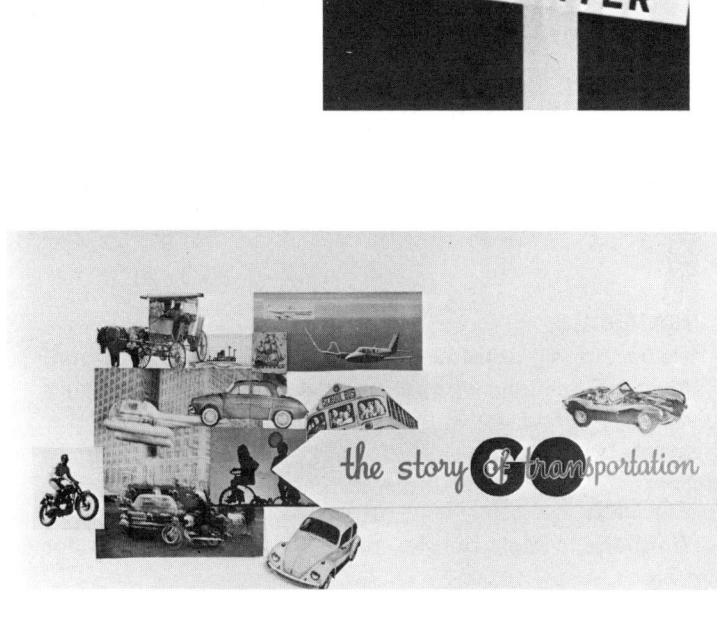

GO: THE STORY OF TRANSPORTATION

MATERIALS:
Construction paper, magazine photographs, glue, pins.

COLORS:
White, blue, green, multicolor magazine photographs.

METHOD:
1. Line Board with white paper.
2. Cut a strip of white construction paper in arrow shape, for the caption.
3. Oversize letters for GO are cut from green construction paper and glued down on strip.
4. The balance of the caption, "The story of transportation," is penciled on blue construction paper in large script letters, cut out, and glued onto the arrow, partly covering the word, GO.
5. Arrange magazine photographs brought in by students in the manner of a collage, one on the other, some whole, some trimmed off, leaving ample white space around the group.
6. Pin caption arrow onto center of display area, pointing left, as seen in illustration.

NOTE:
This Board demonstrates effective handling of a large display with white space as a significant part of the design.

MOVING AIR

MATERIALS:
Tissue paper, construction paper, wool yarn, ribbon, toy items (miniature paper parasol, kite and other flying objects), white cardboard, plastic glue, white poster paint, brush, pins.

COLORS:
Turquoise, violet, purple, pink, white, blue, multicolor objects.

METHOD:
1. Cut cardboard for display area to size required.
2. With two people holding ends, a third cuts tissue sheets of various colors into wavy strips.
3. Lay the strips one over the other to get multihued transparent effect. (Juggle the tissues to obtain most pleasing combination of overlapping colors).
4. Then turn tissue wrong side up onto a flat working area, and brush on a coat of plastic glue.
5. Place glued tissue paper on white cardboard and move around until properly adjusted in the display space (tissue may be moved while still wet).
6. Working quickly, continue to add strips of colored tissue paper one by one, each overlapping the other, as seen in illustration.
7. After all strips are in position, coat whole area with plastic glue for extra sheen and transparency appeal. Let dry to hard, shiny surface.
8. Pin on large, cutout construction paper caption letters to follow wave of air pattern created by overlapping strips.
9. Outline letters with white poster paint to make message stand out against the bright, glossy background.
10. Pin on flying objects—real, toy, or those made by students.

NOTE:
Information typed on white paper could be interspersed among other items. This Bulletin Board would seem particularly appropriate for March, if the caption is changed to MARCH IS A WINDY MONTH. Flying objects might then be spring blossoms, hats, kites, etc., along with shamrocks and high hats for St. Patrick's day (remove the latter items after the holiday). Book jackets, real or simulated, could also fly through the air, to suggest interesting spring reading.

STORM WARNING

MATERIALS:
Construction paper, lightweight cardboard, poster paints, wide-tip marking pen, chalk, sponge, pins.

COLORS:
Blue, purple, turquoise, black, white.

METHOD:
1. Using a large table, or the floor as a work area, wet a full-size sheet of cardboard with a large, wet sponge.
2. Pour small quantities of watered blue, purple and turquoise poster paints in center and rub across the cardboard in sweeping motion.
3. When dry enough not to run, attach to the Bulletin Board so the piece may continue to dry in position. (This will eliminate most of the buckling.)
4. From black construction paper cut out the skyline and affix to bottom.
5. Draw lighting shapes on cardboard, cut around the zigzag pencil lines, then pin away from the background.
6. Black lettering is done with wide-tip marking pen. For sharp contrast, use white chalk lines as a shadow on one side of the caption.

ALTERNATE SUGGESTION:
Also suitable for a library exhibit featuring books about weather and climate. The lightning could be made into larger shapes, extending out over the buildings onto a table below, displaying selected books under discussion. If preferred, the lightning might be placed horizontally across the Board, with photographs, factual pamphlets or written papers pinned at various points.

NOTE:
Students will enjoy creating the skyline, and experimenting with ways of working the lightning into the unit of study to point up related information. The lettering style is dramatic and helps convey the message. On occasion it may be adapted to other subjects.

LOOK AT OUR WILD LIFE

MATERIALS:
Construction paper, posters and/or pictures.

COLORS:
Blue, light green, yellow, turquoise.

METHOD:
1. Have the large caption letters form an arm taking up the left half of the Bulletin Board.
2. Cut hand from green construction paper, as shown, with thumb and forefinger extended. (See pattern section).
3. Mount posters and/or pictures on the "palm" of the hand, and on the yellow portion.
4. The Board is balanced by the turquoise lettering to left and right, plus the turquoise outline around the items on the right.

ALTERNATE SUGGESTION:
Many another subject could be treated in this fashion. Save the letters for LOOK and the hand for future use, changing pictures and caption to suit the new theme.

NOTE:
This is a good-sized Bulletin Board, yet for all the space it covers only a few posters are required. The big, bold letters demand attention. The illustrations are easily seen because of the uncrowded condition of the Board. Balance is obtained, even though the design is not symmetrical.

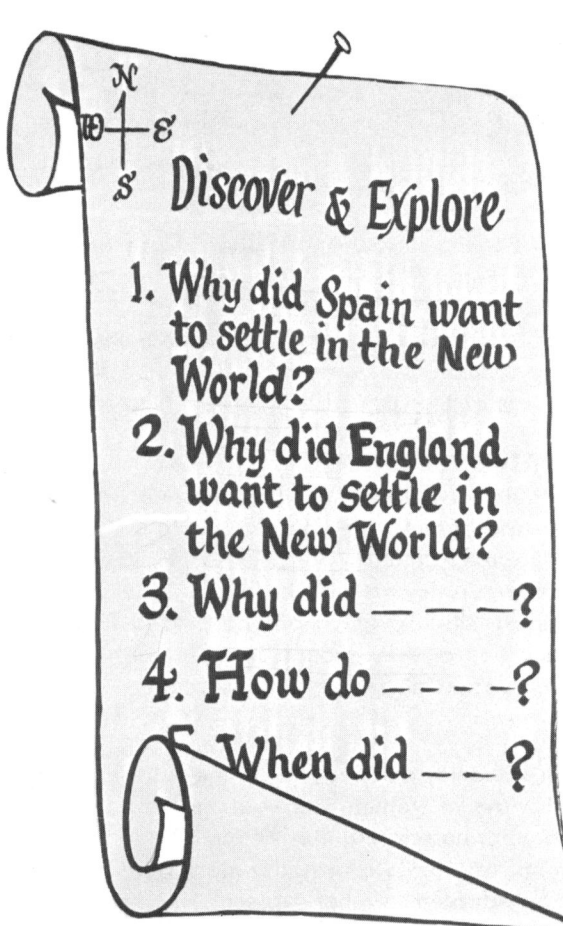

DISCOVER AND EXPLORE

MATERIALS:
Construction paper, brush and paint, marking pen, pins.

COLORS:
Brown, white, black.

METHOD:
1. With a black marking pen draw the shape of a rolled (scroll-type) paper document on brown paper, as seen in photograph.
2. With the same pen neatly print the questions to be covered as the classroom unit is studied.
3. To the inner end of the rolled edge brush on a bit of white paint, to denote the inside.
4. Cut out whole shape, following black lines drawn previously.
5. Add a large cutout nail, top center. Attach document, pinning the rolled paper away from Bulletin Board to produce a shadow, giving dimension to this simple design.

GETTING CLOSE TO NATURE

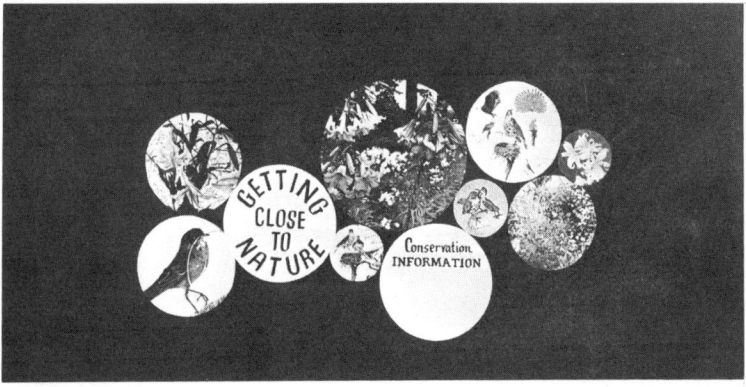

MATERIALS:
Magazine pictures and information, marking pen, construction paper, pins.

COLORS:
Black, white, multicolor magazine pictures.

METHOD:
1. Line Board with black paper.
2. Cut vari-sized circular shapes from natural history pictures in discarded magazines; or use students' art work dealing with the subject.
3. Cut two white construction paper circles for caption, lettered with marking pen, and related information.
4. Pin all circles on backdrop, as shown.

NOTE:
A striking example of how negative (empty) space works well with positive (filled) space to form a well-designed Bulletin Board. The black space surrounding the circles forces the eye to the center of the display, so that the message is quickly apparent. Moreover, the circles give the feeling of looking through a telescope to make faraway objects seem closer, bearing out the theme. Together the caption and illustrations combine to produce a simple, colorful design, easy to prepare and pleasing to view.

MATERIALS:
Floral print fabric, lightweight cardboard, construction paper, marking pen, pins.

COLORS:
Multicolor fabric, deep pink, green, brown, white, black.

METHOD:
1. Line Board with patterned fabric.
2. With marking pen enlarge flower motif from fabric, as shown in this book's pattern section, and cut out.
3. Also use marking pen to draw leaves and trowel on construction paper or cardboard, and cut out. Add the decorative lines to flower, leaves and tool, as seen in fabric.
4. Pin enlarged items on Board away from background, for dimension.
5. The caption lettering, following the style of the fabric design, is also done with marking pen on a cardboard rectangle. Then the sign's left edge is inserted just under the large flower stem.

NOTE:
More flowers taken from the fabric design, or duplicates of the one illustrated, could be exhibited with additional messages if time and space permit.

WE PLANT OUR GARDEN

RAIN - SUNSHINE

MATERIALS:
Floral print fabric, construction paper, marking pen, pins.

COLORS:
Gray, black, white, yellow.

METHOD:
1. Line the Board with gray paper.
2. Cut floral print fabric into shapes of hat, dress, sleeves, sandal decorations, sunglasses.
3. For rain display cut and pin on large yellow half circle, and smaller white inner half circle.
4. Place cutout letters, RAIN, on yellow rim, and day's date, done with marking pen, on white half circle.
5. Add yellow boots and gloves, and black umbrella handle.
6. For SUNSHINE display change raincoat to sun dress by removing sleeves, gloves and boots.
7. Add brown arms, hands, legs and feet, sunglasses under hat brim, and flowered sandal decorations.
8. Pin on full-circle sun shape, with caption, to replace umbrella shape.

NOTE:
This display project may have special appeal for girls, because the figures are feminine and wearing apparel is involved. On the other hand, boy figures could be presented in similar fashion, choosing a more masculine fabric. The display could also go co-ed, with a boy figure standing next to the girl. To coordinate the color scheme, it could be done in yellow and black-and-white stripes.

ALTERNATE SUGGESTION:
Instead of doing one design and changing it, two might be prepared (or as many as local conditions allow) on window shades, and pulled up and down, according to the weather. Then, when there is general class discussion of weather and climate, all decorated shades could be lowered to illustrate points made, and help create a receptive mood.

CLOUDS

MATERIALS:
Cardboard, construction paper, commercial letters, poster paint, sponge, pictures or printed matter pertaining to different types of clouds, pins.

COLORS:
Black, white, purple, blue.

METHOD:
1. Lay white cardboard on several thicknesses of newspaper on a large work table or the floor, and wet with large sponge dipped in water.
2. Mix blue and purple poster paints with water, then pour some of each onto the wet sponge.
3. With sweeping motion rub sponge from side to side across the wet cardboard, repeating until the entire area is coated with color.
4. Cut shapes to resemble cloud formations.
5. On some of the above write the identifying names; on others mount pictures or printed information. Still others may be left as white space to be filled in later with new words pertaining to the subject. Then pin onto backdrop.

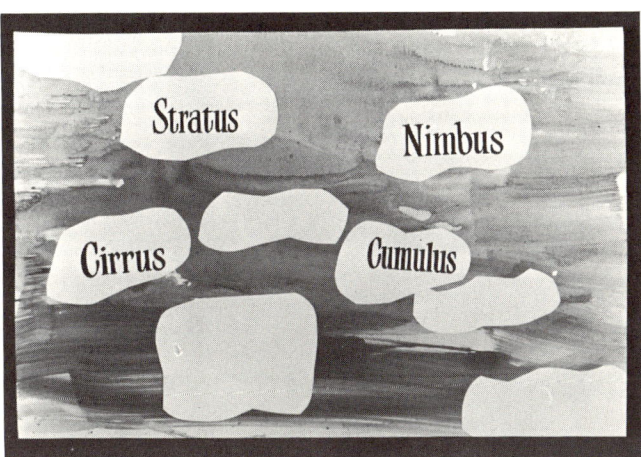

NOTE:
The cardboard cloud formations merely suggest the types under study, and obviously are not scientifically accurate.

BIG FACTS ABOUT LITTLE THINGS

MATERIALS:
Construction paper, tracing paper, chalk, pins.

COLORS:
Black, white, dark blue, dark green.

METHOD:
1. Line Board with white paper.
2. Divide the Board with two large sheets of construction paper, green and blue, as seen in illustration.
3. Place a large construction paper cutout of a microscope done by students, or a magazine photograph of the instrument, in the white area between the panels of color.
4. Cut out the free-form amoeba shapes from tracing paper, to denote small things blown up out of proportion under the microscope, and pin onto blue paper at right.
5. Place related information and photographs, or results of experiments done in class on the dark green construction paper at left.
6. The caption letters, cut from black construction paper, run across the top of the Bulletin Board to link all three areas together.
7. Blue chalk is used to outline the microscope, add

circles to the amoebas, and coordinate the color scheme.

NOTE:
The mats for information mounted on the green construction paper indicate how a small grouping may sometimes prove very effective in a large display space. In this case the blank area balances the filled area, and seems equally important design-wise. Having the three mats at the left touching at the corners, as shown here, forms a good start for a layout. The space created by the touching points provides additional areas for two mats.

DID YOU CHECK YOUR WORK?

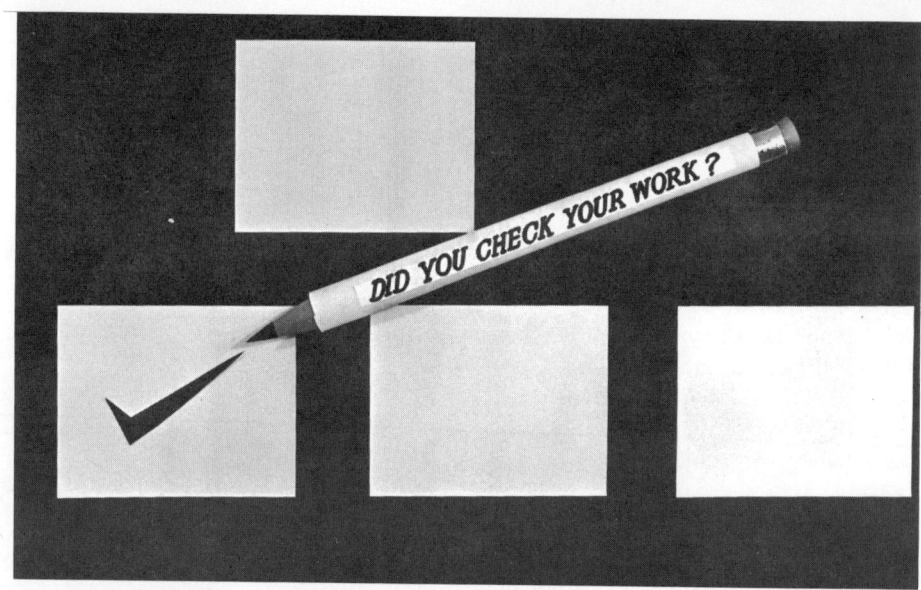

MATERIALS:
Construction paper, students' written work, mailing tube, gold wrapping paper, glue, pins.

COLORS:
Black, white, tan, orange, gold.

METHOD:
1. Line Bulletin Board with black paper.
2. Cover a mailing tube with white construction paper.
3. Cut a triangular piece of brown construction paper to fit into one end of the tube, to resemble the wood surrounding pencil point, and add a small, black triangle for the lead.
4. At opposite end insert a rectangular shape of orange paper, for the eraser.
5. Then wrap a strip of gold foil around the end, leaving the orange "eraser" exposed.
6. With marking pen letter caption on a strip of white paper, and glue onto pencil.
7. Make a large check shape of construction paper, and affix to sheet of white paper, with end of check under point of pencil.
8. Add students' written work to Board, changing papers periodically, rather than crowd too many into the display at one time. (Save pencil for future use).

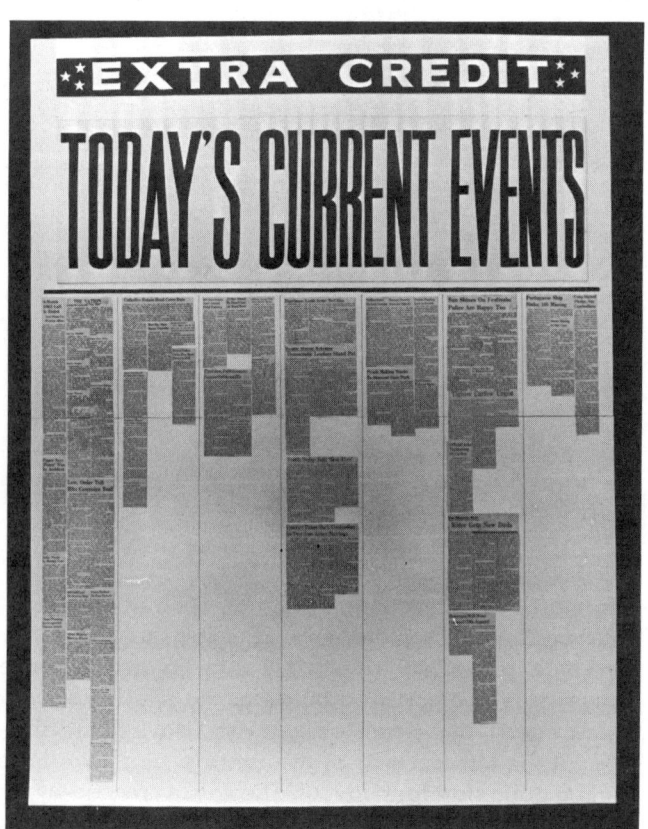

EXTRA CREDIT

MATERIALS:
Construction paper or newsprint, newspaper clippings, commercial stick-on letters and stars, marking pen, pins.

COLORS:
White, black.

METHOD:
1. Line Bulletin Board with white construction paper or newsprint.
2. With the front page of a newspaper as guide, place commercial letters and stars in proper position to form the headline caption.
3. Draw black lines with marking pen and ruler to divide the page into columns.
4. Pin on current events clippings brought in by students, changing frequently to keep them up-to-date.

BACK TO SCHOOL

MATERIALS:
Discarded sweater, hat, jumper; notebook, ruler, pencils, construction paper, white lightweight cardboard, marking pen, masking tape, wire hanger, tack, hammer, pins, glue.

COLORS:
White, brown, red, black, blue, green.

METHOD:
1. Line Bulletin Board with white paper.
2. Cut girl's head and shoulders from lightweight cardboard.
3. Draw face and hair with marking pen, or glue on child's face taken from a magazine photograph.
4. Hang sweater and jumper on wire hanger and insert girl's head at neckline.
5. Hammer onto the Board a tack strong enough to hold the weight of the hanger and three-dimensional figure.
6. Pin hat on girl's head; tuck books, ruler under her arm and pin arm at wrist of sweater into left pocket; add pencils to latter pocket; pin other arm to other pocket, thus avoiding the extra work of drawing and cutting hands.
7. Cut out and place oversized construction paper red apple on girl's head.
8. Caption letters should be slanted, to give Board a lighthearted air.

NOTE:
Discarded clothing and wire hangers may be contributed by students for various display purposes. Students would find it fun to fashion the figures in their own image, using their own clothing. A row of such figures in a school corridor could be arranged successfully as a welcome-back-to-school device. Add heavier winter apparel as the season advances, with appropriate caption. Since human figure representations generally increase interest in Bulletin Boards, use these "hanger people" often.

TAKE GOOD CARE OF YOUR PET

MATERIALS:

Mitten, pants leg, sock, drawing of sneaker, real shoelace, egg cartons, fringe, ribbon, print fabric, construction paper, patterned paper, chalk, gold foil, pins, glue.

COLORS:

White, yellow, tan, brown, olive green, light green, blue, black, orange, red.

METHOD:

1. Line Board with white construction paper.
2. Pin on leg of discarded pair of pants in striding position.
3. Tuck sock under trouser leg and into sneaker. (For the latter use a large newspaper advertisement as a pattern. Stitching is done with white chalk. Punch holes for eyelets, and tie on real shoelace).
4. Attach mitten for hand.
5. The dog's body is constructed from egg cartons.
6. Glue or pin on tail, rectangles for legs, and a triangular shape rounded at one end, for dog's face. Add round, black nose, eye and ears.
7. Cover the visible front portion of the cartons with construction paper, completing the dog's body.
8. Use print fabric for dog's sweater and boy's knee patch.
9. A construction paper strip will serve as the dog's collar. Have a license tag of gold foil hanging from it.
10. Attach ribbon to collar, pull to mitten and tie.
11. Add the simple, circle-shaped flowers, stems, leaves and butterflies; also, a sun of patterned paper and a row of fringe for the grass.
12. Neatly print the caption in sentence form on construction paper, cut out and attach.

NOTE:

The flowers can be larger, if size of Bulletin Board permits, with information about pet care written on them.

LETTERING

In addition to the more familiar lettering styles associated with school and library exhibits, it is occasionally rewarding to employ novel styles for unusual treatment. These are often effective even without accompanying art renderings. Following are three examples, suitable for Bulletin Board captions, case displays, or library bin strips. (The letters may be cut from paper, lettered with marking pen, or done with paints by an experienced calligrapher).

JOIN CLUB 100

MATERIALS:
Construction paper, students' work, glue, pins.

COLORS:
Red, white.

METHOD:
1. Line Board with white paper.
2. Cut a large 100 from construction paper, using the largest red sheets available. Trim off corners of the zeros to give a rounded look.
3. The caption letters, cut from white construction paper, are glued to a strip of red paper and pinned above the 100.
4. Pin 100% classroom papers onto the oversize numerals.

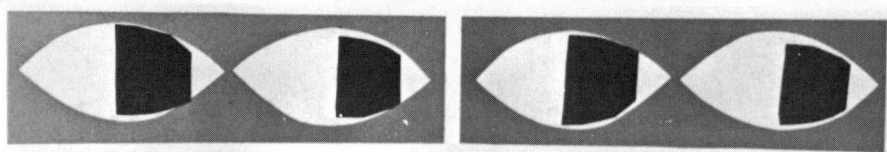

LOOK

MATERIALS:
Construction paper, glue, pins.

COLORS:
Turquoise, magenta, black, white.

METHOD:
1. Line Board with white paper.
2. Cut construction paper rectangles to fit display area, then place two side by side at upper left, and one at lower right.
3. To the upper rectangles add construction paper cut-outs of stylized eyes, with pupils glued to right corners.
4. Pin oversized caption letters cut from construction paper to lower rectangle.
5. Use remaining space on Board for displaying information and notes of importance to the class.

BIN STRIPS

MATERIALS:
Paints, brush, cardboard, construction paper, pins, glue or paste.

COLORS:
Let's draw and paint—white, red, black.
Bat and Ball—white, red, blue.
ALL ABOUT BIRDS—light green, dark green, white.
Let's eat good food!—white, dark green.
Pick a good book—white, turquoise, yellow-green.
Decorate your house with the help of books—white, orange, black.

METHOD:
1. Paint letters, cut out paper letters, or obtain commercial letters to pin or paste on.

NOTE:
Wherever possible, convert an occasion letter into a decorative part of the design, adding interest and humor. Such strips have considerable versatility. In addition to their usefulness as captions for book bins, they may also serve as subject headings for Bulletin Boards, or titles for table displays.

LOVE

MATERIALS:
Same as EAT (see below).

COLORS:
Same as EAT (see below).

METHOD:
Same as EAT (see below), with changed caption.

NOTE:
No special subject matter was required here, so the illustrative magazine pages were chosen purely for their beauty of design and color. The O was cut exactly as it appears from one of the pages, eliminating the need for a pattern to obtain a true circle. Two different pages contributed to the V.

EAT

MATERIALS:
Construction paper, discarded magazines, pins.

COLORS:
White, multicolor magazine pages.

METHOD:
1. Line Board with white paper.
2. Cut and pin on each oversized letter made from an illustrated page of a magazine (in this case the pages appropriately concerned food), using as much of the picture as possible for the intended purpose. The E and T were cut from full pages, while the A was pieced at the crossbar.)

NOTE:
Here is an excellent way to obtain pleasing color and design with minimum investment of time and labor. No measuring is necessary, because the letters are as large as the pages will allow. Students may wish to assemble a sufficient number of discarded magazines with color illustrations to provide a complete alphabet with extra, often-used vowels and consonants, so that they can be brought into play time and time again.

WELCOME BACK TO SCHOOL

MATERIALS:
Construction paper, chalk, patterned paper cut from a magazine, pins.

COLORS:
Black, white, orange, brown.

METHOD:
1. Line Board with white paper.
2. Cut uneven blocks of black paper and pin to lower section of display area to create a floor for the teacher.
3. With pattern in this book as a guide, cut out teacher figure from construction paper, as large as the display will accommodate, rearranging left arm so that it will point to caption when attached.
4. Pin the blackboard (a sheet of black construction paper with chalk lettering) above the floor area. Draw a marking pen line around blackboard to represent wood frame and add a wider line for the wooden ledge.
5. Dress the teacher in a photograph of fabric found on a magazine page, piecing it if necessary to fit size. Add sleeves of outfit in orange construction paper, plus earrings, hair, and pert facial expression with marking pen. When teacher is pinned against blackboard in proper position, outline part of hair in white chalk so that it will show up against the blackboard.

NOTE:
The same type of treatment might present classroom rules, procedural information, and homework assignments for students to copy. The latter, of course, would be changed daily. Occasional costume changes for the teacher might be arranged by the students. Teachers with humorous bent on occasion may wish to substitute their own photographs for the drawn figure faces.

DENTAL HEALTH WEEK

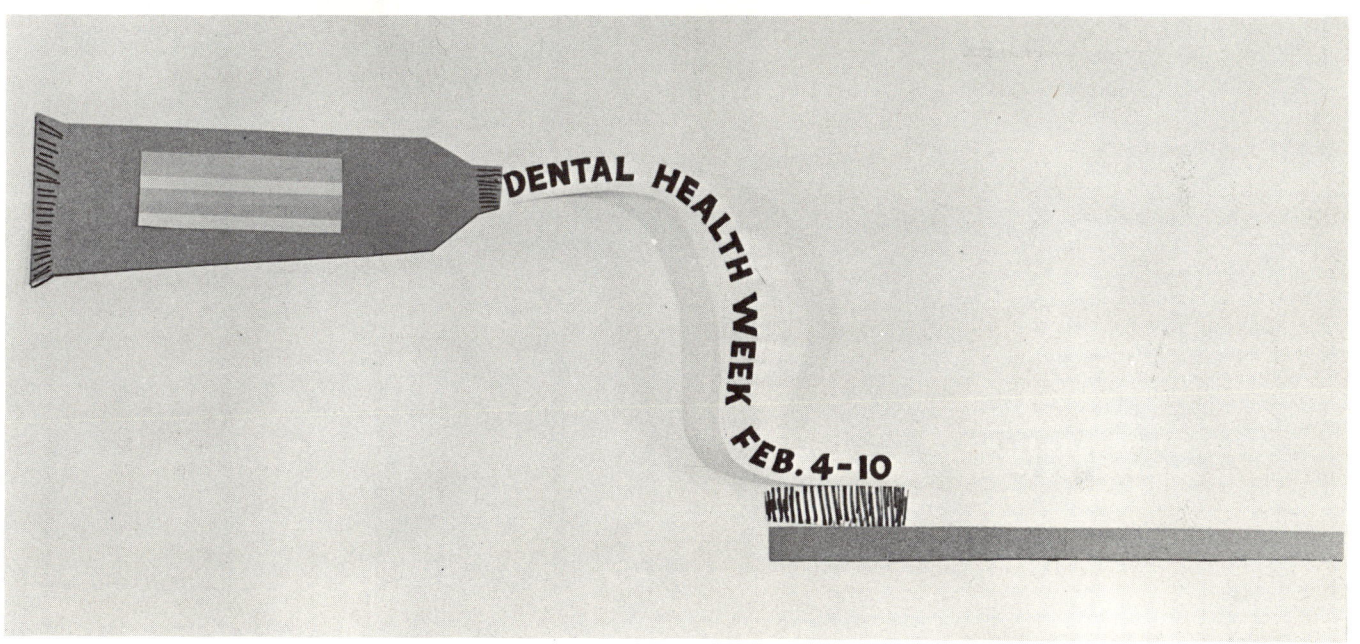

MATERIALS:
Construction paper, marking pen, glue, pins.

COLORS:
Green, black, white, blue, pink, purple.

METHOD:
1. Line Board with white paper.
2. Using a magazine rendition of a tube of toothpaste as a guide, enlarge and cut an oversized tube from construction paper.
3. Add marking-pen lines for end of tube, and colored construction paper decoration for the label.
4. Make toothbrush with strip of construction paper for handle, and marking-pen bristles.
5. The cutout or commercial caption letters are glued to a strip of paper flowing from the tube opening to toothbrush, and pinned away from Board for dimension.

NOTE:
Caption letters should be as large as display area will allow.

PRACTICE GOOD WRITING

MATERIALS:
Cardboard, construction paper, students' work, marking pens, pins.

COLORS:
White, orange, red-orange, blue.

METHOD:
1. Make an enlarged replica of a sheet of notebook paper, drawing the horizontal blue lines and vertical red margin line with marking pens.
2. Cut out small circles from left margin, to represent holes in notebook paper. Pin sheet to Board.
3. Attach students' attractively penned classroom papers, mounted on blue and red construction paper mats, to backdrop.
4. On the lines of the oversized notebook sheet, letter the caption in well-formed script, using black marking pen.
5. Add to the exaggerated spirit of the display by pinning on a pencil made from a mailing tube (in accordance with instructions for illustration, DID YOU CHECK YOUR WORK?). Cover mailing tube with orange paper.

NOTE:
PRACTICE GOOD WRITING is applicable either to handwriting or creative writing. Students' work should be changed often, to allow the showing of all papers deserving recognition. It is well to bear in mind that virtually any simple, familiar object can be blown up to outsized proportions, often serving as the focal point for an amusing, decorative, dramatic, or imaginative Bulletin Board.

BANK DAY

MATERIALS:
Construction paper, lightweight cardboard, polka dot wrapping paper, marking pen, glue, pins.

COLORS:
Pink, orange, black, white.

METHOD:
1. Line Board with white paper.
2. Using pattern of pig in this book, draw and cut out cardboard pig shape.
3. Draw and cut pig shape from polka dot paper, and glue to cardboard.
4. With marking pen add animal's hooves, nostrils, coin slot and other lines, as shown; also, cent marks on some of the polka dots.
5. Pin piggy bank to Board away from background, for dimension.
6. Cut various size circles to represent coins and attach to Bulletin Board, with one coin inserted in deposit slot.
7. Letter part of caption on background, and remainder on largest coins.

NOTE:
Any decorative paper may serve for the pig pattern, but the polka dot type seen here was chosen to harmonize with the coin shapes, resulting in a more pleasing design.

TAKE ONE

MATERIALS:
Green cardboard, construction paper, pink box of facial tissues, pink tissue paper, narrow pink ribbon, pins.

COLORS:
Green, pink, orange, white.

METHOD:
1. Line display area of Bulletin Board with green cardboard.
2. Using the hand pattern in this book, or outlining one's own hand, the worker may cut out a hand shape and glue to a strip of white construction paper or cardboard, to serve as an arm.
3. Cover the arm with a piece of pink tissue paper gathered at the wrist with a piece of narrow pink ribbon, to form the sleeve.
4. Fasten arm to top of green cardboard.
5. Affix pink tissue box to bottom of green board.
6. Decorate sleeve with the caption, TAKE ONE, repeated as an overall design, and a few simple flowers at wrist line.
7. Add a strip of paper with same style caption, and pin on facial tissue as if it were being withdrawn by the hand.

NOTE:
This arrangement would also do well as a table or shelf display, with easel support glued to back of green cardboard.

PLEASE DON'T SPREAD GERMS

MATERIALS:
Construction paper, tissue paper, pins.

COLORS:
Olive green, white, black, purple, magenta, tan.

METHOD:
1. Line Board with olive green paper.
2. Cut two white circles for heads, add scraps of black paper to form hair, and black-white exclamation point.
3. Pin on two sheets of tissue paper, overlapping the purple and magenta to obtain the effect of transparency.
4. Using an actual hand as a guide, cut two hands somewhat larger than lifesize if Bulletin Board seems to require it.
5. Affix hands to bottom of the Board and pin palms away from backdrop, for added depth.
6. Cut caption letters from construction paper, or purchase from display supplier. Letters should follow head lines to fit into design.

NOTE:
The sheets of tissue paper representing the handkerchiefs are effective not only for their oversize quality, but also for their vivid colors. Against the olive green they compel attention. Another advantage is that they eliminate the need for drawing features on the faces. Projected from the bottom and being darker, the hands give the illusion of quick action to prevent the spread of germs so prevalent in schools. This is a good subject to repeat periodically, as a general reminder, or as part of a health study unit.

DON'T FORGET

MATERIALS:
Construction paper, wool yarn, pins.

COLORS:
Black, tan, white, orange, hot pink, off-white.

METHOD:
1. Line Board with black paper.
2. From a sheet of tan paper trim away just enough to form the oversized shape of a hand, with thumb and pointing index finger in evidence.
3. Pin onto the Board, leaving enough space at left for construction paper jacket sleeve and cuff, with paper buttons below the sleeve end. (This arrangement creates large, bold color areas with a minimum of cutting).
4. Place a sheet of construction paper at finger point to display a list of rules pertaining to matters of moment. (The rules may be changed as occasion arises, leaving the remaining elements intact).
5. Add a strip of black paper to which the caption, consisting of cutout letters, has been glued.
6. Pin this across the sleeve and forefinger. At its end wrap a strand of brightly-colored wool yarn around the finger and tied in a bow, to go along with the caption.

NOTE:
A shocking color scheme, especially the shocking pink wool tied to the finger, tends to strengthen the admonition not to forget.

GOOD TEETH

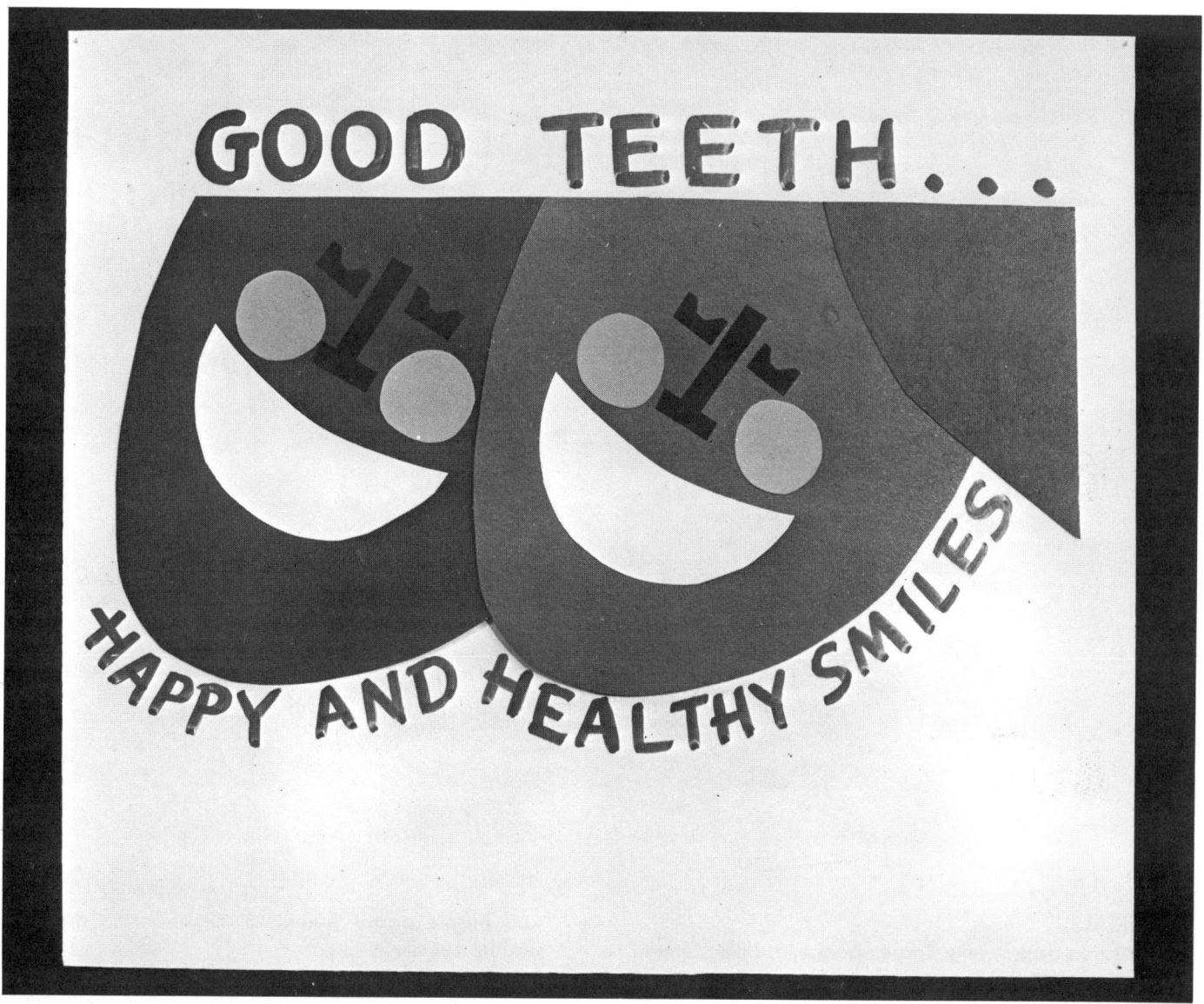

MATERIALS:
Construction paper, glue or pins.

COLORS:
White, black, purple, brown, turquoise, pink.

METHOD:
1. Line Bulletin Board with white paper.
2. Using two large sheets of construction paper, cut duplicate oval shapes for children's heads, ending at top edge.
3. Overlap heads, and add a piece of paper at upper right for hair, and to round off the design, or suggest boy-and-girl arrangement.
4. Add simple facial features of construction paper, and oversized smiles.
5. Have caption letters straight at top, and curved at bottom, in conformity with design.

DRESS FOR THE WEATHER

MATERIALS:
Construction paper, inks, large sponge, rubber cement, marking pen, fabric, mitten, fur, tissue paper, chalk, magazine photograph, cardboard, poster paints, brush, pins.

COLORS:
Light blue, dark blue, white, purple, red, turquoise, black, gray.

METHOD:
1. Working on a large table or floor, and following the snow slope shape, draw basic house shapes, tree and curls of smoke on upper part of large sheet of white cardboard (which constitutes the snow slope).
2. Brush rubber cement on roof tops, house at extreme left, trees and smoke (wherever white is desired). Let dry.
3. With water and sponge dampen lightly the area above snow line.
4. Moisten sponge with water and diluted blue, green and purple poster paints, and rub across the sky section. Let dry.
5. Across the dry sky rub a pickup (dried rubber cement formed into a small ball) and it will remove all paint from the cemented areas, leaving white roof-tops and other white background bits, as shown in illustration.
6. Affix entire work to Bulletin Board.
7. Cut picture of child's face from discarded magazine and mount on cardboard. Roll slightly in pinning to backdrop, thereby enhancing three-dimensional effect.
8. Place fabric scarf, fur-trimmed hat, and mitten in position and pin.
9. The caption is done in icy blue, to resemble curly letters in the snow.
10. To add to the wintry feeling, the wisp of cold air curling from the child's mouth is made with tissue paper. Chalk lines and pen decorations further accent the area.

ALL LIVING THINGS NEED AIR*

MATERIALS:
Same as illustration, THE GREAT OUTDOORS.

COLORS:
Same as illustration, THE GREAT OUTDOORS.

METHOD:
Same as illustration, THE GREAT OUTDOORS, except for additional caption message, top and bottom.

NOTE:
As demonstrated here, Bulletin Boards may serve different purposes at different times, except for their captions, and minor changes. This particular design, almost identical with illustration THE GREAT OUTDOORS, offers concrete evidence of this fact.

Citing a number of living things in a typical outdoor setting, is a good way to introduce one facet of ecology. Through the asterisk following the upper portion of the caption, the lower explanatory portion ties in with the concept of conservation implied overall.

*Clean air.

WHICH ONE ARE YOU ?

MATERIALS:
Construction paper, assorted discarded items (ball fringe, stuffed bird, colored cord, ribbon, crepe paper, artificial flowers, fabric, wool yarn), pins.

COLORS:
Pink, dark blue, white, tan, multicolor items comprising hair.

METHOD:
1. Line Board with white paper.
2. From a sheet of dark blue construction paper cut shapes representing hair of girl on the left.
3. Cut two ovals of tan construction paper for girls' faces.
4. Pin hair and face shapes in position.
5. Add bangs with narrow ribbon bow, cutout construction paper features and happy expression to neat girl at left.
6. Pin assortment of discarded items in a tangled hodgepodge, cutout construction paper features with sad expression onto disheveled girl at right.
7. The large caption letters, cut from white construction paper, are pinned to the hair of the girl at left.

NOTE:
Observe that the head on the right is placed to fit into the contour of the other girl's hair shape, which makes for improved design. Moreover, the caption lettering is an integral part of the design, rather than an afterthought. Many students will enjoy creating disheveled hairdos like the one pictured, from discards accumulated in their homes.

WASH YOUR HANDS

MATERIALS:
Construction paper, blue cellophane, cardboard, marking pen, pins.

COLORS:
White, blue, green, black, brown.

METHOD:
1. Line Board with white paper.
2. Cut out two oversized hands, one brown, the other black.
3. From white cardboard cut out a large soap shape, and with marking pen identify the cleansing agent with carved-type letters spelling out the word, S O A P.
4. Cut out vari-sized cardboard bubble circles, and with marking pen letter the main and auxiliary caption messages—WASH YOUR HANDS—GOODBYE GERMS—FOR GOOD HEALTH, KEEP CLEAN.
5. Draw some outline circles with marking pen, to go under black hand.
6. Pin on hands and bubble circles, as shown, covering the latter with blue cellophane, for transparent look.
7. Place soap with left end inserted between the hands, as seen in illustration.
8. Add a small cluster of bubbles at lower right corner of soap, for more sudsy effect.

NOTE:
Trash can lids, pot lids, jar lids and paint can lids may serve as guides for the various-sized circles. The blue bubbles appear sharp and clean against the white Board, setting the right subject mood.

LOOK AT ME—
WHAT DO I SEE?

MATERIALS:
Construction paper, patterned wrapping paper, clear cellophane, marking pen, pins.

COLORS:
White, black, hot pink, orange, brown, black.

METHOD:
1. Line Board with white construction paper.
2. Cut girl's face from brown construction paper or a discarded magazine.
3. Fashion back of girl's head from black construction paper, using the straight edge toward left side of display, to show only a portion of the figure.
4. A triangular piece of the patterned wrapping paper forms the top part of the girl's dress, with the point of the triangle covered by the hair.
5. The arm is cut from the same paper, in rectangular shape.
6. The pink ribbon and brown hand are cut from paper and pinned away from backdrop, for dimension.
7. Affix front view of the girl to Board in position illustrated.
8. To make the hand mirror, cut from white construction paper a circle larger than the head. Then cut away inner section, leaving only rim to go around girl's head. Cover mirror with cellophane circle. Add handle to mirror, to fit into girl's hand.
9. The upper lettering, done in script with a marking pen, forms the decorative motif around the mirror.
10. Cut strips of pink paper—some patterned, others plain—to represent the pile of books at girl's right, and with marking pen letter in the balance of the caption, BE WELL GROOMED WITH THE HELP OF LIBRARY BOOKS above the volumes, and on some of the spines.
11. To indicate dimension, use marking pen for books' pages, as shown.

NOTE:
The mirror extends beyond the prime display space, stretching it somewhat—a good way to treat a small area, by adding interest and dimension.

GOOD GROOMING

MATERIALS:
Wallpaper or gift wrapping, marking pen, construction paper, clear and turquoise cellophane, dried flowers, wood-grained contact paper, corrugated box, smaller carton, buttons, white lace paper doilies, glue, pins.

COLORS:
White, brown, black, hot pink, yellow, green, turquoise.

METHOD:
1. Cut apart a large, flat corrugated box, leaving the front and back to stand free.
2. Cover the corrugated board with wallpaper or gift wrappings.
3. Use student art work or an appropriate magazine picture for basic figure of the girl.
4. Cut two heads (for girl and her reflection), dress, arm and hair band, from construction paper.
5. Add paper doily collar, and affix girl to left side of Board.
6. Cover carton, in proper proportion to the display, with wood-grained contact paper.
7. With marking pen draw a rectangle on "dresser" to simulate drawer. Add buttons for pulls.
8. From the wood-grained paper cut a circle a little larger than the girl's head, for the mirror, and two strips for the mirror supports.
9. Cut a white construction paper mirror slightly smaller than the wood-grained circle, and glue on the second head cutout, in the position illustrated. Then cover with same-size cellophane circle, attaching with pins.
10. From the turquoise cellophane cut a vase and pin to wall behind dresser, to look as though the container were sitting on the top. Pin dried flowers above vase.
11. The script caption is done with a marking pen to match the hot pink flowers in the wallpaper.

NOTE:
This makes an attractive table display, if Bulletin Board space is scarce and books on the subject are available for the foreground. The idea might also be adapted where two Bulletin Boards join in a corner arrangement.

FOLLOW THE LEADER – KEEP YOUR SCHOOL CLEAN

MATERIALS:
Contact paper, lined paper, printed and plain fabrics, toy brooms, construction paper, marking pens, cord, pins.

COLORS:
Black, white, green, purple, red, tan, multicolor fabrics.

METHOD:
1. Line Board with white paper.
2. Cover floor section with marble contact paper, extending into classroom as shown at right.
3. Use a sheet of lined paper, simulating classroom wall seen from a distance, and strips of black construction paper for doorway opening.
4. Based on pattern contained in this book, enlarge and cut figures to suitable size, rearranging feet and arms to marching posture, and clothing figures as if they were strutting through the school corridors toward the outdoors.
5. The black, construction paper blackboard in the classroom mounted on the striped wall (seen through doorway), bears a list of statements written in chalk on how to keep one's school clean.
6. The desks and chairs seen through the doorway are cut from construction paper.
7. The lead figure carries his broom (tied with cord) upright at the extreme left (in contrast to the others, which have their brooms pinned on extending from hand to floor). From it flies a pennant bearing the caption, done in cutout letters in flowing style, and running across the top of the Board to the doorway.

NOTE:
Such a marching group could depict many different subjects, with the caption changed to suit the circumstances.

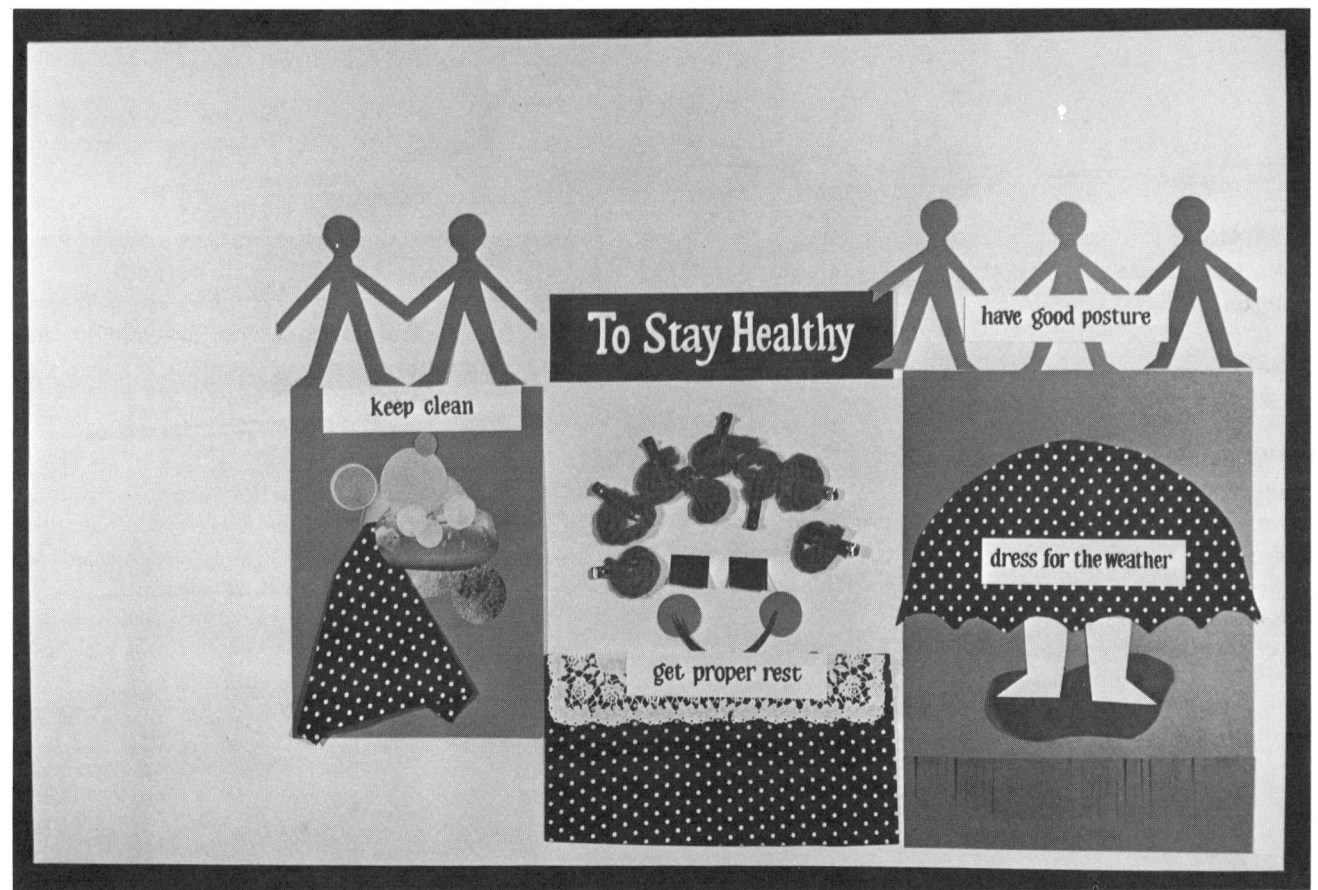

TO STAY HEALTHY

MATERIALS:
Construction paper, fabric, square white lace paper doilies, hair clips, wool yarn, magazine photograph, cellophane, chalk, pins.

COLORS:
White, black, light green, dark green, turquoise, pink, yellow, dark blue.

METHOD:
1. Line Board with white paper, leaving a wide white margin on left and top, and a narrow border at right and bottom edges when colored paper is attached.
2. Pin blue and green sheets of construction paper to backdrop, as shown, leaving center section temporarily undecorated.
3. With white chalk letter main caption on a strip of black paper, and pin onto central white space in line with top corners of blue and green panels. The four supplementary captions are done on white paper strips with marking pen.
4. On the blue panel, with its "keep clean" sign pinned to the top, add a magazine picture of soap, construction paper bubbles, and a real polka dot fabric washcloth.
5. On the white center section place a head fashioned by: a pair of eyelashes cut from black construction paper into fringe; two turquoise circles for cheeks, with dark blue construction paper smile; hair coils of turquoise wool yarn, held together with hair clips.
6. The blanket is fashioned from the same fabric as the washcloth and pinned to the bottom of the center section, while the bed sheet, bearing the "get proper rest" admonition, is made of paper doilies.
7. A large umbrella shape in the same dotted fabric hides the body of the child on the green panel, so that only the boots show, eliminating the need to represent the whole figure. The boots are cut from construction paper and placed on a free-form cellophane water puddle. At the bottom of the panel is a strip of green paper, fringed to simulate grass. The sign, "dress for the weather," is superimposed on the umbrella.
8. A string of paper dolls cut from the various shades of construction paper are used in the display to coordinate the color scheme as well as the design. The last three figures, standing atop the green panel, carry the last sub-caption, "have good posture."

NOTE:
The wide margin on the left may remain empty, or be used to line up a list of vocabulary words related to the subject.

ALTERNATE IDEA:
If arranged at a library, the same area might offer a list of books on the featured subject.

MATERIALS:
Construction paper, silhouettes of Washington and Lincoln, pins.

COLORS:
Red, white, blue.

METHOD:
1. Line the Board with white paper.
2. Cut circles from centers of sheets of red paper.
3. Alternate rectangles and circles as shown, in an allover pattern, making the design as long and as deep as necessary.
4. Cut silhouettes of Lincoln and Washington from blue paper (commercial silhouettes are available for purchase, to serve as patterns, if desired).
5. Pin the caption letters between the rows of rectangles and circles, further emphasizing the allover disposition of the design.

NOTE:
The repeat pattern, projecting the large, bold shapes as well as the letters, results in a design of simplicity. Its message is quickly conveyed. Some workers may wish to place biographical or historical information in the circle areas. Many other subjects could be treated in this same, easy manner.

MATERIALS:
Crepe paper ribbon, construction paper, marking pen, pins.

COLORS:
Red, white, blue.

METHOD:
1. Line Board with white paper.
2. Make the whole display resemble the top of a birthday gift package by pinning on red, white and blue crepe paper ribbon from one end to the other horizontally slightly above center, and from top to bottom toward the right side, caught at the meeting point by a stylized bow of cutout construction paper.
3. The caption is written in script casually at an angle in the lower left area, with blue marking pen.

NOTE:
This seems a somewhat different way to handle the birthdays of America's great Revolutionary and Civil War presidents. The oversized gift box is dramatic in appearance, and the patriotic color scheme effective, simple and easy to do.

*"From Guess Who" is not strictly grammatical, but has been used because it is a generally accepted phrase.

MATERIALS:
White lace paper doilies, cardboard, last year's valentines, ribbon, cellophane, chalk, pins.

COLORS:
Black, white, red.

METHOD:
1. Line Board with black paper.
2. Glue a collage of last year's valentines to cardboard and cut into a heart shape.
3. Pin red cellophane over collage to unify all cards, and trim to conform to heart shape.
4. Attach heart to center of the Board, using doilies around the edges.
5. Add ribbon bow to top of heart for a further decorative touch, as well as dimension.
6. The caption is written with white chalk.

NOTE:
A pleasant way for the teacher to give a valentine to the class, involving a minimum of work.

FEBRUARY BIRTHDAYS

IN FEBRUARY
WE CELEBRATE
THE BIRTHDAYS
OF GEORGE
WASHINGTON AND
ABRAHAM LINCOLN

VALENTINE

FROM SEA TO SHINING SEA

MATERIALS:
Construction paper, cellophane, pins.

COLORS:
Turquoise, purple, magenta, green, golden yellow, amber, blue, white.

METHOD:
1. Line Board with turquoise paper.
2. Cut and pin to background jagged shapes from colored construction paper—purple and magenta for mountains; green, golden yellow and amber for land, and blue cellophane for the sea.
3. Cut caption letters from white construction paper, attaching the first three words at upper left, and the last two at lower right, thereby drawing viewers' eyes across the entire display.

NOTE:
If space permits, this is a good mural-type arrangement for the whole class to work on together, stretching from one end of the room to the other. Yet it is equally effective in a small area, because of its simplicity of style and unusual color combination. The latter, obviously, derives from the song, "America, America," but could be adapted to almost any subject. Many songs and poems may inspire color plans and ideas on which to base displays appropriate for use throughout the school year.

ALTERNATE IDEA:
The construction paper mountains could be used to display pictures, information and maps about this nation's mountain ranges; the section below could present information about the plains, while the bottom section could feature America's great water resources. Strings of coordinating colors could run from the designated areas to their related maps, pictures and information.

READ ALL ABOUT IT

MATERIALS:
Brown paper bag, fabric, newspaper, colored string, commercial letters, construction paper, thickly dotted patterned paper box, glue, pins.

COLORS:
Black, blue, white, orange, red, yellow, purple, gray.

METHOD:
1. Line Board with white paper.
2. Cut a discarded, thickly-dotted (small dots) patterned paper box into an oval, for the boy's freckled face; add a construction paper oval mouth, and marking pen lips, cheeks and nose.
3. From orange construction paper cut longish hair, then glue face and hair to upside-down brown paper bag.
4. Cut out fabric cap and glue to hair and bag bottom. Pin onto left side of Board. The bag's thickness holds head away from backdrop, creating feeling of dimension. Allow part of the bag to show below the face, appearing as the boy's neck.
5. Cover the bottom section of the Board with sheets of construction paper positioning boy's body and arm.
6. Adjacent to boy's mouth and resting on his arm, pin a newspaper megaphone, caption strip down the center. Bold commercial letters comprise the message.
7. Pin colored strings from beginning of caption area to ends of Board, as illustrated, to emphasize shouted declaration.

NOTE:
Boy's construction paper body and open space beyond megaphone's wide end afford space to pin on news clips or important classroom announcements. The display could also serve to introduce library books on any given subject.

ALTERNATE IDEA:
Save this freckle-faced newsboy for repeated later use. With proper change of cap he could be transformed into a baseball figure shouting a message devoted to SPRING SPORTS or PLAY BALL! THE SAFE WAY.

JAPAN

MATERIALS:
Construction paper, magazine photographs, students' drawings, travel posters.

COLORS:
Black, white, red, multicolor photographs, posters and/or art work.

METHOD:
1. Line Board with black paper.
2. Divide the area as shown in illustration:
    a) White construction paper rectangle with red circle, simulating Japanese flag.
    b) Caption letters cut from travel posters and discarded magazine photographs featuring Japan, to correlate with other design elements.
    c) A large photograph of a Japanese scene cut from a magazine or travel poster.
    d) A collage of photographs and students' art work, matted with construction paper to fill out horizontal arrangement of the display. The short, white vertical strip on the left, and red strip on the right, help balance and co-ordinate the color design.

NOTE:
The well-proportioned effect of this simple display is due largely to the even alignment, on both sides, of its component parts.

ALTERNATE IDEA:
Should the teacher need to arrange a case display along similar lines, its floor could be covered with black paper or fabric. Then books about Japan and Japanese objects might be set on sheets of red and white construction paper.

HOW WE USE MONEY

MATERIALS:
Patterned wallpaper, construction paper, marking pen, pins.

COLORS:
White, dark red, light green, turquoise, black, gray, copper.

METHOD:
1. Line Board with white paper.
2. Using the worker's own hand as a guide, cut out a much larger hand.
3. Cut and pin on sleeve conforming to bent arm position, from dark red patterned wallpaper.
4. From a large sheet of turquoise construction paper cut away the inside area and round off the edges, to stimulate an oversize pocketbook. Add strap handle.
5. Use the cutout area to pin on circles representing coins of various denominations, and a dollar bill, lettering the value of each with marking pen.
6. The large caption letters are cut from black paper and pinned on.
7. The shopping list is done on white paper with black marking pen, and pinned on with hand.
8. Outline the pocketbook with black marking pen.

SHAPES

MATERIALS:
Large, flat, gray box top, American flag, construction paper, fabric, pins.

COLORS:
Gray, navy blue, red, white.

METHOD:
1. Make a display area of a large, flat box top.
2. Pin on shapes shown (triangle, circle, square, rectangle) and their name letters, cut from construction paper, and arranged as seen in illustration.
3. Add a small figure coming out of the triangular wigwam. (She combines all the shapes featured: circular head, triangular body, rectangular arms, square feet).
4. Add decorations on ball (triangles with curved edges, to fit circle).
5. Use cutout of fabric print for field of stars on American flag, made with red and white strips of construction paper. (Or acquire a real flag).
6. Rectangular strips and triangular bows adorn the square package.

NOTE:
The color scheme derives from the flag, set against the gray backdrop. (For another box top display, see illustration, YOUR FLAG AND MINE).

HAPPY CHANUKAH

MATERIALS:
Metallic gold paper, construction paper, wrapping paper, marking pen, glue, pins.

COLORS:
Gold, white, blue, purple, turquoise, magenta, green, yellow, pink, black.

METHOD:
1. Using the largest sheet of metallic gold paper available, fold at bottom to create a ledge, in accordance with a real menorah (seven-branched candlestick).
2. Glue black, cutout construction paper caption letters across the part of the ledge that protrudes, then pin the entire sheet of gold paper to Board.
3. Pin into place blue, purple, and turquoise paper Chanukah candles, with pink, magenta and purple flames cut from brightly-colored wrapping paper.
4. Add the large white Star of David, formed by putting together two triangular shapes (previously outlined with marking pen and cut out).

NOTE:
For a portable exhibit along similar lines, use a sheet of gold cardboard, score and bend bottom ledge, glue on the various symbolic items, and attach an easel support on the back. The piece can then stand on a table, bookcase or shelf, with appropriate books. Here is another instance illustrating how an oversized version of a familiar object, very simple to do, may prove an effective and exciting display.

THANKSGIVING

MATERIALS:
Square white paper doilies, construction paper, lightweight white cardboard, plastic fruits and vegetables, a newspaper or magazine cutout of a holiday turkey, stipple brush, poster paint, chalk, green tissue paper, pins.

COLORS:
White, brown, orange, gold, yellow, olive green, light green, red—shades associated with autumn.

METHOD:
1. Line Board with white lace paper doilies.
2. Using a newspaper or magazine Thanksgiving food advertisement as a pattern, cut a turkey from brown construction paper (drumsticks should be cut separately).
3. With white poster paint and a stipple brush, simulate highlights on the turkey, and add frilled paper "panties" from doilies to the drumsticks.
4. Cut a large, oval cardboard platter. The edge of the platter could be decorated with chalk or paint, or left white. Crumple shaded green tissue paper all over a large inside area of platter, to extend beyond the turkey.
5. Pin turkey and drumsticks away from the background, to give three-dimensional effect. Some extra tissue paper may be affixed under the turkey breast, providing a more rounded, plump look.
6. Pin (or glue) on the plastic fruits and vegetables, along with some fruits and vegetables cut from construction paper.
7. Add two paper cutouts of festive candle holders, with lighted candles.
8. The word *Thanksgiving* may be done in the teacher's (or student's) best penmanship, with chalk on a strip of red construction paper cut at both ends to resemble a ribbon. Pin away from the backdrop for dimension.

NOTE:
Interesting contrast is achieved by combining the plastic and paper fruits and vegetables. Students may be given this assignment, as well as the privilege of locating the picture of the turkey to serve as a pattern.

ISRAEL

MATERIALS:
Construction paper, posters, pictures, information pertaining to the subject, pins.

COLORS:
Purple, turquoise, yellow-green, black, white.

METHOD:
1. Line Board with white paper.
2. In accordance with illustration, cut and pin strips of colored construction paper to form a large menorah (candlestick with seven branches) onto display area, leaving space for large, bold, cutout caption letters to fit within the design.
3. Use the parts of the candelabrum for mounting related posters, pictures, seals, and written work done by students.

ALTERNATE IDEA:
Two menorahs could be presented side by side, contrasting the ancient Israeli area with the little democracy in the Middle East as it is today.

MEXICO

METHOD:
1. Line Board with khaki paper.
2. Cover the upper portion of display area, except for narrow border, with a Mexican print fabric.
3. Pin large, bold cutout caption letters, MEXICO, over main body of fabric, with smaller letters, THE LAND AND ITS RESOURCES, inscribed on a strip of white paper above it with marking pen.
4. Bright sheets of construction paper, picking up the colors of the print fabric, form the balance of the design, as shown in the photograph. They may be used as mats for information or photographs related to Mexico.
5. A cutout construction paper hat is pinned onto the letter, M, to heighten the Mexican mood.

ALTERNATE SUGGESTION:
Depending on size of display area, a real or miniature sombrero may be substituted for the construction paper hat.

NOTE:
This type arrangement would adapt well to any foreign land. Instead of fabric students might prepare a decorative panel by printing appropriate designs on construction paper, tying in with the country under discussion. The nation's native-style headgear could replace the Mexican hat.

MATERIALS:
Construction paper, fabric, marking pen, pins.

COLORS:
Khaki, tan, dark blue, light blue, white, yellow-green, hot pink, orange, yellow, yellow-orange.

SPAIN

MATERIALS:
Construction paper, various items representative of Spain (real or students' art work), pins.

COLORS:
Black, yellow, red, white, green, orange.

METHOD:
1. Line Board with white paper.
2. Arrange sheets of construction paper as shown, providing brightly colored panels for the display of maps, pictures, articles of clothing, musical instrument, etc. The seal of Spain may be rendered by a student. All items are pinned onto backdrop.
3. Affix strips of black construction paper to resemble poles from which the exhibit panels are hung.
   Add strips of colored paper bearing explanatory notes for the various things on view.
4. Caption letters may be cut from black construction paper, and pinned onto a white paper strip mounted on the Board.

AUTUMN
HALLOWEEN
THANKSGIVING

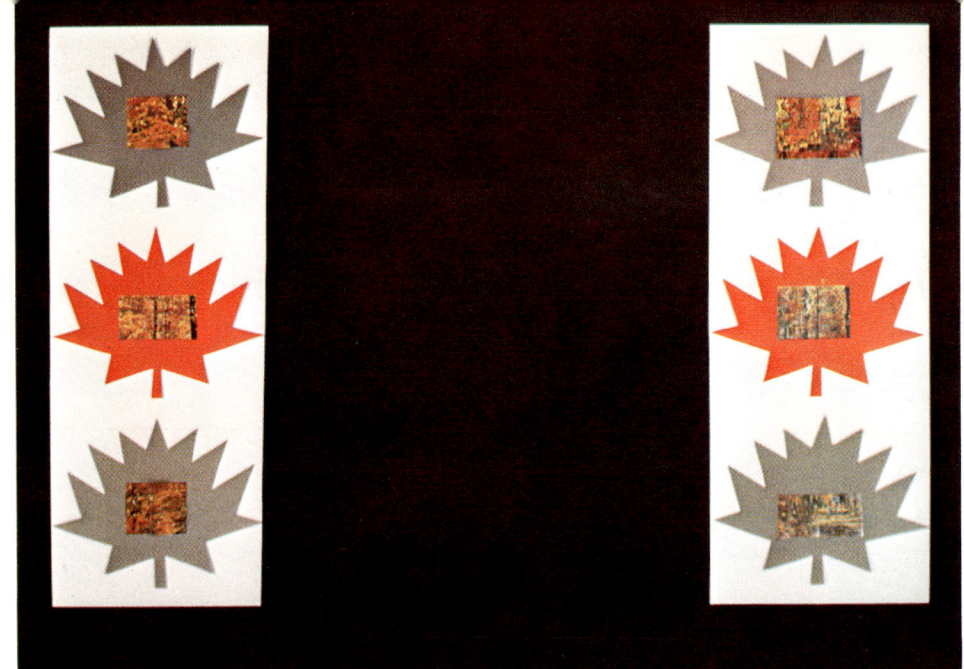

(This design adaptable to all three subjects, with slight changes.)

MATERIALS:
Construction paper, marking pen, magazine photographs or posters of autumn scenes, students' written work, novelty pencil with broom attached to eraser, pins.

COLORS:
White, black, orange, tan, gold.

METHOD:
1. Line Board with white paper.
2. Cut decorative construction paper leaf shapes (see pattern section) large enough to accommodate the pictures to be displayed.
3. Pin photographs or posters of autumn scenes on the leaves. These comprise attractive border panels for the first Bulletin Board of the school season.
4. As Halloween nears, an oversized witch's hat cut from a large sheet of black construction paper may be placed in the center area between the leaves.
5. Cut strips of paper and arrange them in the hatband space for the main caption, HALLOWEEN.
6. Cut blocks of construction paper for mounting students' papers, coordinating the colors with pictures seen on the leaves.
7. The supplementary caption, Poems and Stories, designating the students' writings, is done with a marking pen.
8. Add the pencil broom at hatband.
9. The mounted pictures may be changed to point up Halloween, or left as they are.
10. As Thanksgiving approaches, remake Halloween symbols by turning down the point of the witch's hat to form a pilgrim's hat, and use the O from the main caption for its buckle.
11. Change mounted photographs or posters to Thanksgiving pictures, or leave the original autumn scenes, which would also seem suitable in observance of the holiday.
12. Change Poems and Stories to THANKSGIVING.
13. Replace students' former written papers with either stories or art works related to Thanksgiving.

NOTE:
Save the hat's triangular shape to use as a Christmas tree mounting for student work later on, changing the end panels to Christmas pictures and ornaments.

FRESH FROM THE GARDEN

MATERIALS:
Construction paper, cardboard, felt marking pen, lavender cellophane, pins.

COLORS:
Hot pink, orange, red-orange, light blue, dark blue, lavender, green, gold, khaki, purple.

METHOD:
1. Line Board with white paper.
2. Cut large, irregular circles for flowers, and to some of these add stylized petals.
3. Draw the stems with marking pen, using a yardstick to help keep lines fairly straight.
4. The leaves may be done freehand.
5. Cut a vase from lavender cellophane to fit over stem area, and pin to Board.
6. Cut strips of cardboard to represent book spines, and letter with actual titles of selected books on gardening. Pin these to Board "piled up" near vase.
7. The large leaves balance the design and provide an excellent place for the caption.
8. Add dewdrops cut from cellophane and tiny circles in abundance around the flowers and vase, to denote a light, fresh air.

ALTERNATE TITLE:
READ BEFORE YOU PLANT

NOTE:
Students will enjoy designing and preparing the floral arrangement.

LIGHT READING IS FUN

MATERIALS:
Construction paper, cardboard, jump rope, marking pen, chalk, pins.

COLORS:
Black, white, orange, red-orange, yellow, yellow-orange, green.

METHOD:
1. Line Board with black paper.
2. Cut books from the largest sheets of construction paper available, based on pattern in this book.
3. Also cut out clowns, following pattern in this book.
4. Pin a jump rope from one end of Board to the other.
5. Balance clowns and books as pictured, decorating book spines and drawing page lines with marking pen and chalk. Add construction paper bookmark to center book.
6. The caption letters are cut from construction paper and affixed to book spine at right.

NOTE:
The bright colors against the black and oversized books help imply that lighthearted fun is associated with summer reading.

ALTERNATE SUGGESTION:
A vacation reading list may be appended to the book spine at left.

IN DAYS OF OLD WHEN KNIGHTS WERE BOLD

METHOD:
1. Cut corrugated board in the shape of a shield, proportionate with the size of the Bulletin Board.
2. Cover diagonal quarter sections in brightly colored felt and black construction paper, as seen in illustration.
3. Caption is done in Old English type lettering, with white chalk or poster paint on strips of black paper, and glued to black background.
4. Pin related book jackets or students' book reports on the black area.
5. Decorate the colored felt quarters with a simple, appropriate design, as shown.

NOTE:
With an easel back support this display could stand on a table of books devoted to the featured subject, along with book reports in folders coordinated with those on the shield.

ALTERNATE IDEA:
Students might do a series of such decorative shields in exciting color combinations, using a different symbol for each. As a result more book jackets and more student works would be displayed, and the repeat pattern of bold design all around the classroom would be especially attractive.

MATERIALS:
Corrugated board, felt, construction paper, chalk or poster paint and brush, book jackets, glue, pins.

COLORS:
Black, magenta, orange, white.

SHIPS THAT SAIL THE SEA

MATERIALS:
Cardboard, crepe paper, white poster paint and brush, miniature ship, tissue paper, plastic glue, chalk, pins.

COLORS:
Light blue, white, dark blue, green, yellow-green, multicolor ship.

METHOD:
1. Coat top half of cardboard to be used as Bulletin Board with plastic glue, then cover with sheets of light blue tissue paper, to produce the sky.
2. Next coat the entire area thus treated with the plastic glue, to contrive sheen.
3. Cover the lower portion of the display with alternating blue and green tones of crepe paper.
4. With yellow, green and blue chalk draw wavy lines on the crepe paper.
5. Pin a model of an old sailing vessel to the backdrop, with the bottom of the hull behind the top strip of crepe paper.
6. The white caption letters (style optional) are painted onto a green strip of crepe paper. Puckering of the paper caused by the wet paint will create an interesting effect, giving an underwater look to the caption.

ALTERNATE IDEAS:
The sailing ships representing those used by Columbus and his crew could be affixed effectively to a crepe paper sea.
A line of book jackets with white paper sails, on a crepe paper sea, might indicate cool summer reading.

IN THE DAYS OF LINCOLN

MATERIALS:
Construction paper, chalk, patterned wrapping paper or wallpaper, ball fringe, metallic gold paper, round and square paper doilies, velveteen, magazine cutouts, marking pen, pins.

COLORS:
Red, black, white, gold, green, yellow.

METHOD:
1. Line Board with black paper.
2. With chalk and ruler draw vertical lines on the black paper, to resemble striped wallpaper.
3. Leave top and bottom areas plain, for caption letters cut from white construction paper.
4. Cut the Victorian curtain shape from patterned wrapping paper or wallpaper and pin just below lettered area at top, and above lettered area at bottom, using the ball fringe to edge valance and tiebacks for curtains.
5. To duplicate the Victorian setting illustrated:
    a) Use a round white paper doily for the tabletop.
    b) Cut triangular shape from a square paper doily, tucking point of triangle under the circle, for tablecloth.
    c) Cut curly-shaped legs from metallic gold paper, and pin under tablecloth.
    d) Cut two heart shapes for chair backs and two circles for chair seats from patterned paper. Cut two smaller chair pads from red velveteen and add legs to match those of table.
    e) Add chandelier, a pile of books, and a vase of flowers, either made from paper or cut from a discarded magazine.

NOTE:
The caption lettering is a simplified version of Victorian style letters.

ALTERNATE TITLE:
READ THE VICTORIAN NOVELS.

BOOK WEEK NOVEMBER 10-16 (DATES CHANGE ANNUALLY).

MATERIALS:
Construction paper, marking pens, feathers, pins.

COLORS:
White, green, turquoise, dark green, deep pink, orange.

METHOD:
1. Line Board with white paper.
2. Place a dark blue strip of construction paper across bottom of display area in the shape illustrated, to represent front, back and spine of book as it appears when opened flat.
3. Form the pages with marking-pen lines.
4. Cut circles to indicate happy readers, and two hands for holding the book. (This treatment suggests the whole figure, but obviates the necessity of executing it.)
5. Add pieces of construction paper for the hats, use the hatband on the larger hat for the caption message and, if desired, the smaller hat space to fasten a reading list.
6. For decorative touches pin on the construction paper bird with real feather tail, and feathers to the right side of hatbands.
7. Add marking-pen eyes and smiles.

USING MATH IN THE KITCHEN

MATERIALS:
Construction paper, measuring spoons, measuring cup, cookbook, bowl, cake pan, wooden cooking implements on a rack, potholder, plastic flowers, checked tablecloth, tea towel, marking pen, ribbons, pins.

COLORS:
White, blue, yellow, purple, green, orange.

METHOD:
1. Line Board with white paper and cover table in front of Board with checked cloth.
2. Pin ribbons across the Board to simulate shelving on a kitchen wall.
3. Place on the shelves (by pinning) apothecary jars cut from sheets of colored construction paper, and paper sugar bowl filled with plastic flowers, along with paper book spines.
4. Add dish towel, potholder, measuring spoons, and attach rack of wooden implements in manner best suited to type of Bulletin Board involved.
5. The caption is lettered on the apothecary jar occupying the top shelf, while measuring tables (or other related mathematical information) appear on the jars below.
6. Ready on the table are the cookbook and cookery equipment likely to be used by students learning to measure ingredients.

NOTE:
Depicted here is a way to relate math to everyday experience. The simulated items are presented in sizes proportionate to the real ones handled during the lesson.
The small check pattern of the tea towel, the larger check of the tablecloth, and the gay print of the potholder all combine to heighten interest and help create the impression of a homey kitchen, where learning to measure for the purpose of cooking or baking would be a pleasurable event.

167

GEORGE WASHINGTON

MATERIALS:
Construction paper, American flags, photographs, drawings, wrapping paper, poster paint, glue, pins.

COLORS:
Red, white, light blue, dark blue, light khaki, dark khaki, black, gray.

METHOD:
1. Line Board with white paper.
2. Lightly affix a large, black silhouette of Washington (cut from a newspaper advertisement or construction paper; also available for purchase in varying sizes) in center of Board.
3. Slip a large sheet of construction paper under profile of the first President, extending out to the left, and pin on to form mounting space for information.
4. Using a small sheet of dark khaki paper, extend from back of silhouette to provide additional mounting space on the right.
5. Pin on flags, photographs, drawn sketches and any descriptive notes needed, as shown.
6. Draw and cut out three eagle silhouettes (see pattern section), and with marking pen inscribe Washington's birth and death dates on each. Follow placement of all items as pictured, thus pulling the design together.
7. Caption letters in plain, bold style are cut from black construction paper, and pinned or glued toward top of Bulletin Board, to command attention. Complementing the heading is the small lettering at lower right, done in light khaki poster paint.

NOTE:
While photographs, maps, graphs and similar items are often improved by mounts of harmonizing or contrasting color, it is not always necessary to provide such edges. Observe here the minuteman photograph and blue construction paper under it. Since the photo is mounted on the dark khaki paper, and the latter appears directly above the blue background paper, the surrounding area serves the same purpose as a special edge of blue, and results in better design. However, the small oval sketch of Washington seen at the hairline would be lost without the oval shape of light blue paper mounted on the black silhouette. A mount may not be essential for the hand and quill drawing, but since part of it extends onto the white paper, the edge of blue prevents the piece from seeming to blend into the Bulletin Board backdrop.

This type of layout—using oversized silhouette of related picture or symbol—could apply to almost any subject under discussion. For example, a silhouette of an enlarged butterfly might provide needed display space for information, photographs and drawings devoted to a science program.

(The blue construction paper could offer more space for information. But it appears mainly as a block of color, to help achieve balance).

NATURE STUDY

MATERIALS:
Binoculars, feather for quill pen, nature book, nature pictures, shallow box top, pins.

COLORS:
Red-violet, white, yellow.

METHOD:
1. Using a shallow box top for the display area, pin construction paper hands, binoculars and bird pictures as seen in illustration.
2. Add a reference book about birds, enhancing the bird-watching atmosphere; also, a quill pen, and paper pad for jotting down observations.

NOTE:
The box top display is lightweight, therefore can be carried from room to room. It is also a useful device for creating display space where Bulletin Board space is inadequate.
This would make an attractive arrangement for a library or classroom science corner, where students could view pictures relating to the subject, look up needed information, and write their notes. The binoculars lend a three-dimensional touch of realism to the exhibit.

FEED OUR WINTER FRIENDS

MATERIALS:
Construction paper, raw cotton, soap flakes, lightweight cardboard, tree branch, wool yarn, bird cutouts from magazine or students' art work, milk cartons, index cards, marking pens, tinfoil, tin can to hold the branch, pins, glue, stones or gravel.

COLORS:
White, black, silver, red, yellow, multicolor birds.

METHOD:
1. Line Board with white paper.
2. Cut caption letters from black construction paper, mount on strip of white construction paper, and pin onto Board.
3. Set a tree branch into a can filled with small stones or gravel, to weight it down. Place can on stand or table covered with tinfoil, just below Board.
4. Glue cutouts of birds taken from discarded magazines (or rendered by students) to tree.
5. Add index cards with bird names lettered with marking pens, and tied to tree with wool yarn. The reverse side of each card bears information about the bird it accompanies, easy to read by turning the card.
6. Also with wool yarn, tie on milk cartons, which would be filled with bird seed if children chose to feed their feathered friends during the cold weather months.
7. A piece of white cardboard with scalloped top, cut to resemble mounds of snow, leans against the stone-filled tree holder.
8. Add a mound of cotton snow in front of the cardboard, and sprinkle on soap flakes to give a realistic wintry touch.

NOTE:
The silver (tinfoil) tabletop, cotton, white cardboard and snowflakes may be used in connection with other display subjects related to winter.

HAWAII

MATERIALS:
Construction paper, sandpaper, corrugated board, photograph, map of Hawaii, pins.

COLORS:
White, green, brown, red-orange, multicolor photographs.

METHOD:
1. Line Board with white paper.
2. Pin to lower half a sheet of sandpaper to serve as a mat for photographs, maps and information pertaining to the subject. (If no sandpaper is available, brown paper will do quite well).
3. Cut out a large figure, with arms and feet extended (see pattern section), and dress as a Hawaiian girl, adding chalk lines to skirt, and a ley of flowers around her neck.
4. Cut a palm tree trunk from corrugated board, and above this pin fronds made from green paper.
5. Add the red-orange, paper sun in the sky at upper right, and large, bold letters cut from brown paper for the caption at the base of the design.

NOTE:
The maps, pictures and information relating to Hawaii can be changed often, leaving the remainder of the arrangement intact. This is a good way to introduce a unit, creating interest in the area to be studied. Then, as more information is acquired, the display gathers momentum with each change of material, and the interest is heightened. Such a display may be accompanied by a table display of related books and pamphlets.

171

T. V. SET

MATERIALS:
Wood-grain contact paper, magazine cutouts, cardboard box, lightweight cardboard, construction paper, masking tape, mat knife or single-edged razor blade, thumbtacks.

COLORS:
Tan, wood-grain, red-orange, black, white.

METHOD:
1. With mat knife or single-edged razor blade cut the center from a box front in familiar shape of a television screen.
2. Cover the remaining portion of the box with wood-grained contact paper.
3. From a discarded magazine cut a picture representative of the lesson topic and place in cutout screen area, taping to back of box.
4. Add the caption—a message bearing on a forthcoming television program—lettered on lined paper, with the corners trimmed to follow the screen shape.
5. Mount a magazine picture of fruit in a bowl on a piece of lightweight cardboard and cut out. Place an easel support on back and stand on top of box (T.V.).
6. Add channel and tuning knobs toward lower right using small white construction paper circles.

NOTE:
Often television programs with educational value are assigned to students as homework. This is a fun way to introduce the project. The bowl of apples pictured here adds realism to the arrangement. A cutout of a vase of flowers, or books, would also enhance the homey atmosphere.

PATTERNS FOR DRAWINGS

HOW TO ENLARGE ILLUSTRATIONS

On occasion when original art is unavailable, display workers may wish to "blow up" patterns presented in this book, or pictures contained in magazines, pamphlets, advertising leaflets and other sources.

Proceed as follows:
1. Draw a rectangle around the area to be enlarged, then with pencil and ruler divide it into small squares, as shown in the following examples.
2. Using a proportionately larger rectangle to accommodate the size of the illustration desired, draw larger squares equal in number to the smaller ones.
3. Next duplicate in each of the larger blocks that portion of the drawing seen in the corresponding smaller one, so that the required enlargement is obtained. Credit for the idea should appear on a card somewhere in the display whenever the source can be identified.

BASIC FIGURE

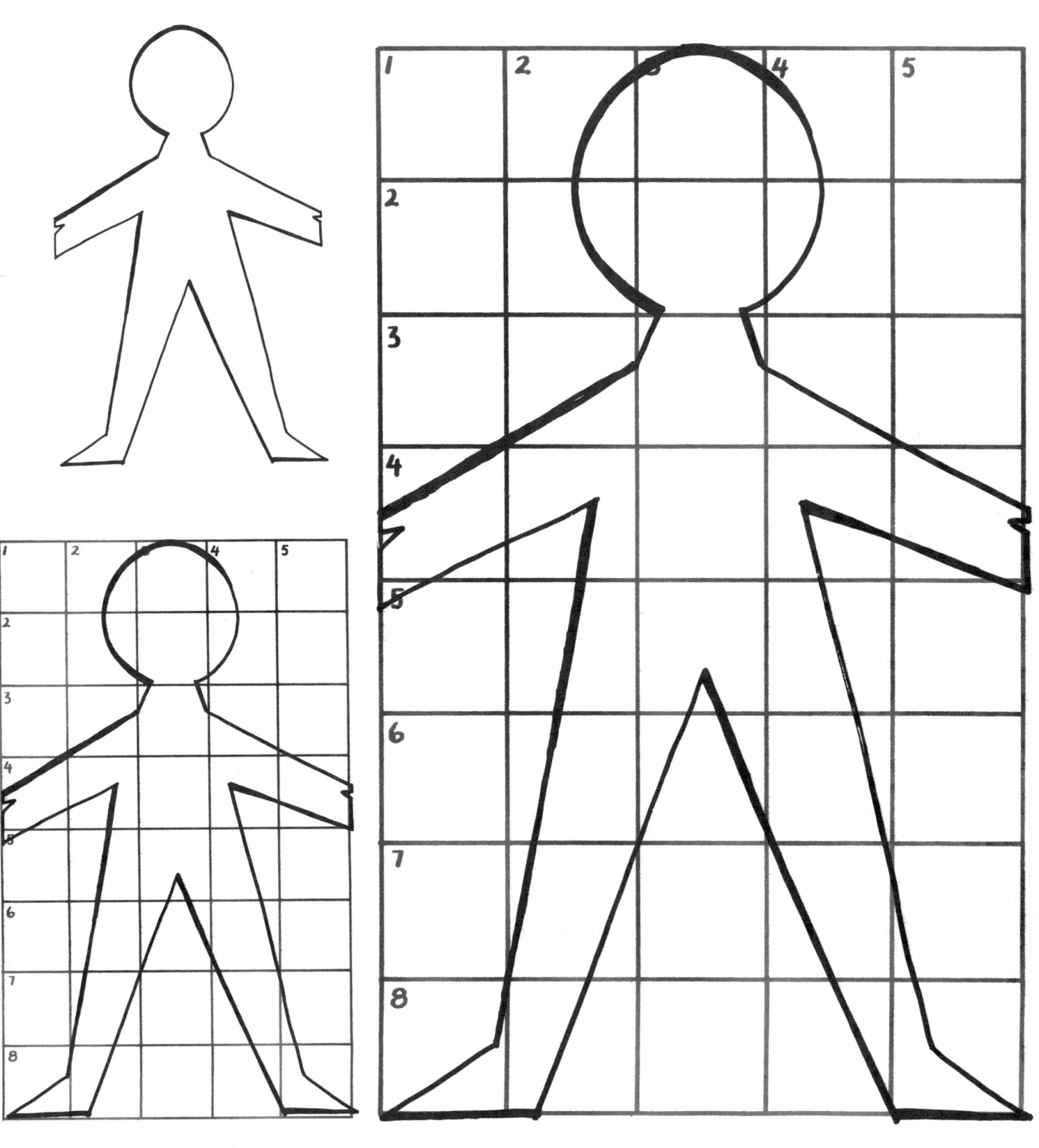

175

SIMPLE ALPHABET STYLE

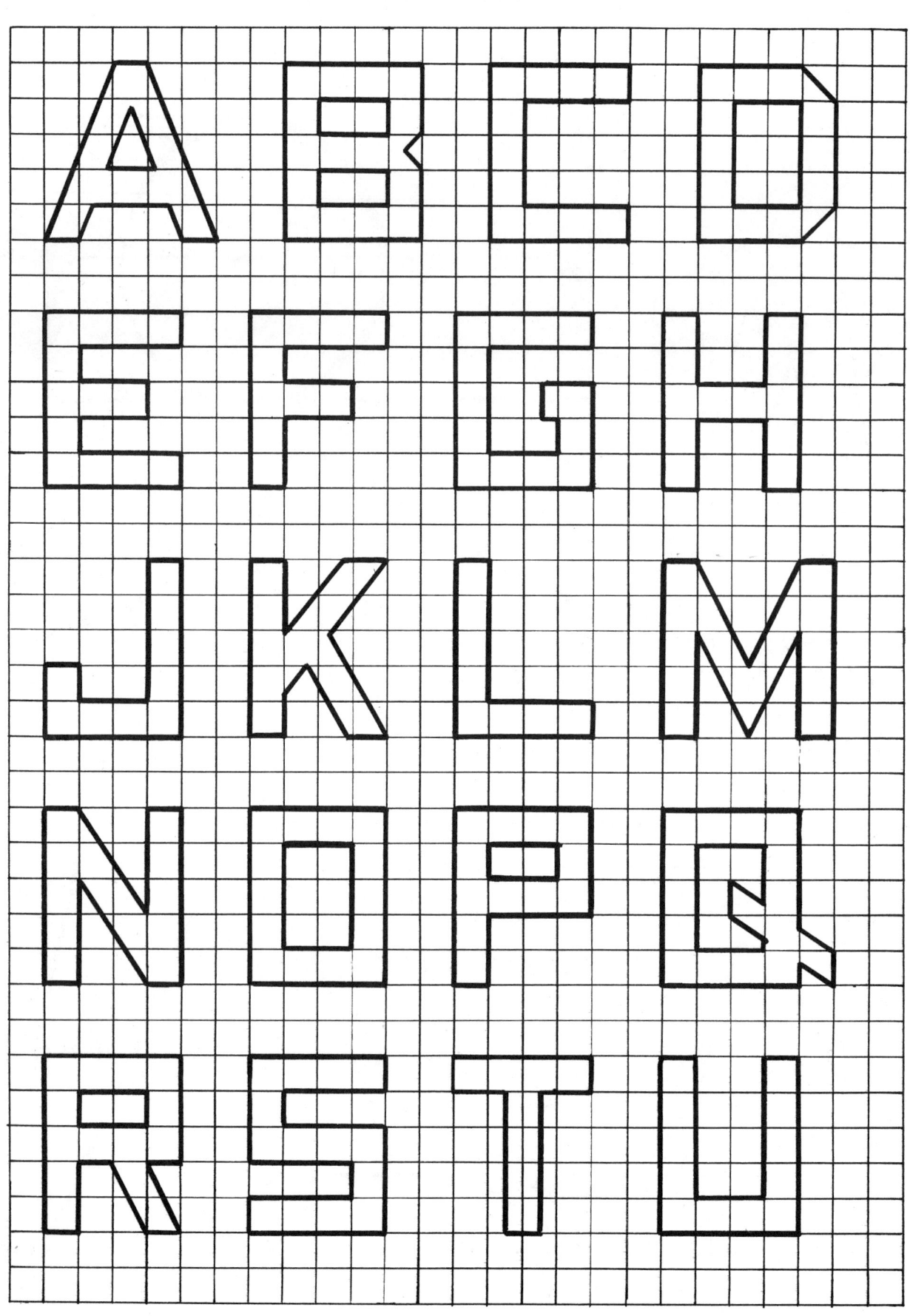

LETTERS, NUMBERS, DECORATIONS

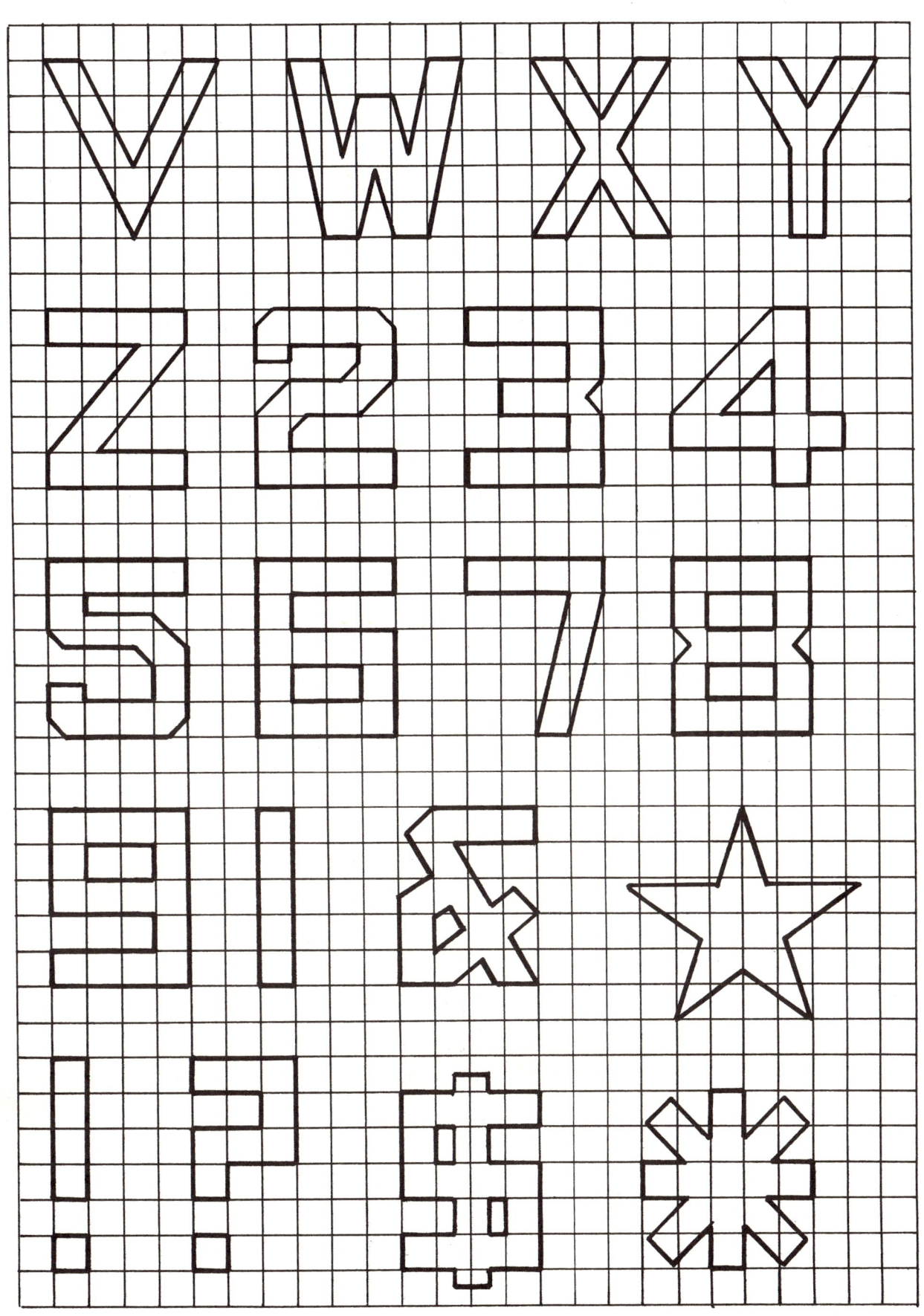

BOY

GIRL

GROUP OF BOOKS

OPEN BOOK

CLOWN

STYLIZED HAND

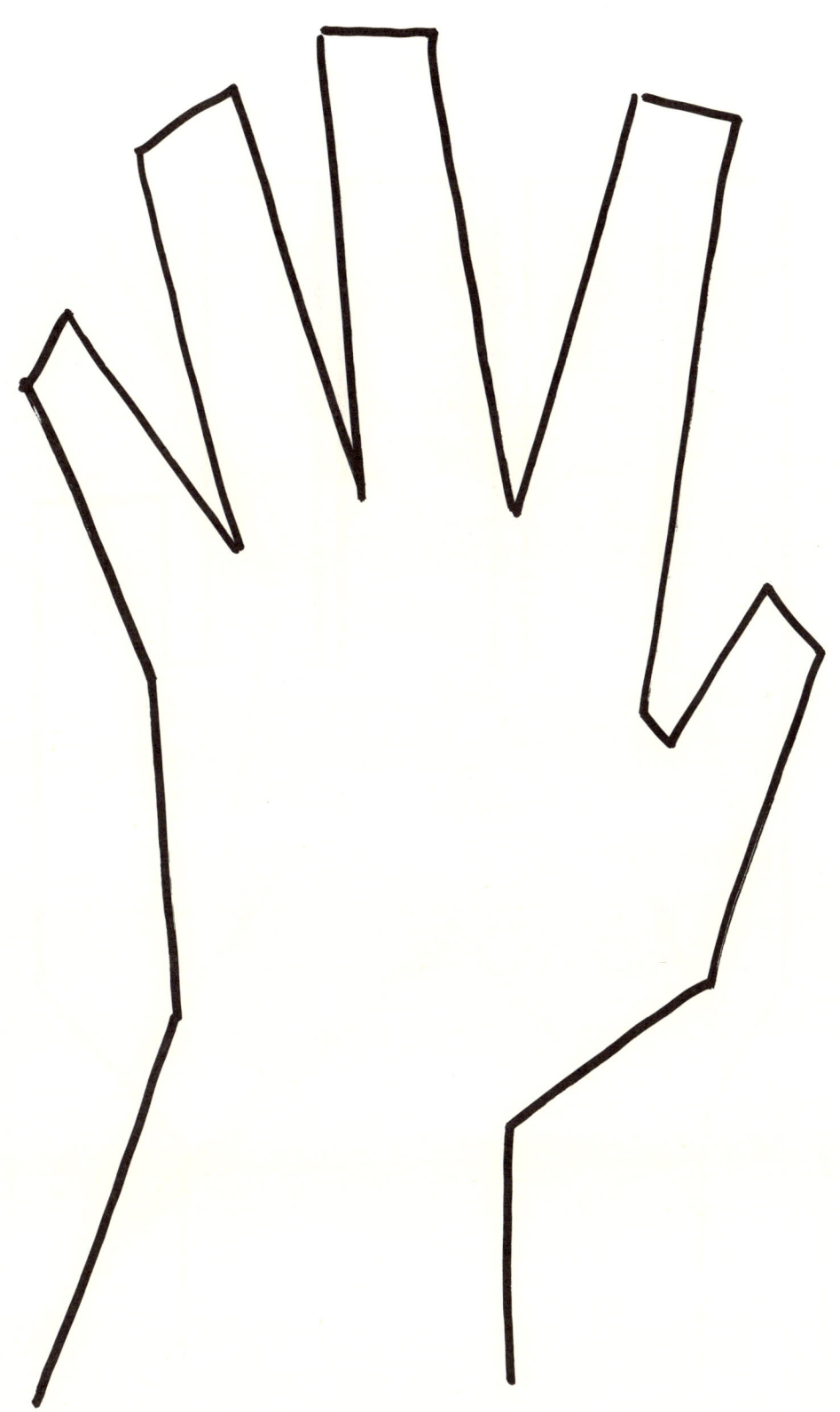

STYLIZED HAND

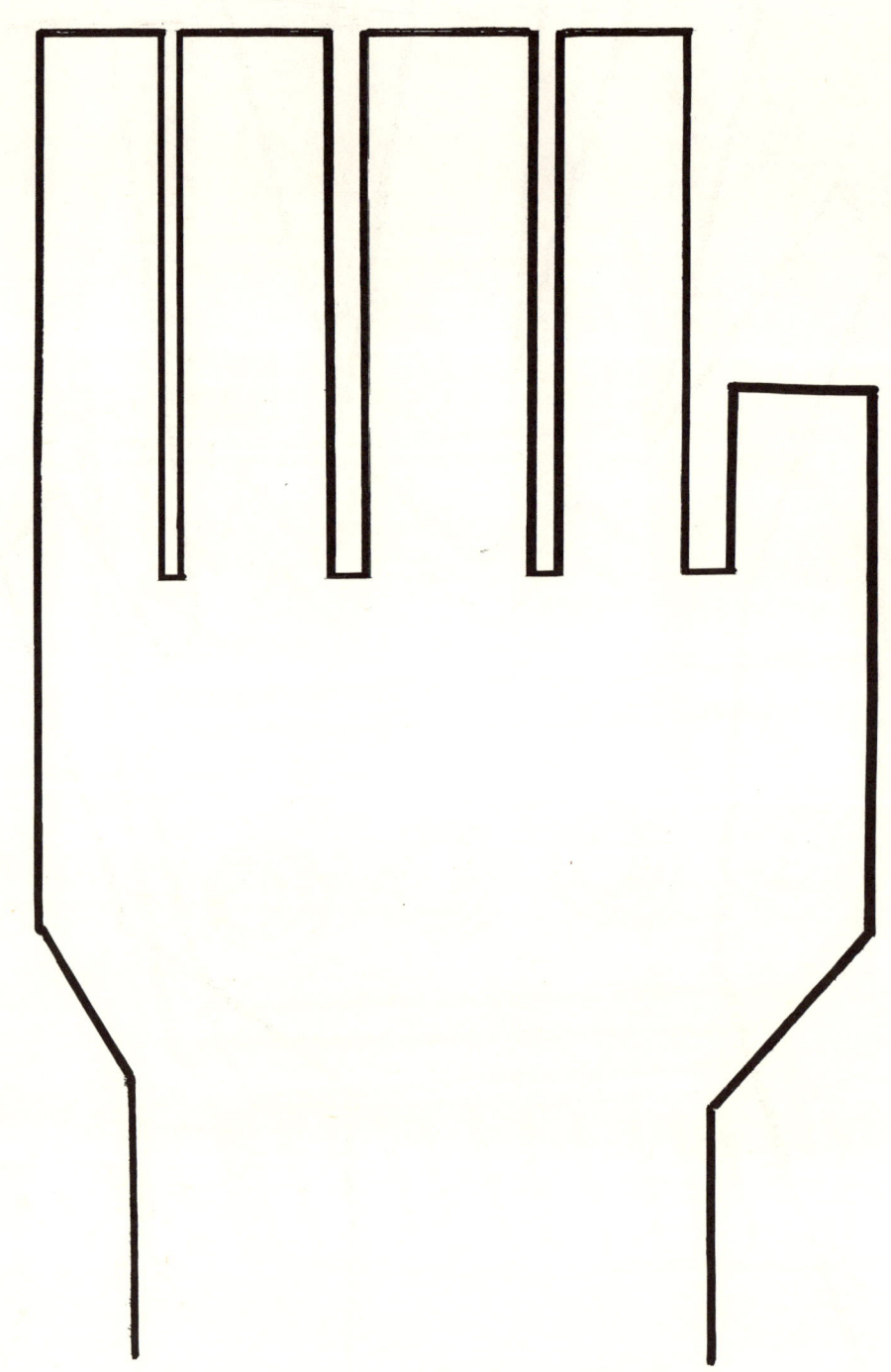

MITTEN

POINTING HAND

ELEPHANT

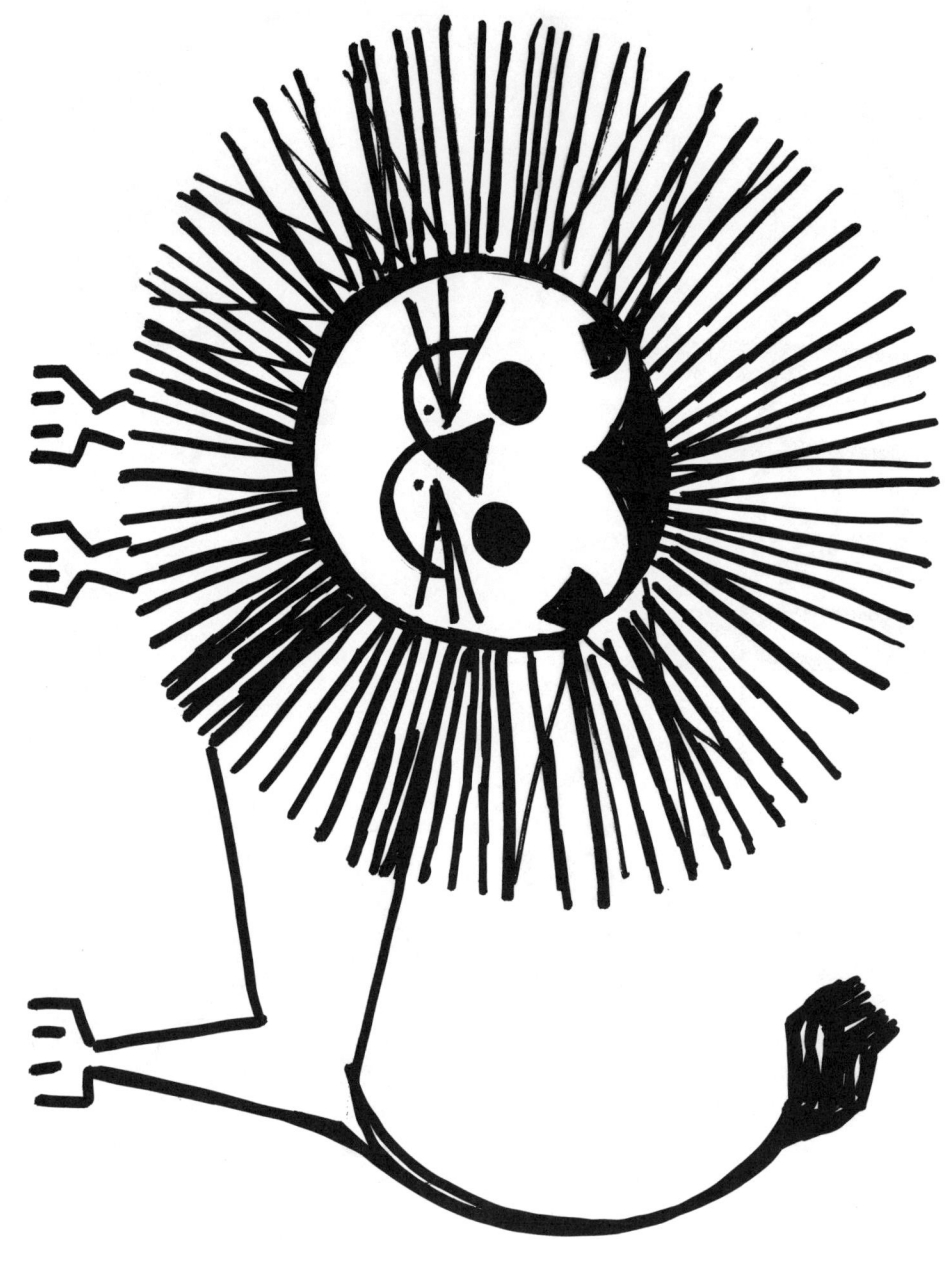

LION

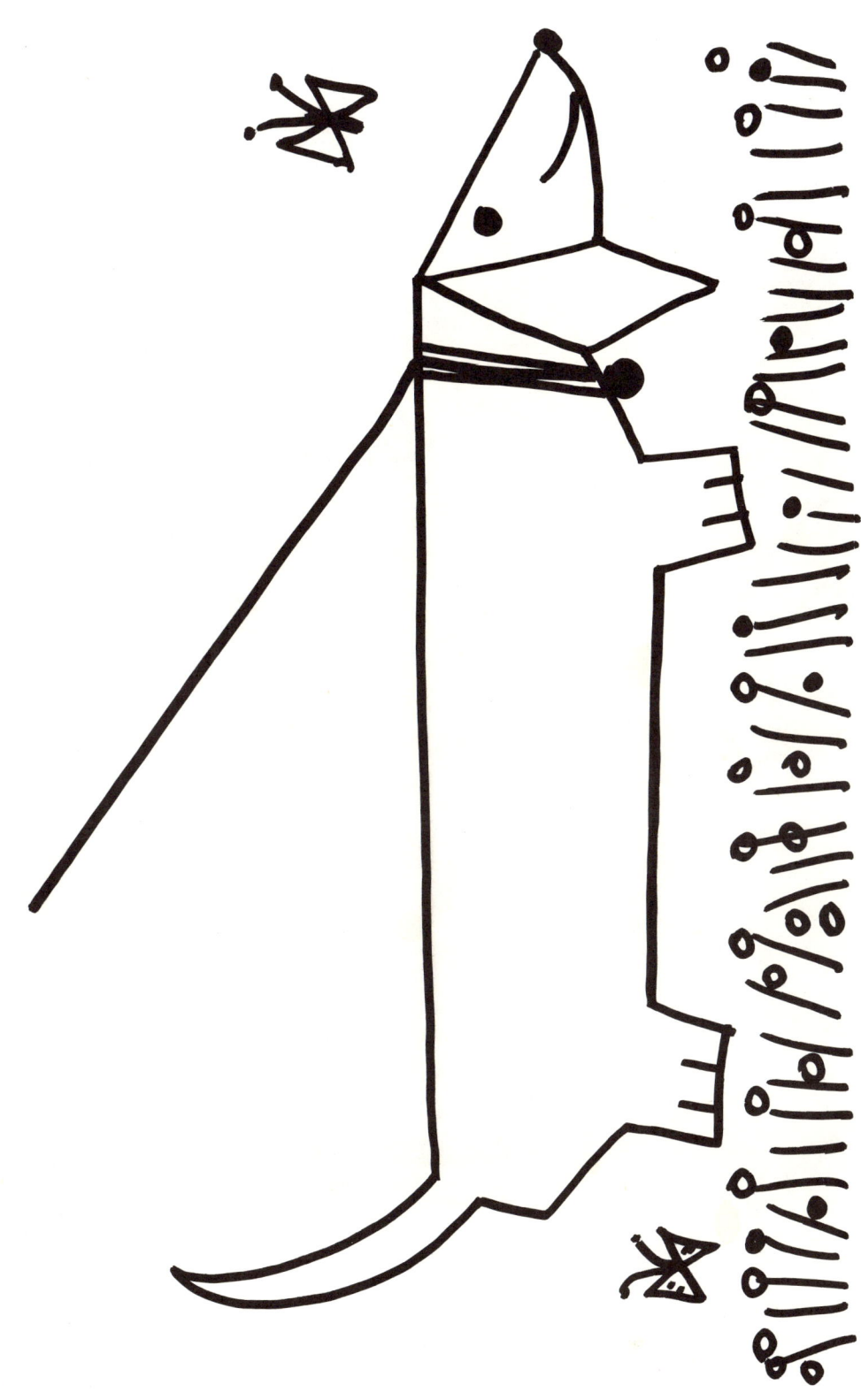

DOG

CAT

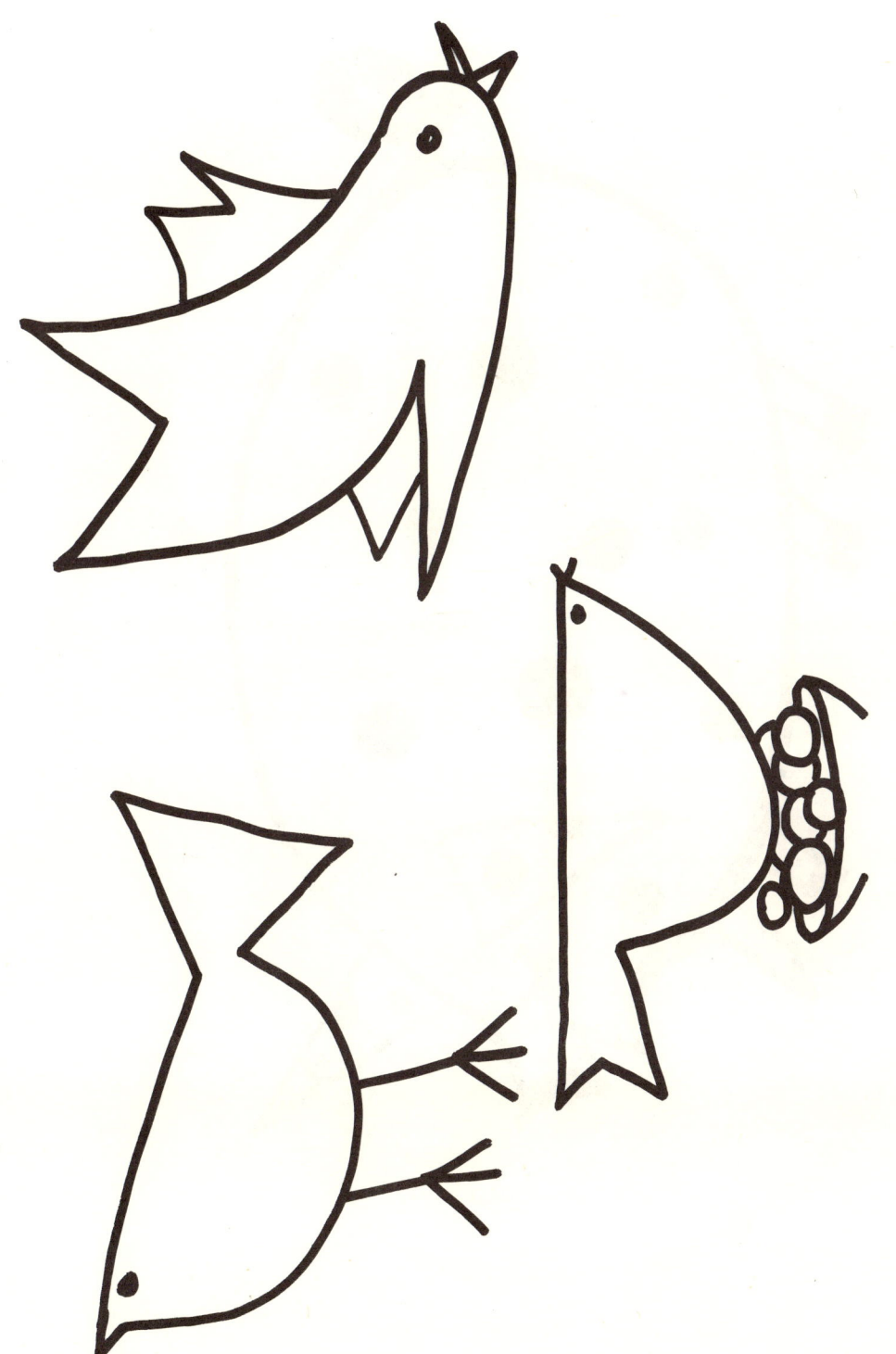

STYLIZED BIRDS

PIG

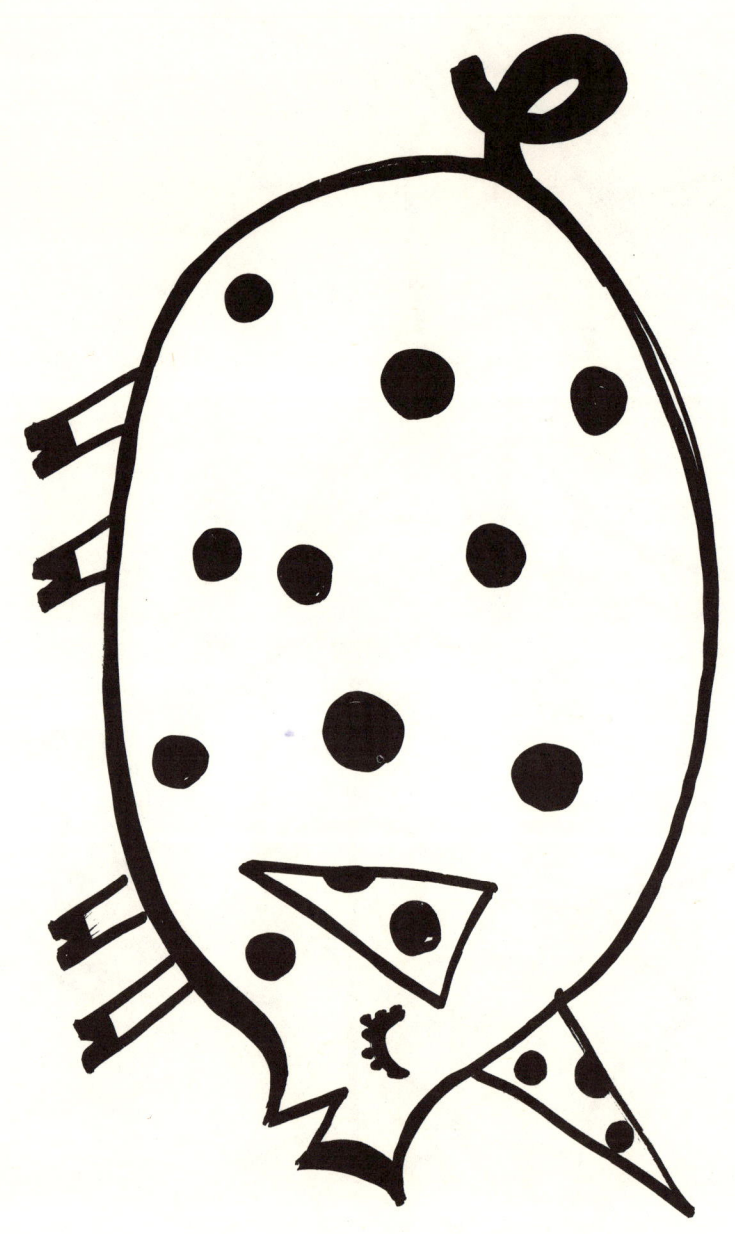

FISH

TURKEY

BUTTERFLY

EAGLE - STAR

196

SUN

FLOWER

TULIP, WOODEN SHOE

FLORAL ARRANGEMENT

TREE

STYLIZED TREE

STYLIZED LEAF

UMBRELLA

TRAIN

AIRPLANE

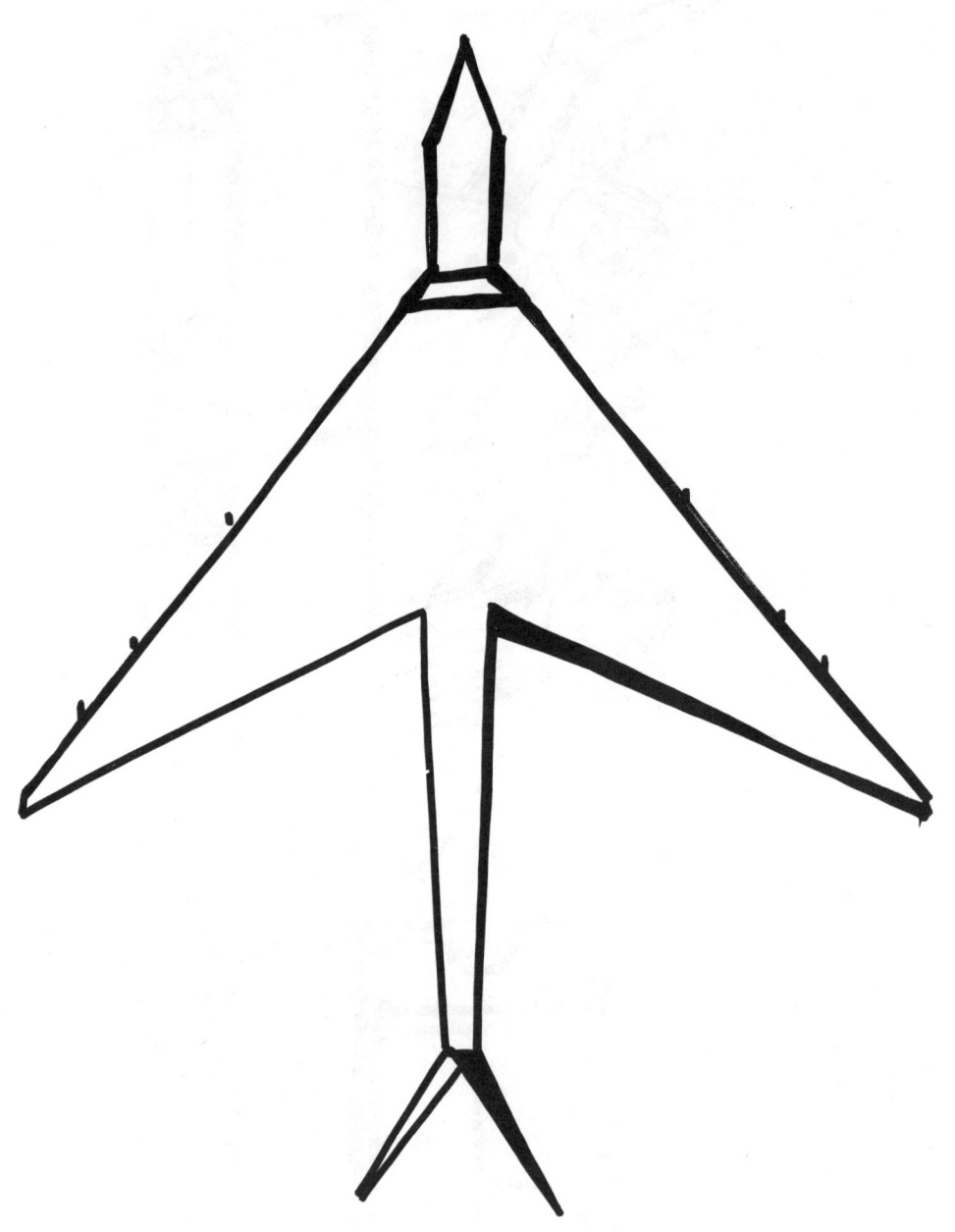

CAR

SHIP

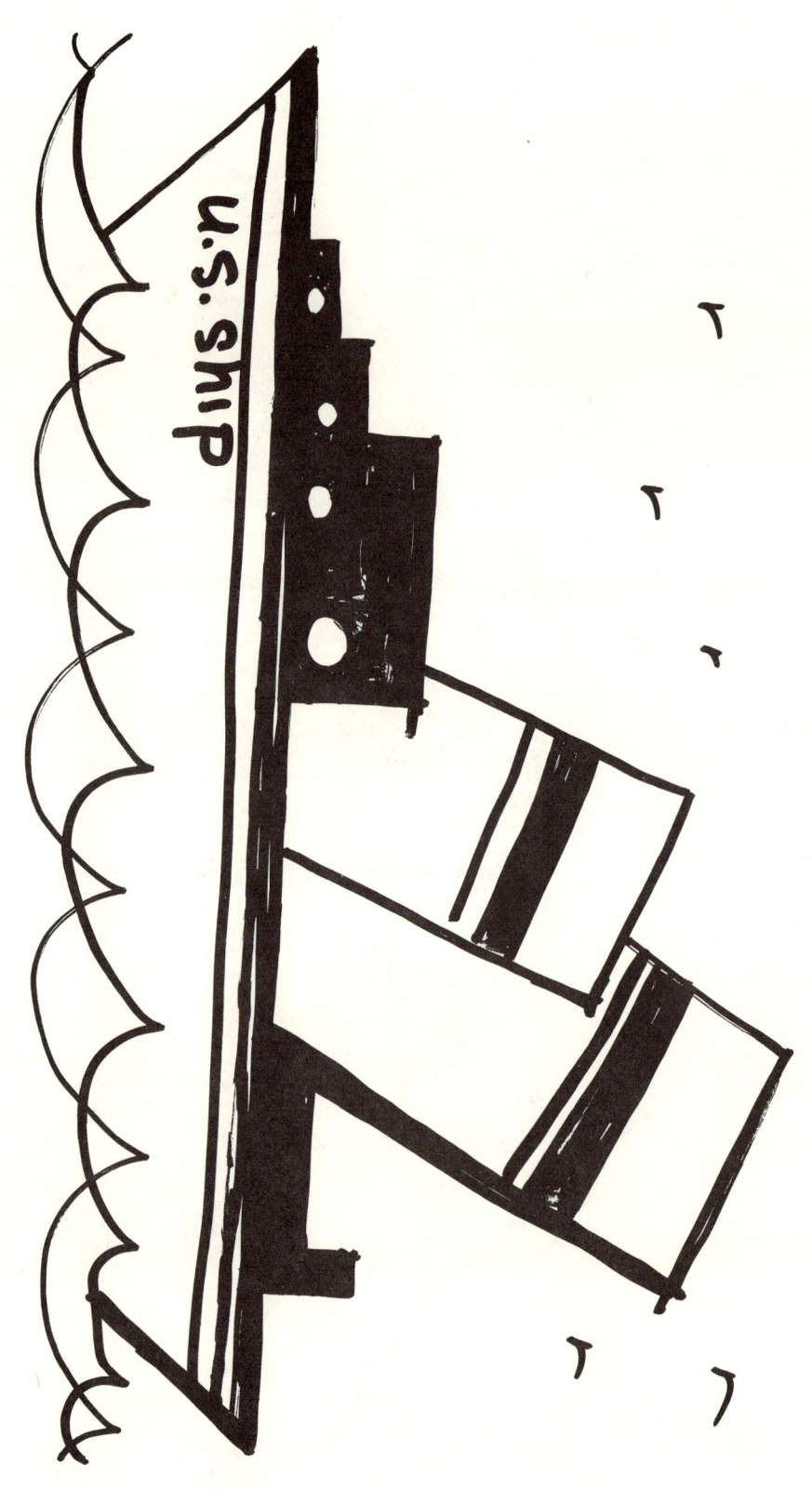

SAIL BOAT

TRUCK

HOUSE

TABLE AND CHAIRS

212

APOTHECARY (OR CANDY) JAR

HORN

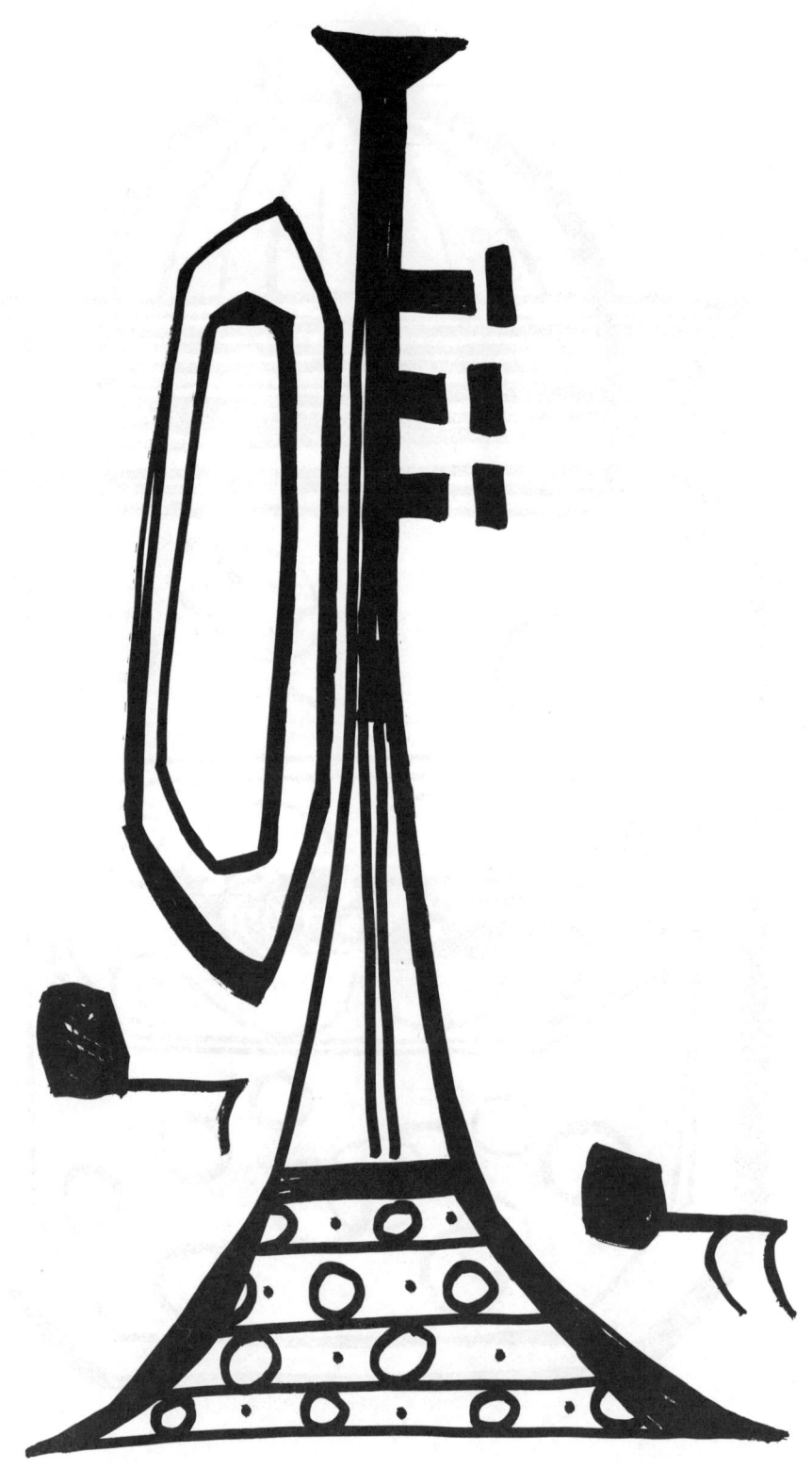

APPENDIX

SUPPLIERS

NOTE: When suitable discards are unobtainable, exhibits workers are likely to find many needed display items in the five-and-dime stores. However, for the convenience of teachers and librarians interested in commercial suppliers of art and display materials, and who have no access to such, we list the following establishments, used from time to time by the authors:

ART & ARCHITECTURAL SHOP
1058 Chapel Street
New Haven, Conn. 06510

ARTS & CRAFTS, INC.
321 Park Avenue
Baltimore, Maryland 21201

BALTIMORE DISPLAY INDUSTRIES, INC.
33 S. Charles Street
Baltimore, Maryland 21201

BECKER SIGN SUPPLY COMPANY
321 N. Paca Street
Baltimore, Maryland 21201

BRATER'S
259 State Street
New London, Conn. 06320

CLIPPER SHIP BOOKSHOP
59 Main Street
Essex, Conn. 06426

HIRSHBERG DIVISION—KEUFFEL & ESSER COMPANY
214 W. Franklin Street
Baltimore, Maryland 21201

KAY'S FASHION FABRICS
1196 Farmington Avenue
Bristol, Conn. 06010
and

926 S. Quaker Lane
W. Hartford, Conn. 06107

NYBORG'S
505 Cathedral Street
Baltimore, Maryland 21201

THE PAINT SHOP, INC.
59 Main Street
Old Saybrook, Conn. 06475

ROGERS ARTISTS' SUPPLY COMPANY
225 W. Mulberry Street
Baltimore, Maryland 21201

For paper turkeys, chickens, rabbits, wigs, masks, etc., try:

RECREATION NOVELTY COMPANY
221 Park Avenue
Baltimore, Maryland 21201

For historic documents try sharp photographic enlargements or:

HISTORIC PLAQUES
P.O. Box 735
Evanston, Ill. 60204

RELATED READINGS

(Issued approximately within the decade prior to publication of this work)

BOOKS AND BOOKLETS

Bowers, Melvyn K.
   Easy Bulletin Boards for the School Library
   Scarecrow '66

Burgert, Robert H. and Meadows, Elinor S.
   Eye-Appealing Bulletin Board Ideas
   Owen '60

Coplan, Kate
   Poster Ideas and Bulletin Board Techniques: For Libraries and Schools   Oceana '62

Currie, Dorothy H.
   Making Dioramas and Displays
   Owen '65

Fabri, Ralph
   Sculpture in Paper   Watson-Guptill '66

Grater, Michael
   One Piece of Paper, for Children and for Teachers   Mills & Boon (London) '63

Grubola, Marion R.
   How to Use a Bulletin Board
   Nat Council for Soc Stud '60

Horn, George F.
   Bulletin Boards   Reinhold '62

Hornick, Joanne
   Creative Bulletin Boards: For Junior High English   Citation Pr '68

Johnson, D. A. and Lund, C. H.
   Bulletin Board Displays for Mathematics
   Dickenson '67

Kelley, Marjorie
   Classroom-Tested Bulletin Boards
   Fearon '61

Kendall, Lloyd
   Bulletin Boards for the Classroom
   Owen '64

Lee, Carvel and Lorita
   The Bulletin Board Guide Book Series (Kindergarten through high school)
   Denison '60s

Lockridge, J. Preston
   Better Bulletin Board Displays: Bridges for Ideas   Tex Univ Div of Extension Vis Instr Bur rev. and enl. '61

Mary Caroline, Sister
   Bulletin Boards for New Math
   Owen '65

Mathre, T. H.
   Creative Bulletin Boards   Denison '62

Miller, Ray
   Bulletin Boards, High, Wide and Handsome
   Bruce Miller (Box 369) Riverside Calif. '66

Phillips, Ward H. and O'Lague, John H.
   Successful Bulletin Boards   Owen '66

Randall, Reino and Haines, Edward C.
   Bulletin Boards and Display   Davis '61

Ruby, Doris
   4 D Bulletin Boards That Teach
   Fearon '60

Weseloh, A. D.
   E-Z Bulletin Boards   Fearon '59

ARTICLES

Beitler, E. J. and Lockhart, B. C.
   Basic Ingredients for Effective Bulletin Boards Prac Home Econ 8:32-3* S '62

Beitler, E. J. and Lockhart, B. C.
   You Can Design Effective Bulletin Boards
   Prac Home Econ 7:24-5* F '62

Buchanan, M.
   Motivate by Board Ariz Teach 49:12-13 Ja '61

Burgert, Robert H.
   Bulletin Boards Instr 72:27-30 S; 64 0; 28 N; 18 D '62; 79 Ja; 49 F; 115 Mr; 96 Ap; 62 My; 32 Je '63

Cochell, S.
   Bulletin Boards As Teaching Aids (Alexander Hamilton High School) Sr Schol 87: sup. 6 N 4 '65

Dement, S.
   Look What Charley Did! (The right way to display papers) Bsns Ed World 49:18-19* O '68

Donley, Marshall O., Jr.
Our Bulletin Board Nat Educ Assn J 48:40-1 '59

Dye, C. F.
Redecorate Your Bulletin Board J Bsns Ed 44:40 O '68

East, M.
Methods for Creating Persuasive Bulletin Boards Prac Home Econ 4:13* Mr '59

East, M.
What Students Learn When They Create Bulletin Boards Prac Home Econ 4:26* Ap '59

Epstein, Edward B.
Tips for Tacks Grade Teach 81:62-3* N '63

Falke, Mary
New Ideas for Bulletin Boards Lib J 85:818-21 F 15 '60

Fine, Edith
Bulletin Boards, Springboards to Catch a Student's Eye Grade Teach 86:133-6* F '69

Fox, W.
Care and Feeding of Bulletin Boards Sch Activities 35:172-3 F '64

Greenwood, Colleen and Others
Say It Fast! Tex Outl 44:16-17 Je '60

Hall, Donald E.
Bulletin Boards for Elementary School Arithmetic Arith Teach 11:114-15 F '64

Harbage, M.
Sharing Time: Suggestions for Teachers of the Elementary Grades Sr Schol 74:13 T AP 17 '59

Horn, George F.
Bulletin Boards: How to Make Yours Come to Life Design 64:28-30* S '62

Jahnke, Jeanne
Bulletin Board Displays Wilson Lib Bul 33:499-503 Mr '59

Kendall, Lloyd
Brighten Up Those Social Studies with Your Bulletin Board Grade Teach 83:132-3 O '65

Kendall, Lloyd
Bulletin Board Ideas for Those Three Big Special Days Grade Teach 83:50 — 1 F '66

Kendall, Lloyd
Little People: Bulletin Boards Just for Kindergartners Grade Teach 83:98-9 D '65

Kendall, Lloyd
Problem-Solving Displays for Those First Few Days Grade Teach 83:124-5 S '65

Knirk, Frederick G.
Bulletin Boards Are a Waste of Time! Instr 77:21 My '68

Lees, Margaret M.
Bulletin Boards, Anyone? Try These Tips Bsns Ed World 44:14-15 S '63 (Followed by illustrations by Cunningham, G. S.; Graver, V. R. and Beede, R. C. Gallery of Bulletin Boards Bsns Ed World 44:16-19 S '63)

Lutz, Hazel P.
Attractive Bulletin Boards Boost School Activities Sch Activities 34:12 S '62

McMahan, Marie and Dickerman, Stella
Arranging Your Bulletin Board Instr 71:43 O '61 (These writers contributed Bulletin Board suggestions monthly, Ja '61 to D '62)

Madsen, Edna
Let's Exhibit the Children's Pictures Sch Arts 67:12-15 Mr '68

Marvey, M.
Bulletin Board Display: Using Large Circles As Background Design Wilson Lib Bul 43:776-7 Ap '69

Ramsay, Katharine S.
Is Your Bulletin Board Becoming a Dropout? Bsns Ed World 43:22-4 D '62

Robbins, Irene
Displays with a Tree Motif Instr 77:41 D '67

Wagner, G.
What Schools Are Doing; Preparing Attractive Bulletin Boards Bibliog Ed 83:124-5* F '62

Weisjohn, Rhyllis
Bulletin Board Display Wilson Lib Bul 34:569-83 Ap '60

White, James B.
Bulletin Board Exhibits Bibliog Ed 84:373-6 F '64

Wike, V. S.
Foolproof Bulletin Boards; Principles for Arrangements Grade Teach 83:100-1 N '65

BIBLIOGRAPHY

Rudolph, Belah Counts
Bulletin Boards and Displays to Publicize Books and Reading; bibliography of books, pamphlets and articles on techniques, ideas, sources El Engl 44:37-9 Ja '67

INDEX
TO ILLUSTRATIONS

INDEX TO ILLUSTRATIONS

A

Africa, 89, 90, 120
Airplanes, 49
America, 62, 154
Animals, 8, 61, 93, 94, 111
Arizona, 10
Art work: finger painting, 101; hanger people, 131; string pictures, 16; wool pictures, 4
Authors, 14
Autumn, 20, 162

B

Baby, 77
Banking, 139
Bicycles, 113
Bin strips, 134
Bird watching, 122, 169
Birds, 8, 111, 123, 170
Birthday cake, 22
Black Americans, 13, 14
Book week, 166
Breakfast, 12
Brother, 75
Building a house, 53
Butterflies, 58

C

Chanukah, 26, 27, 158
Child care, 77, 78, 79
Christmas, 11, 26, 27, 76
Chivalry, 164
Circles, 52
Circus, 51, 59, 60, 118
Citizenship, 71, 110
Climate, 68, 120-1, 125, 129
    see also   Weather
Clean: air, 145; community, 17, 110; hands, 147; school, 150
Club, 100, 133
Communication, 70
Congo, Belgian, 120
Continents, 66
Community relations, 17, 92, 110
Cookery, 22, 29, 30, 167
Cowboys, 45

Credits, 130
Current events, 91, 104, 155

D

Dairy products, 37
Daytime, 21
Dental health week, 137
Displays, 19
Dress, 144, 147, 150-1
    see also   Grooming

E

Eating, 12, 15, 35, 36, 134
Ecology, 145
    see also   Nature studies
Electricity, 115
Elephants, 51
Exhibitions, 19

F

Fall see   Autumn
Family life, 53, 56-7; members, 73-5, 77
Famous people, 13, 14, 41, 153
Farms, 34, 37
Father, 73, 74
February events, 153
Finger painting, 101
Flags, 46, 62, 85
Flowers, 8, 32, 65, 95, 96, 111, 163
Food, 12, 22, 35, 36, 37, 117, 134
Foreign lands, 87: Africa 89, 90; Congo, 120; France, 3; Greece, 88; Holland, 81, 82; India, 86; Israel, 160; Japan, 156; Lapland, 120-1; Mexico, 160; Sahara Desert, 120-1; Spain, 161
Forest, 8-9
France, 3
Free material, 140
Freedom, 71

223

G

Gardens, 95, 96, 127, 163
Geography, 66, 120-1
Germs, 141, 147
Giveaways, 140
Greece, 88
Grooming, 144, 148, 149, 150-1
Group relations, 20, 23, 48, 50, 56-7, 103

H

Halloween, 31, 162
Hanger people, 131
Hawaii, 171
Health, 12, 15, 35, 36, 141, 147, 151-2
    see also   Hygiene
Hearing, 99, 100
History, 62, 90, 164, 165
Hobbies, 58, 68
Holidays, 12, 27, 28, 29
    see also   individual events
Holland, 81, 82
Home life, 23, 56
Homework, 130
Horns, 100
Housekeeping, 79
Houses, 23, 53
Hygiene, 15, 137, 141, 147

I

India, 86
Indians, 47, 71
Insects, 8
Israel, 160

J

Japan, 156

K

Knights, 164

L

Lapland, 120-1
Leaves, 20
Lettering, 69, 133, 134, 138
Library use, 41, 119
Lincoln, Abraham, 153, 165
Litter, 17
Lost and found, 114
Love, 134

M

Marketing, 117
Mathematics, 38, 39, 40, 98, 107, 108, 167
    see also   Numbers; Roman numerals
Measuring, 38, 107
Mexico, 160
Money, 139, 157
Mother, 74; helper, 79
Museum visit, 8
Music, 98, 100, 102

N

Nature studies, 40, 121, 122, 124, 127, 169
New Year, 28
News, 91, 104, 155
Nighttime, 21
Noise, 99, 100
Novels, 109
Numbers, 38, 39, 108

O

Oceans, 66
Outdoors, 19
    see also   Nature studies

P

Party giving, 22, 42
Patriotism, 46, 62, 71, 154
Peace, 25, 84
Pets, 53, 93, 132; housing, 94

Play, 43, 44, 49, 56-7
    see also   Recreation
Pollution, 17, 110, 145
Puzzles, 66

R

Rain, 49, 65, 80, 128
Reading programs, 2, 14, 64, 68, 78, 82, 83, 87, 103, 116, 121, 155, 163, 166
Recreation, 5, 6, 43, 49, 56-7, 80, 85
Reminders, 142
Roman numerals, 38

S

Safety, 5, 43, 44, 59, 63, 106, 113
Sahara Desert, 120-1
Scales, 40
School opening, 106, 131, 136
School work, 130
Science, 124, 129
Seasons, 7
    see also   individual names
Self knowledge, 48, 148
Ships, 164
Sickness, 141
Sister, 75
Skiing, 6, 42, 64
Sky, 49
Sorting, 24
Spain, 161
Spring, 5, 65, 68, 112, 124
Stories, 45, 72; Indian, 47
Story hour, 72
Storms, 125
String pictures, 16
Summer, 95, 106, 116

Sunshine, 8, 128
Supermarkets, 117

T

Teeth, 15, 137, 143
Television, 172
Thanksgiving, 33, 159, 162
Togetherness, 20, 48, 50, 56-7, 103
Touch, 97
Toys, 44
Traffic lights, 59
Transportation, 123
Travel, 1, 2, 10, 83, 87, 123
    see also   foreign lands
Trees, 55, 114
Turkey, 33
Turtles, 94

U

United Nations, 84, 85
Vacations, 63
Valentine's day, 30, 153
Vocabulary, 53, 54, 105

W

Washington, George, 153, 169
Weather, 125, 128, 129, 144
The West, 45, 47
Wild life, 126
Winter, 6, 42, 67, 170
Witches, 31
Wool pictures, 4
Writing, 69, 138

MEMO

MEMO

MEMO

MEMO

MEMO

MEMO

MEMO